COACHING
The Art and the Science

The complete guide to self-management, team management, and physical and psychological preparation

Dave Chambers

FIREFLY BOOKS

A FIREFLY BOOK

Published by Firefly Books Ltd. 2013

First printing

Publisher Cataloging-in-Publication Data (U.S.)
Chambers, Dave.
   Coaching : the art and the science / Dave Chambers.
[176] p. : ill. ; cm.
Includes bibliographical references and index.
Summary: Information on developing positive coaching strategies, using principles collected from sport psychology, pedagogy, and physiology. Also includes fundamental coaching techniques as well as advanced mental and physical training methods.
ISBN-13: 978-1-77085-184-9 (pbk.)
1. Coaching (Athletics)—Handbooks, manuals, etc. I. Title.
796.077 dc23   GV711.C536   2013

Library and Archives Canada Cataloguing in Publication
Chambers, Dave, 1940-
   Coaching : the art and the science / Dave Chambers.
Includes bibliographical references and index.
ISBN 978-1-77085-184-9
1. Coaching (Athletics). I. Title.
GV711.C42 2013   796.07'7   C2012-906730-X

Published in the United States by
Firefly Books (U.S.) Inc.
P.O. Box 1338, Ellicott Station
Buffalo, New York 14205

Published in Canada by
Firefly Books Ltd.
50 Staples Ave.
Richmond Hill, Ontario L4B 0A7

Printed in Canada

The publisher gratefully acknowledges the financial support for our publishing program by the Government of Canada through the Canada Book Fund as administered by the Department of Canadian Heritage.

First published: Toronto: Key Porter Books, 1997 (ISBN 1-55013-877-4)
Second edition: A revision of the 1997 edition printed in limited quantities by the York University Bookstore, 2012

PHOTO CREDITS
Front Cover
Stop Watch © Shawn Hempel / Shutterstock.com
Whistle © Africa Studio / Shutterstock.com

Back Cover
Clipboard © Feng Yu / Shutterstock.com

Contents

iv

Introduction

Coaching—a science or an art? The obvious answer to this question is that it is both. The science of coaching is involved with the physical and mental training of the athlete using modern methods verified by research by sport physiologists, sport psychologists, biomechanics, and nutritional experts and so on. The art of coaching is to take all this information, apply it to the particular coaching situation, and adjust and modify when necessary. The art of coaching also includes communicating, problem solving, decision making, and generally being able to lead, manage, and motivate a group of athletes toward a common goal. Coaching is not just having the expertise about training methods, tactics, and strategy, it is also about dealing with people. The successful coach is skilled in both the art and the science of coaching.

This book is divided into five sections: self management, team management, physical preparation, mental (psychological) preparation, and sport quotations. The self-management section deals with the coach's role as a leader of a group of athletes. The team management section deals with the many aspects of the daily, monthly, and yearly operation of a team. The physical preparation section includes the various physical training methods used while the mental preparation section deals with the psychological and mental training strategies used by today's modern athletes and coaches. The sport quotations are designed to motivate both coaches and athletes.

Part 1: Self-Management

PHILOSOPHY

Coaching is a very complex and demanding profession. It requires many technical and personal skills and a very sound philosophy. Most good coaches discover early that their philosophy, beliefs, and principles serve as a guide for the many decisions that have to be made daily in the training and supervision of athletes. The best coaches realize that these basic philosophical concepts must be applied in a skillful way to develop the essence of team work in the pursuit of excellence and success.

The philosopher Will Durant once said, "Science gives us knowledge, but only philosophy can give us wisdom." It is therefore important for every coach to have a well-thought-out philosophy of coaching that will guide his or her decision making, determine the coaching aims and objectives, and define the direction the team will take. The coach must develop a philosophy of competition, winning and losing, the value of athletics, criticism, and interacting with and motivating athletes.

The coach has an undeniable effect on the athletes he or she is associated with:

It is impossible to underestimate the importance of the coach in the development of an athlete. From the youngest peewee player to the elite athlete, the coach is a pivotal character in the moral as well as the physical development of his or her charges.

The more intensive the training, the greater the opportunity for moulding the athlete's character and personal philosophy as it pertains to his or her athletic career. Elite athletes appear to cleave to their coaches as mentors, guardians, and, in some cases, almost as surrogate parents. They are fortunate indeed if their coach is concerned with their moral and intellectual development as well as their athletic training. (Dubin)

One of the most important philosophical decisions a coach must make is how he or she will treat the athletes. An approach that is firm but fair appears to be the most successful, but athletes must feel that the coach cares about them. The age of the athletes and the type of coaching situation are also important considerations. Young, developing, amateur athletes may be treated differently from older professional athletes, but, regardless of age, athletes benefit from a sound coaching philosophy.

Two letters from parents and one from a young athlete serve to illustrate the responsibility the coach has when handling young people.

Letter 1

Dear Coach:

Tomorrow morning my son starts hockey. He's going to step out on the ice and his great adventure, that will probably include joys and disappointments, begins.

So I wish you would take him by his young hand and teach him the things he will have to know. Teach him to respect the referee, and that his judgment is final. Teach him not to hate his competitors, but to admire their skill. Teach him it is just as important to be a playmaker and get an assist as it is to score a goal. Teach him to play as a team and never to be selfish. Teach him never to blame his goaltender when a goal is scored against him, because five mistakes were made before the puck got to the goalie. Teach him that winning is not everything, but trying to win is. Teach him to be a competitor. Teach him to close his ears to the howling mob and to stand up for himself if he thinks he is right. Teach him gently but don't coddle him, because only the test of fire makes fine steel.

This is a big order, Coach, and I place my son in your hands. See what you can do for him. He is such a nice little fellow.

His Dad (Argue)

Letter 2

Dear Coach:

We hardly know each other, and yet very shortly we will have quite a lot in common, namely, my son Mike. Now that your season is about to begin, we are "loaning" you one of the greatest possessions the Good Lord has seen fit to give us—our son, and make no mistake about it, coach, during these next few months he is yours.

To his mother and me he is still a little boy in many respects, but of course we wouldn't dare let him know we felt that way since he thinks he's quite grown up at age 15. To most coaches, he and his buddies are looked upon as young men because they have the backbone to come out for the team and to stick with it. Little boys couldn't do this, only "men" can take it. But I guess most parents are hesitant to want to see their sons in this light because these youngsters seem to grow up so quickly anyway.

You know, Mike has been a hero worshipper ever since he was little more than a baby and I'm happy to say that at one small point in his life he even included me, but now, you are number one! In his eyes, you are the man. He believes in you. He believes in what you do. He believes in what you stand for and what you say. He doesn't miss a thing where you are concerned, and most importantly he believes in what you are! This, my friend, makes you a very special person fulfilling a very special role, with very special responsibilities, which far outweigh the limited message any scoreboard might tell.

Some of us have only one son to guide and enjoy, but you, coach, will literally have hundreds of "sons" to guide and enjoy over the years. In this respect, especially, you are a very lucky man indeed. Now, I'm not naive enough to believe that our son and his teammates won't keep you awake nights, make mistakes, frustrate you, lose some, win some, and cause you other kinds of problems, but in the final analysis it might be that this is because they are boys, not men. This might come as a surprise to you, but in some ways these things hurt the boys more than it hurts you since they are so anxious to please you. It might not show, but deep down they are disappointed when these things happen because they feel that they have let you down.

Ever since I can remember, this boy of ours has dreamed of the day when he would have his chance to "make the team." At the moment this is his one burning desire. He wants to be an athlete and be part of the team, and at this time and in this place he is ready to do what you tell him in order to accomplish this goal. As you might expect, like every boy, he dreams of glory and of becoming a superstar who always manages to come through when

the team is on the brink of disaster! I guess this isn't too bad, for the moment, at least, since the hard facts of life bring us face to face with reality all too soon anyway.

Please do not misunderstand me, coach. I am not suggesting that he be treated any differently than anyone else because I feel that basically our boy is just like all the boys on your team. I don't know if he will ever be good enough to "make the first team," or whether he has any real athletic ability or not, but to us this is not our primary concern. I believe that I speak for most parents when I say that we are more concerned about what happens to our youngster through this experience and because you are his teacher. We hope that in spite of your busy schedule you will be able to see these boys as something other than X's and O's on a play sheet, or "tools" to be used in furthering your ambitions for that really "big job."

We hope, too, that our boy will not only learn the fundamentals of the game from you but also a respect for authority, the necessity of following rules and the penalty for violating them. He needs to learn that discipline is important to an individual and to a group in order to prevent chaos. He needs to develop an appreciation for hard work and the fact that this is still a good guideline for success in any endeavor. We think he should learn that loyalty is not a bad word and that being loyal to his team, his coach, his school, his family, his church and his country is good and necessary. Through athletics he should develop an understanding of the importance of taking care of his body and not abusing it by using tobacco, alcohol, or drugs. His experiences with you in athletics should also teach him to accept his fellow man for what he is and what he can do rather than the color of his skin or his nationality. No one enjoys losing, but youngsters need to get a taste of it in order for them to learn that the important thing is the necessity of "getting off the floor" and trying again. These are the little things that begin to make young men and good citizens out of little boys and I'm convinced that they can be taught through athletics without sacrificing any mechanical aspects of the game.

I realize that every community has its corps of "super-critics" who only have eyes for the scoreboard. But I am suggesting to you, coach, that if you teach "boys" instead of just a "sport," the boys and the parents will rarely, if ever, be numbered among the leather-lunged experts in box X and your personal scoreboard will record so many young men out of so many boys.

Good luck to you and the team.

Sincerely,
A Father (Sabock)

An eleven-year-old boy, the grandson of a former professional player, expressed his hopes this way:

Letter 3

Well, here it is another sport season,
So I am writing you for just one reason!
Please don't scream or curse and yell,
Remember I'm not a professional
I am only 11 years old
And can't be bought or traded or sold.
I just want to have fun and play the game
And am not looking for fame!
Please don't make me feel I've committed a sin
Just because my team didn't win!
I don't want to be that great, you see
I'd rather play and just be me! (Cosentino)

As these letters illustrate, the coach must decide early in his or her career how athletes are to be treated. In many ways, these early decisions will determine whether a coach's career will be successful.

PHILOSOPHIES OF WELL-KNOWN COACHES

We can learn from the philosophy and thoughts of prominent coaches.

Vince Lombardi (Former professional football coach, two Super Bowl championships)

Winning isn't everything, but making the effort to win is.

Lombardi's success lay not only in his inspirational personality, but also his ability to teach. He could communicate an idea to his players, explain it so they understood it—not only how to execute it but why.

Three things make a winning team
1. Players have to know their roles
2. The "we" is bigger than "me"
3. Players must respect each other

He never expected more from us than he was willing to give of himself.

The philosophical basis of the Lombardi legend was total dedication to the pursuit of excellence.

Success is not a sometimes thing. In other words, you don't do what is right once in a while, but all the time. Success is a habit. Winning is a habit. (Walton)

Woody Hayes (Former university football coach, five national championships)

I never talked down to the players.

Even when I thundered at the players, I thundered that they could do better.

They may outsmart me, or be luckier, but they can't outwork me. (Walton)

John Wooden (Former university basketball coach, ten national championships)

He made them winners, winners with character, not characters with wins.

Wooden's greatest achievement was his gift to others, his teaching on how to find the best in oneself, and how to find peace of mind.

Success is peace of mind which is a direct result of self satisfaction in knowing you did your best to become the best you are capable of becoming. (Walton)

Bill Walsh (Former professional and university football coach, three Super Bowl championships)

The stylish, graceful, accommodating, easy-going, affable coach will get 80% of the job done. The final 20% can be directly attributed to making tough decisions, demanding a high standard of performance, meeting expectations, paying attention to details, and grabbing and shaking when necessary. (Walsh)

Joe Paterno (Former university football coach, two national championships)

I feel that certainty of winning only when I know that we've done all the preparation, when we've practised intelligently and thoroughly.

Success is perishable and often outside our control. In contrast, excellence is something that's lasting, dependable, and largely within a person's control. (Paterno)

Phil Jackson (Former professional basketball coach, eleven NBA championships)

He makes you think about more than just basketball. He makes you look at the larger picture.

One of his strengths is that he likes a debate. He wants us to express our ideas on things, even to the point of an argument. (Jackson)

Scott Bowman (Former professional ice hockey coach, nine NHL championships)

The most important job as a coach is to get the right players on the ice at the right time.

His practices were in constant motion, shooting, passing, everything done on the go, with speed, every drill rooted in high-pace skating. (Dryden)

Pat Burns (Former professional ice hockey coach, one NHL championship)

If you're not playing well you're not going to play. That is the bottom line. The players are responsible for themselves and the reward or punishment is going to be whether they play or not. It's just that simple. (McKenzie)

Steve Yzerman (Former all star and Hall of Fame professional ice hockey player and general manager, National Hockey League)

"I always try to do what is best for the team."

Mike Krzyzewski (University basketball coach, three national championships)

"You develop a team to achieve what one person cannot accomplish alone. All of us alone are weaker, by far, than all of us are together."

Guy Boucher (Head coach, Tampa, National Hockey League)

"I don't coach players, I coach people, that's how I see it."

"I don't like to be a slave to any routine. I always tell the players I don't want to be right. I want to get it right. If the players had an idea and we feel it is a good one, we go with it."

Nick Saban (University football coach. Three national championships)

"The process is more important than the result. Our commitment, character, conviction and attitude allow us to do what we needed to do as a team to achieve at the highest level."

"Remember that success is never final and failure is never fatal."

"There is no I in team."

Coaching is a great challenge, and not for the faint of heart. It requires long hours and intense interaction with people who are in competition with themselves and others. It runs the gamut of emotions, involving success and failure, joy and despair. It involves wanting and trying to win, and learning how to accept defeat. It also involves the opportunity of participating, having fun, and learning to work with others toward a common goal.

Walter Gillet probably summarized the job of a coach best in "What Is a Coach?"

A coach is a politician, a judge, a public speaker, a teacher, a trainer, a financier, a labourer, a psychologist, a psychiatrist, and a chaplain. He must be an optimist and yet at times appear to be a pessimist, seem humble and yet be very proud, strong but at times weak, confident yet not overconfident, enthusiastic but not too enthusiastic.

He must have the hide of an elephant, the fierceness of a lion, the pep of a young pup, the guts of an ox, the stamina of an antelope, the wisdom of an owl, the cunning of a fox, and the heart of a kitten.

He must be willing to give freely of his time, his money, his energy, his youth, his family life, and his health. In return he must expect little if any financial reward, little comfort on earth, little praise but plenty of criticism.

However, a good coach is respected and is a leader in his community, is loved by his team, and makes lasting friends wherever he goes.

He has the satisfaction of seeing young people develop and improve in ability. He learns the thrill of victory and how to accept defeat with grace. His associations with athletes help keep him young in mind and spirit, and he too must grow and improve in ability with his team.

In his heart he knows that, in spite of the inconvenience, the criticism, and the demands on his time, he loves his work, for he is the coach.

QUALITIES OF A GOOD COACH

Successful coaches do not seem to fit a specific personality type. They are as individual as members of the general population, but they do have specific leadership qualities. Many good coaches are outgoing and extroverted, while others are quiet and somewhat withdrawn. Some coaches are autocratic and hard-nosed, while others are democratic and accommodating. Here are some of the characteristics good coaches have in common:

Knowledge of the Sport

To be effective, the coach must have a sound knowledge of the sport. However, in most cases, participation alone is not sufficient to supply that knowledge. A good coach will continually read, observe, and use any other methods to further his or her knowledge of the sport. Most good coaches attend at least one coaching clinic per year and participate in any coaching certification program that is available.

Communication

A good coach is an effective communicator. Good communication with the athletes leads to mutual understanding. Problem areas between coach and player should be dealt with to avoid lasting misunderstanding, and an athlete should feel that the coach is approachable.

Ability to Understand and Handle the Athlete

The ability to communicate is related to the ability to handle and understand people. In order to be an effective communicator, a coach must understand the athlete and be able to relate to him or her. A lack of understanding of the athlete's motivation and/or problems is one of the major reasons for a breakdown in the coach–athlete relationship.

Organizational Skills

One common characteristic of all good coaches is that they are highly organized in all areas of team operation. A well-organized team gives the athletes confidence and pride in the team and the coach. A coach who spends the time to become highly organized will generally be respected by the athletes. Today's coach should have a yearly, monthly, weekly, and daily plan for the organization of his or her team. The physical, technical, tactical, and psychological preparation of the athletes should be part of a year-round training plan.

Knowledge of Training and Conditioning Methods

A coach should have an up-to-date knowledge of various training and conditioning methods. This knowledge can be applied in the day-to-day training of a team or individual athletes. The coach should have the ability to develop a plan for improving and/or maintaining his or her athletes' conditioning levels throughout the year, including off-season training programs.

Effectively Run Practices

One of the most important aspects of coaching is the ability to run effective practice sessions, which most coaches believe are the key to the success of teams and/or individual athletes. The coach should have the ability to run organized, active practices, stressing well-thought-out drills and the techniques used in competition.

Evaluation of Athletes

A good coach should be able to evaluate the ability of the athletes. This is an ongoing process for the coach, but it is most important in the initial selection of team members. Good coaches have an ability to evaluate an individual's performance based on previous observations of athletes and techniques in their sport. However, most good coaches also rely on other factors such as specific drills, reports by other observers, skill tests, potential, physical attributes, and personality traits to make their final selection. Character is a key factor in selection by most coaches.

Strategy

The ability to prepare a team for an opponent is an important attribute of a coach. The skill is developed through experience, learning, and the ability to analyze an opponent's strengths and weaknesses. As well as preparing a team for a contest, the coach should be able to improvise and adjust strategy during games.

Effective Use of Personnel

In team sports a good coach has the ability to make effective use of certain athletes at certain times. The coach must have a good understanding of what athletes can do in certain situations and must be able to react quickly and use good judgment during games to select the right players for critical situations.

Fairness

It is important that the coach give fair treatment to the athletes on a team. Athletes can turn quickly against a coach if they feel his or her treatment of the team is unfair or that he or she favors certain individuals over others.

Motivation

Good athletes should be self-motivated, but a coach should also be able to motivate in order to be effective. Not all coaches have this ability, but it appears to be a quality shared by those whose coaching is outstanding.

Dedication, Enthusiasm, Maturity, Ethics

Good coaches display dedication to the task, which has a positive effect on the athletes. A lack of dedication can seriously affect the athletes' view of the coach, and can be extremely detrimental; the coach may even be viewed as lazy and uncaring.

Enthusiasm is an important quality in a coach, and it is important that he or she maintain it throughout the year, especially at times when the athletes appear fatigued and/or unmotivated.

As well, the coach should act in a mature manner. Immature behavior, such as harassing officials, can affect the athletes, leading them to imitate this behavior or to lose respect for the coach.

It is important for a coach to conduct him- or herself in an ethical manner both with and away from the athletes. The coach is a role model and should realize the importance of this position and be aware of the effect that he or she has, especially on the more impressionable, younger athletes.

Knowledge of How the Body Works (Exercise Physiology)

The coach should have a basic knowledge of exercise physiology in order to understand how the body works. This knowledge will allow the coach to understand the science behind various training techniques, such as work-to-rest ratios during training and games. A coach should also be able to interpret scientific articles on various training methods and conduct and interpret the outcomes of various types of fitness testing.

Knowledge of Growth and Development Principles

Many coaches are working with younger players who are still growing and developing. It is important that the coach have a knowledge of both the physical and the emotional stages that younger players go through. In some cases, growth spurts may affect a younger athlete's coordination and create certain emotional problems. This, in turn, may affect his or her athletic performance.

Ability to Teach

The coach is in many ways a teacher, and as such he or she must have an understanding of basic learning principles and teaching techniques. A good coach needs the ability to teach fundamental skills as well as team play. Factors such as voice, appearance, teaching formations, and planning are as important to the coach as they are to the classroom teacher.

Concern for the Athlete

Concern for each individual athlete is very important for a coach. Athletes must feel that the coach cares about them and that each individual is important to the team. The coach should also show concern for athletes after they have moved on. Some coaches receive a great deal of satisfaction by keeping in touch with their athletes after they have stopped participating for their team or organization.

Knowledge of the Rules

An effective coach should have a thorough knowledge of the playing rules. This knowledge should be passed on to the players and is important in both practice and game situations.

Discipline

Most good teams have a basic discipline code that sets down guidelines for behavior. Team rules are more likely to be followed when the athletes have input and agree with the coach on rules such as those related to punctuality for practices and games, and general conduct on and off the playing surface.

Media

A coach should have a good relationship with the media, as publicity can greatly affect the support the team receives. It is important for a coach to be available and cordial, no matter what the circumstances, when dealing with the media. Regular reporting of game results and of interesting team information can help the coach develop a good relationship with the media.

Humor

Not all situations in sports are serious. A good coach should have a sense of humor. Athletes will feel more relaxed if the coach is able to see humor in some situations. A coach who is always serious may put added pressure on the athletes and may not be able to relate to them. It is also important that the coach not take him- or herself too seriously and start to believe that he or she is the only reason for the success of an athlete or a team.

Ability to Recruit and Build a Program

Most good coaches have the ability to relate and sell both themselves and their program to a prospective athlete. When recruiting athletes, coaches should have a recruiting plan in which they are able to identify and relate information about themselves and the program to the potential team member.

Generally it is important to realize that each coach is an individual. Coaches should attempt to study and emulate the techniques of successful coaches rather than imitate their personalities. Be yourself, but do attempt to make yourself better by working hard at improving your coaching techniques.

COACHING RESPECT FACTORS

Halliwell, a sport psychologist at the University of Montreal, and a consultant for many professional and elite amateur athletes, developed twenty respect factors that make an excellent self-evaluation checklist for coaches:

1. Previous playing experience and success.
2. Previous coaching experience and success.
3. Good appearance—neatly dressed, fit.
4. Good living habits.
5. Good work habits—puts in the hours, is efficient.
6. Well-organized—practices, meetings, travel, and so on.
7. Good communicator—explains things clearly, good listener.
8. Availability—always has time for the athlete.
9. Knowledgeable—demonstrates knowledge of the game, both technical and tactical aspects.
10. Teaching ability—displays ability to correct technical and tactical errors.
11. Highly motivated—displays intensity, commitment, involvement.
12. Positive, upbeat, enthusiastic, optimistic—gives lots of praise and reinforcement.
13. Good bench coach—makes adjustments, reads and reacts, gets last change.
14. Good sense of humor—can keep things loose.
15. Good leadership skills—in the dressing room and during the games.
16. Good self-control skills—displays composure, emotional control.
17. Desire to improve—seeks new knowledge, attends coaching clinics, self-evaluates.
18. Honest and fair with players—doesn't show favoritism, is "tough but fair."
19. Open to suggestions—displays some flexibility, listens to players' and assistants' suggestions.
20. Shows a genuine interest in players as individuals—demonstrates knowledge and interest in their life away from the sport situation.

Knowledge of the sport, being a good communicator, being honest but fair with the players, and showing an interest in them, as well as being positive and upbeat, were deemed the most important of the twenty factors. These respect factors can serve as a useful checklist for periodical self-evaluation for coaches.

THE COACH AS LEADER

Coaches are in leadership positions with their athletes and teams, and quite often hold similar positions within the community.

Some coaches adapt to the leadership role rather well. Others, although they may be knowledgeable about their sport, have a difficult time with leadership. Many coaches in the high-profile sports such as baseball, basketball, ice hockey, and especially football have been described as not only great coaches but also great leaders. Vince Lombardi (professional football), John Wooden (college basketball), Knute Rockne (college football), and Scott Bowman (professional ice hockey), among many others, are famous for their success in coaching and their ability to lead. These leaders/coaches all possessed the burning desire to be successful, but they also are as different as they are similar.

What makes a great leader, and how can coaches learn to be more effective leaders?

There are many definitions of leadership, but Hemphill and Coons's definition seems to fit best: "the behavior of an individual when he/she is directing the activities of a group towards a shared goal."

Research in leadership has evolved over the years from trait to behavioral to contingency theories.

The trait theory, which began in the 1920s and lasted until after the Second World War, was based on the premise that all great leaders had certain common traits such as intelligence, confidence, motivation to succeed, and responsibility, and would be great leaders in any situation (Stogdill). In other words, leaders are born, not made. The trait theory was discounted by social scientists in the late 1940s because the relative importance of the traits was not confirmed by most studies, and the needs of the followers were basically ignored.

Leadership-theory research moved to a study of the common behaviors of the leaders after the Second World War. This theory was based on the fact that successful leaders have certain common behaviors; it was felt that, if these behaviors could be determined, they could then be taught to potential leaders.

Two research studies, at the University of Michigan and Ohio State University, identified the two essential behaviors of leaders as consideration and the initiating structure. "Consideration" refers to caring, respect for feelings and ideas, mutual trust, and so on between the leader and the subordinates. "Initiating of structure" refers to the leader's ability to create an organization structure and define clearly the roles within it (Kahn and Katz).

The contingency theory advanced by Fiedler proposes that the effectiveness of a group is contingent upon the leader's style or personality, the individuals he or she is leading, and the circumstances that allow the leader to exert influence. Fiedler further postulates that, in terms of personality, leaders are either task-motivated or relationship-motivated.

Task-motivated leaders clearly spell out goals, tasks, and guidelines. Relationship-motivated leaders are concerned with having a good relationship and mutual trust with their subordinates.

Fiedler also refers to "position power," in which the leader's position gives him or her the ability to reward and punish. He points out that position power alone cannot make an effective leader; the support of the group and a well-defined task are necessary as well.

Other leadership theories include the path–goal theory (Carron) and the life-cycle theory (Hersey & Blanchard). In the path–goal theory, the emphasis is on the needs and goals of the subordinates, and the leader acts as a facilitator to help the subordinates reach their goals. In the life-cycle theory, the emphasis is also put on the subordinates. Here, the type of leadership depends on the maturity of those being led.

How does the research on leadership help the coach? In terms of trait theory, it is important to realize that, while good coaches can have some similar traits, more often this is not the case. In terms of behavioral theory, we have already noted (in "Qualities of a Good Coach,") that consideration and initiating structure are the two key components of leadership.

In terms of the contingency theory, it is necessary to recognize the importance of being in the right situation and working with athletes who have the same goals and motivation as the coach. Certain coaches are more effective for certain ages and competition levels, and it is important for the coach to find a situation and level he or she is comfortable with.

Both the path–goal and life-cycle theories place the emphasis on the athlete, putting the coach in the role of facilitator and guide for the athlete. This type of leadership can work well with mature athletes, where the coach sets the training program and acts as an adviser and confidant, and is most effective in individual sports, such as gymnastics and figure skating, and in track and field (athletics).

COACHING STYLES

Every coach has his or her own personality, and consequently there is no one coaching style that fits all coaches. However, as we noted earlier, there are some common successful coaching and leadership qualities and behaviors.

Generally, good coaches have to be organized, demand excellence, care for and communicate with the athletes, maintain team discipline, be knowledgeable and have teaching ability, and be patient. These qualities are the foundation of coaching, regardless of the style a coach selects as suitable for his or her personality.

Percival was one of the first to categorize different coaching styles. He listed them as positive and negative and the names he chose are, in most cases, self-explanatory. Percival's categories are shown in table 1.1.

Tutko and Richards identified five coaching styles and listed their advantages and disadvantages. They identified coaches as hard-nosed authoritarian, nice-guy, intense or driven, easygoing, and businesslike.

The hard-nosed authoritarian coach is described as the autocratic, hard-driven, demanding type who believes there is only one way of doing things—his or her way. Admiration for this type of coach depends upon team success and whether the athlete shares the goals and objectives of the coach. This type of coach believes strongly in discipline, rules, schedules, and plans; is not usually close to the athletes or warm personally; uses threats and punishment to motivate; and may prefer weaker people as assistant coaches. The advantages of this type of coach are that the athletes become disciplined, organized, and usually better conditioned, and the team has good spirit when winning. The disadvantages are that dissension arises when the team is losing; the coach is often disliked or feared; sensitive athletes are unable to handle this type of treatment; and the team is continually driven and tense, and can become fatigued.

The nice-guy coach is the opposite of the hard-nosed coach. This type of coach is well liked, flexible, personable, sociable, and is concerned about the feelings and personal lives of the athletes. The nice-guy coach is mostly positive and involves the athletes in decision making. The advantage of this type of coach is that there

NEGATIVE

Insulter	Whiner	White Cane
Shouter	Fast Mouth	Sulker
Avenger	Blister	Sloppy Joe
Choker	Rapper (knocker)	Hitler
Shaky (nervous)	Black-Catter (superstitious)	Mumbler
Tough Guy	General Custer (only one strategy)	Sad Sam
Molder	Critic	Scientist (genius)
Hero	Super Friend	Jailer (controls)
Rockne		

POSITIVE

Counsellor	Organizer	Explainer
Mr. Cool	Orator	Salesman
Democrat	Planner	Tourist
Appreciator	With It	Supporter
Inspirer	The Doctor	Shrink

Table 1.1: Coaching styles, as identified by athletes.

is usually good team cohesiveness, athletes produce above their expectations, and problem athletes are handled well. The disadvantages of this type of coach are that the coach is often seen as weak; con (deceiving) athletes are usually not handled well; and socially inhibited athletes sometimes cannot relate to a social, personable coach.

The intense or driven coach is somewhat similar to the authoritarian type in that the approach is aggressive and emphasizes discipline. Other characteristics include a tendency to be emotional and worry, and to take things personally; an overemphasis on preparation; and a propensity to push and lead by example. The advantages of this type of coach is that the team is usually prepared and up for the competition, and is supported when it works hard, and the coach is totally committed and dedicated. The disadvantages of this type of coach are that he or she may be too demanding and may sometimes have unrealistic expectations; may be too emotional; may not handle sensitive or lazy athletes well; and may overwork the team to the point that it is mentally and physically fatigued at the final competition.

The easygoing coach is a direct opposite of the intense, driven coach. This type of coach appears to be pressure-free and unemotional, dislikes exact schedules, and does not take things seriously—so much so that he or she may appear to be lazy. The advantages of this type of coach are that the team feels little pressure and does not complain about being overworked, and the athletes feel independent and can question and have more input into the operation of the team. The disadvantages are that the coach is often seen as lazy and inadequate; the team is often not in good physical condition, having been underworked; and pressure may not be handled well by the team.

The businesslike coach is becoming the norm in today's sporting world. This type of coach is well prepared, educated, and continually learning and improving. Other characteristics include approaching the sport in an organized, logical manner, and being intelligent and always a step ahead in preparation and handling problems. The advantages of this type of coach are that the team uses up-to-date techniques and conditioning methods and is always well prepared for competition; and the athletes feel confident they are ready for the contest. The disadvantages of this type of coach are that he or she may seem uncaring and to be using the players as pawns in a game; may be too technical for some athletes; can be hard on disorganized athletes; and may ignore the importance of team spirit and emotion.

Martens outlines three distinct coaching styles: the command style, the submissive style, and the cooperative style.

The command style involves the coach making the decisions and the athlete following the directions. In this style, the coach usually has a great deal of experience and believes that he or she knows the correct way of doing things without input from the athletes. Thus, the athlete must submit totally to the coach in terms of training, discipline, and so on.

The submissive style requires the coach to make few decisions and is a *laissez-faire* approach. In this approach, the athletes make most of the decisions, with the coach acting as a facilitator. The submissive style is usually adopted by coaches who lack confidence or are generally lazy. It is not a recommended style of coaching.

The cooperative style involves the coach sharing decision making with the athletes. The coach serves in a leadership role and guides the athletes in developing their skills and reaching their goals.

The Coaching Association of Canada identifies three leadership styles similar to Martens's: directive, supportive, and participative.

The directive approach is task- and performance-oriented in using rewards and punishment. It is a "we have a job to do and let's get on with it" approach, with less attention paid to the needs and feelings of the athletes, and very little, if any, athlete input.

The supportive approach encourages the athletes to express their feelings, is people-oriented, and uses primarily positive reinforcement. The supportive approach strives for harmony between the athlete and coach, and among the athletes.

The participative approach is democratic and involves sharing responsibility with the athletes for success and failure.

From these many descriptions of coaching styles, it is obvious that no coach fits one category exactly but, instead, each coach is a composite of two or more types or subtypes. It is important for the coach to develop a style he or she is comfortable with and that draws on the strengths of a number of different approaches. But, most important, **a coach must evolve a style that fits his or her personality**. Also, different levels and different situations may require different styles.

Athletes' Reasons for Participating in Sports

Athletes participate in sports for the following reasons:

1. *Desire for achievement*: A wish to master new skills and pursue excellence.
2. *A need for affiliation*: A desire to have positive relationships with teammates and others associated with the sport.
3. *A desire for sensation*: A desire to experience the excitement, sights and sounds of participating in sports.
4. *A desire for self direction*: A wish to feel self-control, decision making, and possible positions of leadership. (Coaching Association of Canada)

THE COACH AS TEACHER

One of the roles of the coach is that of a teacher of physical skills. To be an effective teacher, the coach must understand the learning and teaching process, and how to observe and analyze skills.

The Learning Process

The common saying "I hear, I see, I do" is the simplest way of describing how people learn. Coaches apply it by explaining and demonstrating a skill, and then having the athletes practice. Generally, athletes learn by gathering information about a skill, making decisions about how to perform the skill, practicing the skill, and evaluating the result or being provided with feedback on how the skill was performed.

How athletes learn a skill has been defined in three categories: motor, cognitive, and affective.

Motor learning involves the acquisition of the skills and techniques involved in the physical performance and is the most visible sign of improvement.

Cognitive learning derives from the acquisition of technical, tactical, and strategy aspects of the sport which is involved in competition with decision making individually a team play.

Affective learning involves attitude, perseverance, ethical behavior, self-esteem, and working with others.

In the learning process, the coach must first assess each player's level of skill. Such factors as age, strength, maturity, and motivation influence the learning capability of the athlete. If the skills you teach are too easy, your athletes may become bored; if the skills are too difficult, the athletes may become frustrated with their lack of success.

Feedback

Feedback is an essential part of the learning process. Some guidelines for giving feedback:

- more effective when immediate rather than delayed
- young athletes respond better to visual feedback, i.e., show how
- older athletes can be responsive to verbal feedback as well as visual
- feedback should be specific rather than general
- feedback should be provided in limited amounts
- feedback should be provided only when the difference between the athlete's performance and the desired results require it. Usually when the performance is more than 75 percent acceptable, feedback can be optional (called bandwidth feedback) (Coaching Association of Canada)
- very frequent feedback does not always promote learning
- feedback during the execution of the skill is least effective
- feedback can be individual or general to be effective

Feedback can be defined as evaluative, prescriptive, and descriptive

Evaluative feedback occurs when the coach assesses the quality of the performance and makes some kind of adjustment to the performance of the skill.

Prescriptive feedback involves telling the athlete how to execute the skill next time.

Descriptive feedback is when the coach describes to the athlete what he or she had just done in the execution of the skill.

Feedback is one of the most important aspects of skill development. Generally feedback should be more often positive than negative, specific more often than general and offer a balance of prescriptive and descriptive methods.

Whole versus Part

A complex skill can be learned more easily when it's broken down into separate parts, but the skill should be seen in its entirety first. To make learning effective, each part should be related to the whole skill. An example of the "part" method would be the teaching of the jump shot in basketball, where the skill is broken down and practiced as the following elements: preparation, release, and follow-through. The progressive part method involves putting parts of the skill into integrated larger blocks of the whole skill.

When the skill requires coordination of timing and speed, the "whole" method should be used; that is, the skill should be practiced with all parts together and in sequence. Generally, it is better to finish up by practicing a skill as a whole.

Chaining

"Chaining" refers to learning and connecting the parts that make up a complex skill. When the athlete is learning a skill, he or she learns to link the various, distinct parts of the skill. "Forward chaining" refers to learning a skill by starting with the beginning segment; "backward chaining" starts at the segment at the end of the skill and works back to the beginning. The links are then joined together and the skill is practiced as a whole. An example of forward chaining in the teaching of the golf swing would be starting with the preparation stage, that is, the back swing, and moving through the forward swing, impact, and follow-through stages. An example of backward chaining would be starting with the lay up shot in basketball and moving back to the approach before the shot.

Shaping

Shaping is a learning method where the learning of the skill takes place gradually. The skill is briefly demonstrated, and then simplified to include only the most important parts. The missing parts are added gradually until the whole skill is learned. Shaping differs from chaining in that, in the former method, the learner may start with any link in the chain, rather than with the beginning or end.

Mental Practice (Imagery)

It has been shown that the mental rehearsal of a skill aids the learning process. In this learning method, mental practice is used in conjunction with physical practice, both just before a skill is to be executed and away from the practice situation. The athlete needs some knowledge of the skill before mental practice can be effective. (See the discussion of imagery in Part 4 for details.)

Massed versus Distributed Practice

The total number of trials or total time for quality practice is more important than whether practice is massed or distributed. Practice of a skill that is distributed over a number of training sessions is believed to be superior to massed practice at one training session. Distributed practice is more effective when the skill to be learned is complex or takes a great deal of physical effort, or when the athlete is young or just beginning. Massed practice can be successful in some situations when used with the highly skilled or mature athletes.

Grouping

Athletes with similar skill levels tend to learn faster when grouped together. Lower-skilled athletes tend to learn faster in a mixed-skill group, while superior athletes prefer to work with, and learn faster while practicing with, the highly skilled.

Environment

A pleasant, clean, well-lit practice environment enhances learning. Positive, well-planned instruction with proper teaching aids and equipment supports the learning process.

Short-Term Memory

Usually an athlete can handle and understand only three or four key teaching points at one time, and this information stays with the learner for between twenty and thirty seconds. Therefore, it is essential for the athlete to practice the skill being taught immediately after the teaching presentation.

Classification of Sport Skills

A sport skill is a movement or series of movements performed with precision with a minimum amount of energy expenditure.

Sport skills are movements involved in (i) a stable and predictable environment or (ii) have a clearly defined start and end point.

Some sports are easy to classify as they have well defined skills while others involve a variety of skills executed under different conditions. Sports in a stable and predictable environment can be classified as closed or open skills.

Closed skills include sports such as archery, diving, shooting, and weight lifting.

Open skills are performed in an environment that is unpredictable such as team, racquet, and combative sports.

Some sports are performed in an environment that is predictable but changing. Sports such as skiing, golf, and cross-country running are examples of these sports and fit between a closed and open skill. Sport skills with a distinct beginning and end point are further classified as discrete, serial, or continuous.

Discrete skills have determined beginning and end points such as throwing and catching a ball, swinging a golf club, or shooting a foul shot in basketball.

Serial skills have a series of discrete actions linked together such as a figure skating or gymnastics routine.

Continuous skills are repeated actions but don't have beginning and end points such as running, cycling, and swimming.

Coaches should realize that athletes go through different phases of skill development and the teaching and refinement of sport skills has a definite progression and in many cases is age related.

Stages of skill development can be classified as:
- Beginner—Initiation and acquisition
- Intermediate—Consolidation
- Advanced—Refinement, creative variations (Coaching Association of Canada)

The Teaching Process

Select the Skill

The first step in the teaching process is to select the skill or skills to be taught. Factors such as the athletes' present skill level, age, physical maturity, and motivation are important in deciding on the skill progression.

The skills taught should not be too easy or too difficult for the athlete. The progression should always be from simple to complex, and you should have a plan for the progression. As much as possible, skills and drills should be gamelike and challenging for the athlete.

Once you've selected the skill, the keys to effective teaching are the explanation, demonstration, practice, and feedback and correction.

Explanation

The explanation should be well planned. Start the explanation with the importance of the skill. Choose three to five key teaching points and use short descriptive phrases to present them. The explanation should not take more than sixty to ninety seconds. Remember, learners have short attention spans and start forgetting as early as thirty seconds after an explanation. Speak clearly and concisely, and use direct eye contact with the athletes.

Demonstration

In most cases, demonstration accompanies explanation of the skill. You must decide from what angle the skill is to be viewed and who will demonstrate it. When demonstration is used with explanation, it may be advantageous to have a highly skilled athlete demonstrate the skill. If the coach does not possess the skill, it can be demonstrated by an athlete or an assistant coach. Some coaches demonstrate skills in slow motion (such as the golf swing) when they do not possess an advanced level of the skill themselves.

Set up the teaching formations so that all the athletes have a good view of you and/or the demonstrator of the skill. No athlete should be behind you when you are talking. Formations such as the semicircle and U-formation are best. You must also make sure that the athletes are viewing the demonstration from the correct angle. If outdoors, make sure the athletes are not looking into the sun or are affected by any other distractions. End the demonstration as the explanation began, with a review of the key teaching points. Include time for questions or clearing up misunderstandings. Take a maximum of three minutes for the explanation and demonstration.

Practice

Practice the skill immediately after the explanation and demonstration. Remember, athletes start forgetting shortly after they have had something explained to them. The practice formation or drill should take into account whether the athletes work alone, in pairs, or in groups.

Practice drills can be simple or complex, depending on the level and skill of the athlete. The specifics of practices and drills will be discussed in Part 2.

Practicing sport skills have three general methods: constant, variable, and random.

Constant practice is used when the same movement is repeated many times, such as throwing a ball.

Variable practice is when the same movement is done repeatedly but the speed of movement is changed. A baseball pitcher using various speed pitches is an example of this.

Random practice occurs by not practicing the same skill consecutively. A soccer player moving sideways quickly and then kicking the ball would be an example of random practice. One repetition of one skill followed by a repetition of another skill is also categorized as random.

Two other methods of practice can be classified as blocked or problem solving (decision training) practice.

Blocked practice involves repeating the same task under the same conditions, which leads to the most rapid improvement and is the traditional method. This type of practice may not be the most stable or maintained over time and should be combined with other methods to prevent boredom.

Problem solving type of practice on the other hand may not be as fast but may lead to superior learning and better transfers the skills to the competition environment where the athlete has to react to different situations.

Feedback and Correction

Give feedback and correction during the practice of the skills. Feedback should be given to individuals and should be provided as the skill is being practiced. Correction should be given to the group to highlight common errors.

Observing and Analyzing Skills

Giving feedback and analyzing skills can be learned and improved on. Knowing what to observe and how to observe requires knowledge, experience, and practice.

To be able to give feedback, you must understand the key phases of a skill. By observing or using videos of a skilled athlete, you can understand what a properly executed skill should look like. Break the skill down into the important phases, and understand the key words for correction (e.g., straighten the stride leg in skating—hip, knee, ankle).

Observing

Make sure you're in the correct position on the practice field or arena to observe, and be sure to circulate, along with assistant coaches, in order to give feedback to as many athletes as possible.

Once again, your feedback should be specific and be given as soon after the skill is practiced as possible. Observing and giving feedback to athletes is a skill you must practice and work on. Being able to understand and pick out common errors is essential for good coaching.

Positive and Negative Feedback

As a general rule, use positive reinforcement approximately 90 percent of the time. If you want a movement or behavior to be repeated, positively reinforce it. If you do not want a movement or behavior repeated, don't reinforce it, or reinforce only the positive aspects of the movement. Negative reinforcement can be used to prevent a movement or behavior being repeated, but should not be used on a regular basis. Athletes learn more, and more quickly, in a positive environment.

COMMUNICATION

Communicating with the athlete is considered by many to be one of the most important aspects of coaching. We often hear of a professional coach being fired because of a lack of communication with the athletes. However, communication is a two-way street, and athletes should realize that they also have a responsibility in the communication process.

Communication skills are something that both coaches and athletes can work and improve on. Communication can be in the form of feedback on a skill the athlete is practicing, a comment on behavior, praise, punishment, or a simple daily greeting. Communication is usually verbal, but can be varied by the tone, volume, and speed at which one speaks. Communication can also come in the form of gestures, both facial and body.

Communication is also improved by being a good listener. Many coaches do not listen enough to what their athletes have to say, and the skill of being a good listener is important in the communication process. Paraphrasing what the athlete has to say from time to time, while listening, is an effective method as it not only shows that the coach is listening, but also that he or she is understanding or trying to understand what is being said.

Here are some suggestions for the coach to be an effective communicator:

1. *Try to speak to each athlete every day.* This may be in the form of a few sentences of feedback on a skill or general play, a simple greeting, or a longer conversation or a meeting. If the team is quite large, as with a football team, ask that the assistant coaches share in the communication with every athlete.

2. *Meet with your athletes on an ongoing basis.* Try to have an in-depth meeting with each athlete every two or three weeks to give feedback on performance and to discuss individual and team problems. One professional coach suggests meeting on a rotational basis with three or four athletes a week.

3. *Give feedback to the athlete daily.* The feedback should be immediate, direct, usually positive. Also, elicit feedback from the athlete as to whether the communication was understood.

4. *Be honest.* Athletes appreciate honesty, and they quickly perceive when coaches are not being honest.

5. *Be tactful.* Although honesty is very important, the coach can be tactful and diplomatic when giving feedback or communicating.

6. *Be positive.* Athletes do not like being around or being coached by negative people. Although negative communication is sometimes necessary, effective coaches are positive in their communication the majority of time.

7. *Learn to be a good listener.* Learn to paraphrase what is being said by the athletes and listen to their suggestions. The athletes also must learn to be good listeners.

8. *Communicate clearly and directly.* Make it clear what you are saying, and communicate directly. Don't use assistant coaches to communicate important decisions that have a direct effect on the athlete, such as not playing or being cut from the team.

9. *Remember that gestures, facial expressions, and so on are a form of communication.* The athlete will react to these forms of communication as well.

10. *Manage confrontations.* Confrontations are a part of the coaching communication. Effective coaches are demanding, and this sometimes leads to confrontations with the athletes. Before confronting, the coach should be under control, be clear on the facts, and show respect and care for the athlete. Also, the confrontation should take place shortly after the problem that led to it. The classic confrontations between athlete and coach, on the bench or sidelines, do occur sometimes in the heat of competition, when emotions are running high, but generally confrontations should be thought out and be held in the coaches' room or another more private setting.

11. *Get feedback from the athletes on communication skills.* As lack of communication is one of the more frequent complaints athletes have about coaches, the coach should get feedback from the athletes to the effectiveness of his or her communication skills.

GOAL SETTING

Along with a sound philosophy, coaches, in conjunction with their athletes, should set reasonable, clear, attainable, and measurable goals. Goal setting can give direction and meaning for both coaches and athletes throughout the long competitive season.

It is important that goal setting be done by both coach and athletes. If the coach's and athletes' goals are not compatible, a conflict exists before training begins. If a coach's goal is excellence and hard training, and the athletes' goal is simply recreation, conflict will develop, as it will when athletes who are striving for excellence and wins have a coach without these goals.

Group goal setting can give all persons involved with the team a stronger commitment to the goals. Goal setting should involve both team and individual expectations, and should be for both the short and the long term. Confusion or misunderstandings related to the goals should be addressed by the team and the coach. Goal setting should be done before the training begins, and any limitations that exist, such as budget and facilities, should be made known to the athletes.

Once the goals have been established, they should be communicated to all persons associated with the organization, including parents and administrators. The goals should be reviewed at regular intervals throughout the competitive season, and adjustments made if the goals set are too high or too low. The coach should meet at regular intervals with both the team as a whole and individual members to discuss progress toward both short- and long-term goals.

Botterill gives some guidelines for setting goals:

How to Set Goals with Your Athletes

1. Plan on your own.
2. Plan to involve your athletes.
3. Consider involving them a bit at a time.
4. Share the limitations of the sport program (e.g., facility availability).
5. Set the right climate.
6. Act as a facilitator, not a dictator.
7. Set specific goals.

8. Strive for consensus.
9. Discuss strategies as well as goals.
10. Record all specific goals and strategies.

Here are the reasons that group goal setting makes sense.

Twelve Payoffs in Using Group Goal Setting

1. Clarified goals and priorities.
2. Increased commitment and motivation.
3. Measurable success.
4. Improved confidence and morale.
5. Psychological maturity.
6. Improved "coping" capabilities.
7. Prevention of problem behaviors.
8. More enjoyable and effective leadership.
9. Appreciation of planning and goal setting.
10. Empathy for the rights of others.
11. Improved communication.
12. Happier athletes, better performance, and more fun.

ETHICAL DECISION MAKING

Coaches find themselves often making decisions on questionable behavior and actions their players make during the course of competitions and/or training sessions. In most cases the decision is related to behavior that requires a decision that affects the individual and/or teammates and possibly has a disciplinary aspect to it. In many cases the coaches' ethical and philosophical values are important in the actions taken when problems arise. Before making a decision the following steps should be taken.

1. Establish the facts: What happened, when did it happen, who was involved, and what did the persons involved say about the situation?
2. Determine whether there are legal or ethical issues involved. Legal actions include criminal action, breach of contract, child protection, and discrimination.
3. Identify options and possible consequences.
4. Evaluate the options.
5. Choose the best option.
6. Implement the decision.

The National Coaching Certification Program of Canada (NCCP) code of ethics is a useful guide to assist coaches in making decisions with teams or individuals.

General areas to consider:
1. Physical safety and health of the athletes.
2. Responsibility of the coach.
3. Integrity in relation to others.
4. Respect for the athletes.
5. Honoring the respect for the sport.

TIME MANAGEMENT

One trait all successful coaches share is that they are highly organized. Studies analyzing effective managers in different professions have shown that the behavior they have in common is effective time management (Douglass & Douglass). Time management is important for all coaches, and is especially important for the volunteer and part-time coach, who works at a profession during the day and coaches in the evening. Planning and prioritizing your goals and the activities that lead to the fulfillment of these goals are an essential component of time management for coaches.

Coaches should be aware of which activities save time and which ones waste time. Time savers include setting specific goals, prioritizing activities, setting deadlines, delegating, and planning. Time wasters include doing nothing, being disorganized, spending too much time on unimportant activities, and working on low-priority activities.

Kozell describes five causes of poor time management: relying on mythical time, underestimating demands on time, task creeping, task hopping, and ignoring reality. "Relying on mythical time" refers to believing that you will have more time later and squandering the time you have without getting on to the task. "Underestimating demands on time" involves not being efficient enough to do what must be accomplished in the time allotted. "Task creeping," which is quite common, refers to failing to complete one task before taking on another. "Task hopping," also common, refers to jumping back and forth from one task to another. "Ignoring reality" is failing to recognize your limitations and taking on too much.

In summary, here are some suggestions for a coach who wants to be a more organized and efficient time manager:

1. Set realistic short- and long-term goals.
2. Prioritize goals.
3. Identify priorities and tasks daily.
4. Set and try to keep deadlines.
5. Develop a yearly, monthly, and weekly training plan.

6. Take time each day to plan each training session.
7. Set aside time each day to communicate with your athletes and handle problems, usually before or after the training session.
8. Set aside time to deal with administrators, alumni, and so on.
9. Set up a monthly training and competition calendar for coaches, athletes, and support staff.
10. Don't waste time on the telephone or on idle conversation.
11. Don't take on more than you can do. Learn to say no. Prioritize.
12. Keep an organized desk and file system.
13. Delegate responsibilities, but supervise and follow up.
14. Have meetings organized and managed efficiently.
15. Set aside time to answer telephone calls.
16. Set aside time during which you are not available.
17. Make sure that others are not wasting your time.
18. Set aside time for daily relaxation and fitness.
19. Don't forget your personal life: Take time for family and friends.

STRESS MANAGEMENT

There are very few professions that have as much stress as coaching, especially at higher levels of competition. The expectations for success from athletes, spectators, parents, media, and so on place extra stress on a coach, as do his or her own personal expectations. No profession is more forthcoming about how you are doing than coaching: the scoreboard, and team and individual performances are evident to all. How the coach handles the various stresses is important both on a personal basis and in terms of his or her relationship with the athletes.

A number of studies have been done using heart-rate measurement to determine stress levels experienced by coaches during training and competitions. Gazes, Sovell, and Dellastatious found, with basketball and football coaches, that an average resting heart rate of 68 beats/minute rose to an average of 132 beats/minute during the games. Kolbenschlag found that one coach had a heart rate of 150 beats/minute just before the game and an average of 166 beats/minute during the game, with a high of 188 beats/minute. Husman, studying basketball coaches, found heart rates rising to 114 beats/minute during training sessions and rising to rates as high as those of the athletes during the contest.

In a study on factors causing stress among coaches, found disrespect from the players as the major cause of stress (47.8 percent); not being able to reach the players (20.7 percent); and lack of appreciation by administrators (14.0 percent) were the other major causes. Disruptive and unmotivated players were also listed as factors. (Kroll)

Many coaches suffer from burnout, as discussed by Wilson, Bird, and Haggerty. The researchers defined burnout as "a progressive loss of one's energy, and one's idealism and purpose in sport, and a growing feeling of being locked into a routine that is no longer exciting or pleasurable." The symptoms and stages of burnout include depersonalization, decreased feelings of personal accomplishment, overinvolvement with or isolation from athletes, and emotional exhaustion to the extent that one can no longer give emotionally to others. Here are some suggestions for preventing or overcoming burnout:

1. Take action to overcome negative feelings. Discuss personal differences and problems in an open manner.
2. Cut back on total contact hours with athletes but make the hours of availability quality ones.
3. Establish a good working relationship with other coaches, even those involved in different sports, to discuss common problems.
4. Learn self-regulation skills, such as relaxation, imagery, positive self-talk, and energizing, and practice these skills the same as the athletes do.
5. Improve your physical fitness.
6. Make time to spend with family or friends and take up an outside interest.
7. Take a break or holiday.
8. Seek professional help if burnout and stress signs persist.

It is important to realize that you must be able to handle stress and problems if you wish to lead your athletes. Bob Johnson, the now deceased former successful ice hockey coach at University of Wisconsin and of the National Hockey League Pittsburgh Penguins, used to say, "If you don't like handling problems, don't get into coaching." It is not the problems and stress that get to coaches, but how they handle them. Some coaches thrive on the challenges of stress and problems, while others are unable to handle these situations.

A strong philosophical base, along with an understanding of the role of leadership, will assist a coach in handling stress. Setbacks and losing put a coach to the ultimate test. How the coach responds to these situations greatly affects the athletes and their view of the coach, themselves, their teammates, and their team.

In handling stress, the coach can use some of the same techniques used by athletes (described in Part 4), such as relaxation, imagery, positive self-talk, thinking, and energizing. Taking time for personal fitness and other interests away from coaching are also important for handling stress. A full personal life, with support from a spouse and/or friends, can also be invaluable for the coach.

The coach must be able to deal with problems quickly and thoroughly and maintain communication with the athletes in order to reduce or alleviate the potential causes of stress.

Some sound advice: Look after yourself first before you look after others. Keep a balanced life. Learn to have fun when doing your job. Look at criticism at its source and learn from it. Remember, stress alone is not the issue, but how you handle it.

Part 2: Team Management

BUILDING AN EFFECTIVE PROGRAM

Some sports organizations have a long tradition of success, while others seem to flounder year after year.

The coach's role in building an effective sports program may range from only coaching to being responsible for the operation of the total program. Coaches in schools and those involved with community sports may be responsible for all aspects of the program, while university, college, club, and professional coaches may have a support staff to assist with the various duties of the sport organization. Coaches, although they often complain that they only want to coach, have to be involved with some, if not all, aspects of administration and management of the organization.

The five main steps for a coach in the building of an effective program are: planning, organizing, staffing, leading, and controlling. Associated with these five steps are the resources and funding needed to operate the sports organization.

Planning

As mentioned previously, all successful coaches seem to be efficient at planning and organizing. Most successful organizations, in both sport and business, include short-term, intermediate, and long-term planning as an integral part of their organization.

Planning involves determining in advance what is to be done, how it is going to be done, and who is going to do it. It involves setting goals and objectives and making day-to-day decisions on how these objectives can be reached.

Quotes on Planning

Those who fail to plan, plan to fail.

Luck is infatuated with the efficient.
—Persian Proverb

Chance favors the prepared mind.
—Pasteur

Proper preparation prevents poor performances.
—U.S. Marines

Plan your work and work your plan.
—U.S. Army

Luck is what happens when preparation meets opportunity.
—Darrel Royal, football coach

The will to win is not nearly as important as the will to prepare to win.
—Bobby Knight, basketball coach

First I will be prepared, then my chance will come.
—Unknown

Developing a training program for the athletes is probably the most important aspect of planning for the coach. The yearly plan is the first step. Once it has been established, all other planning can take place. The weekly and daily training plans are the next essential step. All other aspects of the sport organization—such as competition dates, travel and accommodation, selection of athletes, training camps, publicity, and support staff—must be carefully planned as well.

Planning therefore involves:

1. setting overall objectives;
2. setting specific goals;
3. identifying a course of action;
4. developing standards for evaluation; and
5. developing a process to evaluate.

Organizing

Organization is the next step after the short-, intermediate, and long-term plans are established. Organizing involves the details of the plan: who is going to do what, and what is required to allow the person or persons to carry out the task.

It is important in organizing that all details of what is to be done are listed and clearly defined. Clear responsibilities should be detailed for each person, and their interaction should be explained. The dividing up of various tasks, plus establishing the hierarchy of authority (who is responsible to whom), are essential in any sport organization. The roles of assistant coaches, trainers, support staff, parents, and administrators should be made clear at the beginning, before any organizational task is undertaken. If these organizational details are introduced at the outset, conflicts or misunderstandings may be avoided.

Staffing

Selection of all the people involved in a sport organization is one of, or, in most cases, the most important factor for success. Talented people with good character, a strong work ethic, and an ability to get along with others are the key in successful organizations. The selection of assistant coaches, training staff, support staff, and so on should be done methodically, taking the required time to make informed decisions. Expert planning and organizing will be to no avail if staff have been poorly selected.

Quotes on Staffing

How you select people is more important than how you manage them once they're on the job.
—Red Auerbach, Former general manager, professional basketball

We're probably the most careful hirers of employees that you've ever met. We follow the Carpenter's Rule . . . measure twice and cut once, except we measure about four or five times and hire once.
—Dan Fianne, President, professional basketball

There are certain qualities that you look for in people whether you are on a football team or in business. You look for people who are committed, devoted and doing the best job. Talent isn't going to matter either. I'll take the guy breaking his butt over a guy with talent in a close situation every time. I may get my butt beat a few times, but in the long run, I'll win because I'll have a guy with more character.
—Mike Ditka, Coach, professional football

One enemy can do more damage than the good done by a hundred friends.
—Bill Walsh, Coach, professional football

Leading

Coaches are in leadership positions, but many are not good leaders. To become a good leader requires many skills of the coach other than the knowledge of the technical aspects of the sport.

Leaders provide the direction and the vision of the organization. They create an atmosphere to achieve team goals. Good leaders are able to motivate members of the group to achieve the goals set out by the organization.

Leaders are able to communicate with members of the group. A very important aspect of leadership is being able to confront and solve problems quickly and fairly.

Quotes on Leading

Leaders perform management functions but they also determine the direction for the future, then marshall the resources in the organization to pursue that vision. Too many U.S. corporations are overmanaged and underled. Leadership emphasizes interpersonal relationships and has a direct impact on motivation.
—John Kotter, Harvard Business School professor

The main distinction between leaders and followers is not strength or knowledge, but the will, the zeal to win.
—Vince Lombardi, Coach, professional football

It is amazing how much can be accomplished when no one cares who gets the credit.
—John Wooden, College basketball coach

You don't become a leader because you say you are. It's much more what you do than what you say.
—Sparky Anderson, Manager, professional baseball

Coaches should realize that they are the leaders of their team and work toward improving their leadership skills.

Controlling

A very important aspect in developing an excellent organization is controlling and measuring the performance of individuals and the group as a whole. The setting of achievable goals is the first step in directing individuals and teams. However, without a follow-up measure of how the individual and the team are progressing toward the goals, the goal setting lacks meaning. It is important that the coach continually be measuring progress toward goals. Setting standards, and then observing and evaluating, are methods of controlling.

Any significant deviations from the set standards will require corrective action. By holding regular individual and team meetings, issuing and evaluating questionnaires, and seeking the views of assistant coaches and observers, the coach can evaluate progress toward the objectives and goals of the organization and its members.

Resources

Any successful organization must have the resources to build an effective program. Excellent training and competition facilities are an important step to building a successful sports team. The operating budget for equipment, travel, and accommodation must also be sufficient.

The ability to employ excellent coaches and assistants, as well as a competent support staff, is probably the most important aspect of building a sports organization. Without the resources to hire the best people, an organization cannot be successful.

In an age of austerity and tight money, it may be necessary to raise funds to achieve the resources necessary to run the organization. Fundraising may even be a part of the duties of a coach in maintaining the operation of the sports club or school team. Fundraising is a specific skill and it requires staff and organization support.

Most organizations build their success on the basic principles of planning, organizing, staffing, leading, and controlling.

THE ANNUAL PLAN— PERIODIZATION

Periodization, discussed in more detail in Part 3, allows the coach to plan and train an athlete methodically through a twelve-month period. Periodization allows for the physical and mental part of the athlete's preparation to be planned and organized.

The physical preparation is divided into four main categories: the preparation, pre-competition, competition, and transition periods.

Preparation Period

The preparation period of training is extremely important for the athlete. During this period the athlete must attempt to raise his or her conditioning to as high a level as possible. In most team sports, the conditioning level is not improved appreciably during the competitive season, and a maintenance level is usually the goal.

The first step in the preparation period should be to develop a fitness-assessment profile to measure the athlete's strength, power, flexibility, muscular endurance, agility, fat percentage, and cardiovascular endurance. After the fitness-assessment profile has been done, the athlete can begin the training program.

The preparation period is divided into two periods: general and specific. The general period is devoted to building a solid base of strength and aerobic fitness, along with flexibility. The specific period includes more sport-specific training, along with power, anaerobic, and flexibility training, depending on the nature of the specific sport.

Competitive Period

In the competitive period, the goal should be to improve, or at least maintain, the conditioning level achieved in the preparation period. Flexibility should be done daily, and strength and power workouts should be performed at least once per week. The competitive period may include a pre-competition period of a few weeks, as is common in many team sports. A tapering-off period of usually one week to ten days before the final competition or the playoffs is common in team sports.

Transition Period

The transition period is a time when the athlete recuperates from the long competitive period. Rest and relaxation, along with general fitness and participation in other sports, usually characterize this period. It is, however, a period where general fitness should be maintained, with shorter general fitness workouts. An example of a winter team-sport periodization annual plan is shown in figure 2.1.

MAY	JUNE	JULY	AUG.	SEPT.	OCT.	NOV.	DEC.	JAN.	FEB.	MAR.	APRIL
Preparation				Pre-competition	Competition				Ta-per	Playoffs	Transition
General		Specific									

Figure 2.1: Winter-sport periodization annual plan

Monthly, Weekly Plans

An important organizational tool for the coach is the monthly and weekly schedule. The monthly schedule can be of a general nature with practice times, travel, days off and so on as shown in figure 2.2. This type of schedule allows the coach to be flexible in the content of the practices and is ideal for team sports such as basketball and ice hockey where training is adapted weekly and daily to the various situations (i.e. more work on defence, offense, or on recent weaknesses). The schedule shown in figure 2.3 is an exact three weeks of training for sprinting in track. These practices are outlined in detail for the entire three weeks. This type of planning is common in individual sports such as track and field and swimming. Figure 2.4 is an example of a schedule for the team sport of volleyball and illustrates the general planning for the week. Some coaches distribute the weekly plan to the athletes while others prefer to distribute the schedule to the coaches only.

ICE HOCKEY
JANUARY

Monday	Tuesday	Wednesday	Thursday	Friday	Saturday	Sunday
		1 OFF New Year's Day	2 Practice 4–6 pm	3 Practice 4–6 pm	4 Moscow Dynamo @ York 2:00 pm @ Ice Gardens 12:30 pm	5 OFF
6 Practice Dryland 4–6 pm	7 Practice 4–6 pm	8 Practice 4–6 pm	9 Waterloo @ York 7:30 pm @ Ice Gardens 6:00 pm	10 Practice 4–6 pm	11 York @ Laurier 2:00 pm Depart 11 am	12 OFF
13 Practice Dryland 4–6 pm	14 Practice 4–6 pm	15 Practice 4–6 pm Depart for Sudbury 6:30 pm	16 York @ Laurentian 7:30 pm	17 Practice 4–6 pm	18 Laurentian @ York 5 pm @ Ice Gardens 3:30 pm	19 OFF
20 Practice Dryland 4–6 pm	21 Practice 4–6 pm	22 Practice 4–6 pm OUAA All-Star Game @ York Ice Gardens 7:30 pm	23 York @ Guelph 7:30 pm Depart 4 pm	24 Practice 4–6 pm	25 York @ Toronto 7:30 pm @ Varsity 6 pm	26 OFF
27 Practice Dryland 4–6 pm	28 Practice 4–6 pm	29 Practice 4–6 pm	30 Practice 4–6 pm	31 Queen's @ York 7:30 pm @ Ice Gardens 6 pm		

Figure 2.2: General monthly plan for ice hockey (Wise, G.)

	Monday	Tuesday	Wednesday	Thursday	Friday	Saturday	Sunday
Week I	WARM-UP POWER SPEED DRILLS, 3 X 30 X 2 (FROM BLOCKS) 2X60 2X80 1X150 (3-5 MIN. BETWEEN REPS, 10 MIN. BETWEEN SETS) WEIGHTS	WARM-UP TEMPO (75%) 100+100+100 100+200+200+100 100+200+100+100 100+100+100 +=50m JOG WALK 200m BETWEEN SETS MEDICINE BALL	WARM-UP POWER SPEED DRILLS, SPECIAL ENDURANCE 5X110M, 10 MIN. REST BETWEEN REPS WEIGHTS	WARM-UP TEMPO 80% 5 X 300 (WALK 100m BETWEEN REPS) 5X2100m (WALK 100m BETWEEN REPS) CIRCUIT	OFF OR WARM-UP	MINOR COMPETITION 100m & 200m	OFF MASSAGE
Week II	WARM-UP TEMPO (75%) 300⎫ 200⎬ X 3 100⎭ WALK 100m BETWEEN REPS WALK 200m BETWEEN SETS MEDICINE BALL	WARM-UP SPECIAL ENDURANCE 250m 200m 150m ALL OUT FULL RECOVERY WEIGHTS	WARM-UP RECOVERY EASY TEMPO ON GRASS 3X80mX6	WARM-UP POWER SPEED DRILLS STARTS TECHNIQUE WEIGHTS	WARM-UP 3X150m@90%X 2 SETS 5 MIN. BETWEEN REPS, 20 MIN. BETWEEN SETS	WARM-UP LIGHT CIRCUIT OR OFF	OFF
Week III	WARM-UP POWER SPEED DRILLS FROM BLOCKS ON CURVE 2X30 2X50 2X80 1X100	WEIGHTS (POWER)	TRAVEL DAY OFF OR LIGHT WARM-UP	CANADIAN CHAMPIONSHIPS — COMPETITION WARM-UP 3-4X20mSTARTS MASSAGE	100m (1 OR 2 ROUNDS)	100m SEMI-FINAL 100m FINAL	200m HEAT

Figure 2.3: Three-week plan for 100 and 200 meter sprints (Wise, S.)

VOLLEYBALL PRACTICE

WEEK OF OCTOBER 7
OUTLINE

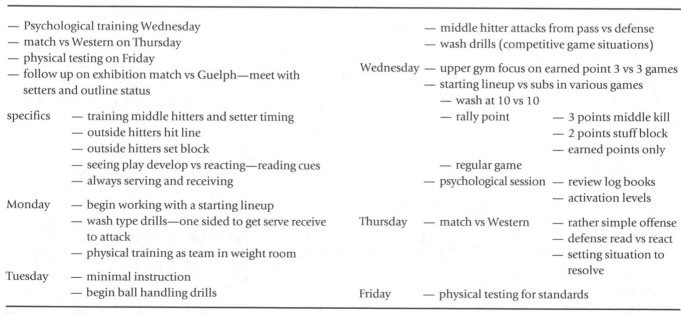

— Psychological training Wednesday
— match vs Western on Thursday
— physical testing on Friday
— follow up on exhibition match vs Guelph—meet with setters and outline status

specifics
— training middle hitters and setter timing
— outside hitters hit line
— outside hitters set block
— seeing play develop vs reacting—reading cues
— always serving and receiving

Monday
— begin working with a starting lineup
— wash type drills—one sided to get serve receive to attack
— physical training as team in weight room

Tuesday
— minimal instruction
— begin ball handling drills

— middle hitter attacks from pass vs defense
— wash drills (competitive game situations)

Wednesday
— upper gym focus on earned point 3 vs 3 games
— starting lineup vs subs in various games
  — wash at 10 vs 10
  — rally point   — 3 points middle kill
                       — 2 points stuff block
                       — earned points only
  — regular game
— psychological session   — review log books
                               — activation levels

Thursday
— match vs Western   — rather simple offense
                          — defense read vs react
                          — setting situation to resolve

Friday
— physical testing for standards

Figure 2.4: Men's volleyball practice outline for one week (Dyba)

PLANNING THE PRACTICE

One day of practice is like one day of clean living, it doesn't do any good.

If I don't practice for one day I know it.
If I don't practice for two days, the critics know it.
If I don't practice for three days, everyone knows it.
    —Ignace Paderewski, famous Polish pianist

How you practice is how you play.

Perfect practice makes perfect.

The game is an opportunity to see the results of your teaching.

The adages quoted above have been around for many years, but they emphasize the importance of practice in the development of an athlete. The improvement of individual skills, tactics, strategy, mental preparation, and conditioning are related to the practice situation. Running effective drills and practices is one of the most important aspects of coaching. Planning the season; the monthly, weekly, and daily practices; and the effective use and progression of drills are intricate parts of the coaching responsibility. Game day, as many coaches comment, is only the result of all the hard work, preparation, and dedication of athletes and coaches.

The individual practice is one part of the total plan. The development of individual skills (technical), as well as team play and systems (tactical) and conditioning, should be part of each practice. In addition, in team sports, the coach can address the strategy part of the game in practice. As well as having a set plan for each practice, consider weaknesses you have observed in previous practices and games.

Plan the practice according to your philosophy of teaching as it relates to the amount of activity and flow. Also consider the skill and physical development level of the athletes and confirm that the equipment and facilities are in proper order to ensure the safety of the players.

Make skill or technical development a part of most practices. A skill-progression and other suitable drills should be part of the plan; vary the drills that teach the same skill to prevent boredom. Systems and team play should be part of the tactical development of the practice for team sports. Make sure that systems fit the athletes' age and skill level, and progress from the simple to the more complex.

Include some physical preparation (conditioning) in each practice. Take into account the conditioning effect of each skill drill and team drill when you design the practice. Consider such factors as energy systems, strength, and flexibility.

Don't forget the mental aspect of practice. Include as part of the general plan tactics and strategy discussed and practiced during the training period.

Evaluate each practice after it has been completed and use this information to plan the next. Although you should plan for the whole year, your daily and weekly planning must be flexible enough to accommodate day-to-day changes and to adjust to the strengths and weaknesses of the athletes and the team.

Designing an Effective Practice

1. Set the goals and objective of the practice. Inform the assistant coaches and players of what you are trying to accomplish.
2. Plan a general progression through the practice from individual skills to team play.
3. Arrive early, be available.
4. Project a good mood, use idle chatter to create a feeling of ease at the beginning of the practice.
5. Teach new skills and drills early in the practice.
6. Keep all the players active in the practice.
7. Give clear, concise instructions throughout the practice, and be in command.
8. Use effective teaching formations, and make sure you have the attention of all athletes when you are speaking to them.
9. Explain and demonstrate skills and drills clearly. Have the players perform the drills immediately after your explanation.
10. Be concise, keeping explanations from thirty to ninety seconds.
11. Keep your assistant coaches informed and use them effectively. Keep them active in all drills, and make them part of everything you do.
12. Keep the players active, and use all the training surface. You may wish to use the full training area for team drills and use different parts of the training surface for individual-skill drills.
13. Observe, evaluate, and give feedback throughout the practice. Assistant coaches should be involved in this process as well.
14. Keep drills effective, competitive, active, and challenging.
15. Be positive and upbeat. Greet the athletes, using their first names, before practice or at the start of practice. Use voice communication throughout the practice at the proper times. Early in the practice, use voice communication more frequently to get the players going and establish a good rapport.

16. Include a warm-up and cool-down in each practice. The warm-up should include stretching, and the cool-down should follow the reverse order of the warm-up.
17. Use mass stretching and/or a fun warm-up drill to get the team together and ready for the main part of the practice.
18. Include a fun drill in most practices.
19. Stop the drills when a common error or lack of effort is apparent.
20. Choose drills for their conditioning features or use a conditioning drill or drills at the end of practice.
21. Speak to players as a group at the end of practice. Discuss the practice, upcoming games, general information, and so on.
22. If time permits, have certain players work on specific skills with the assistant coaches after practice.
23. If possible, after practice provide an area for additional strength, anaerobic, and aerobic conditioning.
24. Conduct individual meetings with players before or after practice, if time permits.
25. Meet with assistant coaches, and possibly the captains, to discuss and evaluate the practice and plan for the next practice or game.
26. Demand excellence. Repeat a drill until the players get it right.

DESIGNING EFFECTIVE DRILLS

The development, designing, and implementing of effective drills is a key ingredient of coaching. How the athletes relate to the coach in many ways determines how the drills and practices are implemented. The coach's knowledge, planning, and communication skills are very evident in the training sessions. As noted above, how you practice is how you play. Effective, well-run drills are the essence of training.

Here are some guidelines for coaches in developing drills:

1. The drill should have a specific purpose and meet the objectives you have set for the practice.
2. The drill should be suitable to the age, skill level, and physical maturity (i.e., strength, size) of the athletes.
3. The drills should be applicable to the skills used in the game. A drill that does not relate to the skills used in the game and does not serve any purpose is meaningless to both the athlete and the coach.

4. Drills should follow a progression, moving from the simple to the more complex. Build on previous drills, and develop a progression of drills for each skill taught.
5. Maximum participation of all the players should be an objective of every drill. All players should be involved in the drills, and the number of trials should be at the maximum, with only an adequate pause for recovery between trials or repetitions.
6. Drills should challenge the skill level of the athletes. If drills are too easy, the athletes will become bored quickly. Conversely, if the drills are too difficult, the athletes will become frustrated with lack of success.
7. Explain the drill clearly and demonstrate it before the athletes practice it. Your explanation should be clear, concise, and, with the demonstration, should take less than three minutes.
8. Explain new drills in the dressing room or on the playing field, using a chalkboard or other erasable board. New drills may have to be demonstrated on the playing area as well, especially if the drill is complex. In general, younger athletes need both an explanation and a demonstration, whereas older, higher-skilled athletes may need only a verbal explanation.
9. Drills should be varied and innovative. Your training program should include a series of drills and a number of different ways of accomplishing the same purpose. Always be aware of new drills, and be innovative in designing drills. With older, mature athletes, you may wish to combine a number of skills and purposes in one drill.
10. Drills should be undertaken at a tempo that simulates the action in the game. High-intensity practices are more enjoyable for the athletes and carry over into the game situation. Teams that practice at high tempo play at high tempo. However, a drill that introduces a complex skill, and thus must be broken down into parts, should be practiced initially at a slower speed, until the skill is perfected.
11. It might seem obvious, but the drills should be done correctly. After you give a clear explanation and demonstration, you have the responsibility to see that the drill is done correctly. If the execution is not correct, stop the drill and emphasize the correct method.
12. The athletes should work with intensity in every drill. Inform the players of the intensity and work ethic required, and remind them that it is their responsibility and yours to ensure that this work intensity is evident in all drills.

13. It is your responsibility as coach to give effective and constructive feedback during and after a drill. The feedback can be general, provided to all the players, and/or specific, directed to certain players. Athletes need to know how they are doing, and only with effective feedback can they correct the errors in their execution of a skill or drill. A complete understanding of the skills and the ability to observe and analyze are areas that all coaches must work on to become more proficient.

14. As much as possible, introduce competition into drills. Any time a race, a battle, or a winner is involved in a drill, the participants' interest and intensity levels are raised. As much as possible, you should try to equalize the competition when there is a large discrepancy in the skill level, size, and strength of the players.

15. Remain flexible in the development and running of drills. Some drills may be too complicated and have to be changed; other drills may not work with certain age groups. Stop drills or improvise when drills are not working.

16. Drills should run for the ideal amount of time—generally, they should last not more than eight to 10 minutes, and not less than three minutes. Coaches should not allow a drill to be overly long. On the other hand, a drill that is too short will not allow enough repetitions for each player. The timing of a drill is a skill that develops with your experience and close observation of the intensity with which the athletes perform the drill.

17. Drills should flow from one to another, with a minimum of time between them. A sequence of drills built on a progressional flow makes an effective practice. A well-planned drill progression gives an overall flow to the practice.

18. The whole training surface should be used for most drills. The ideal drill involves all players and uses the complete area. In some situations, the players may be split into groups, executing different drills on different sections of the training surface.

19. If drills are planned correctly and executed at high tempo, and a proper work-to-rest ratio is used, a conditioning effect should take place. Incorporate into each drill the number of repetitions along with the appropriate rest period for best results.

20. Drills should be enjoyable. Well-planned drills will allow the athletes to enjoy a practice. Make specific fun drills part of every practice.

21. Each drill should be evaluated after each practice. Did the drill accomplish its objective? Was the drill too difficult or too easy? Was the drill too long or too short? Was the drill executed properly? Did all players understand the drill? Were the players motivated throughout the drill? Were there noticeable improvements in the skill level?

22. Use drills that will improve areas of weakness observed during a previous game or practice. A certain drill may be more effective after a weakness was shown in a game. For example, a defensive drill may be necessary at the practice after a game in which there was poor defensive execution.

23. Overall, effective drills should show improvement in individual skills and team play. Teams play as they practice. Individuals and teams should be evaluated on improvement, and effective, properly executed drills should make this improvement possible.

DAILY PRACTICE PLAN		
Practice Number _____	Date _____	
Time	**Drill Name** (Key Points)	**Drill Diagram**
Announcements:		
Notes/Evaluation:		

Figure 2.5: Daily Practice Plan

It is important that the coach vary the drills and practice routine for the athletes over the competitive season. In team sports, practices may be of different types, including offensive, defensive, skill, and fun. The length of the training is also important. Practices lasting longer than ninety minutes tend to drag for the athletes, and learning decreases. Some days a short intense practice of thirty or forty minutes is effective. Competition-type drills, and at least one fun drill per session, add interest. Change the location of the practice, or play a different sport at practice for variety once or twice a year. It is important to have as much activity as possible during the practice. Practices should be a combination of learning, work, and fun. An example of a daily practice plan is shown in figure 2.5.

USE OF VIDEO/DVD

"Pictures paint a thousand words—greatest teaching device in our game if not overused. Players love to watch themselves doing great things."
—Mike Babcock, Coach, Detroit Red Wings, National Hockey League

Most coaches make use of the video in almost all sports if the technology and the time to use the technology are available. The video allows the coach to analyze both individual and team performance and is used in both training and competition situations. It is also effective to analyze top performers and in team sports to analyze the opposition. Visual aids also allow the athlete to better understand their performance and the sport they play. In certain situations videos can be used as a motivational tool to pump up the athlete and the team.

When choosing software the following should be considered:
- cost
- how easy to download and install software
- are commands easy (play, pause, rewind, fast-forward)
- can you rip a DVD or do you need to capture it from a DVD player
- can you sort clips and organize them easily
- can you easily adjust the start/end of clips
- can you add images to the presentation or incorporate PowerPoint
- can you create movies easily
- does it have a telestrator feature
- can you easily display through TV or through projector
- can you upload clips to web (Cooper)

Considerations When Presenting

"A video presentation should be long enough to leisurely drink a cup of coffee."
—Anonymous professional athlete

"His video sessions were so long that if you asked me at the end of it what I learned I wouldn't be able to tell you anything."
—Anonymous Olympic team player about an anonymous head coach.

The amount of video the coaches can watch can be endless if the coach desires. However, athletes in a team session have a limited attention span and a ten to fifteen minute session should be maximum with probably two to three minutes of actual video being shown. Individual video sessions one to one also have to be limited but countless hours may be spent preparing and analyzing the video. In most cases the video should be as positive as possible depending on the situation. A good rule normally is not to embarrass an individual in front of the group and use a one-on-one situation for correction. There are, however, situations where group correction from lack of effort or repeated team errors can be shown.

The video session should be well prepared and the equipment and video should be set up and run through 30 minutes before the session. Meetings should be timed properly depending on the situation before or after training. Periodically humor can be added to the session with funny clips. The number of video sessions per week depends on the coach, sport, and time in the training or competitive season. Many coaches prepare their athletes in team sports with a video/DVD sessions of the opposition and their tendencies.

There are very few sports where video/DVD cannot aid in individual and team preparation and improvement of performances. Money to buy the equipment and the time available to the coach and athletes is a determining factor on how extensive video sessions can be used. For professional and full-time coaches video is essential. For part-time and amateur coaches time available and motivation are key factors but all athletes and teams can benefit from this aspect of coaching.

EMERGENCY ACTION PLAN

Coaches should have a well-defined plan when an emergency situation arises in a training session. Most sport organizations have emergency plans for competitions but the coach should check to make sure that each competition is covered for accidents and emergencies, e.g., first aid, medical personnel available.

The following are guidelines for an Emergency Action Plan:

1. Assess the injured person
   (i) breathing
   (ii) pulse
   (iii) bleeding
   (iv) consciousness
   (v) injury to back, neck, or head—cannot move arms and/or legs
   (vi) visible trauma
2. Access to a telephone, cell phone, pay phone
3. Emergency phone numbers should be available
4. Directions for medical services to reach the site as quickly as possible
5. First-aid kit available
6. In advance, an emergency call person

RETURN TO ACTIVE TRAINING AND COMPETITION

The most important factor for an athlete to return to training and/or competition is medical clearance by a doctor. The athlete must also feel that they are psychologically ready to return first to training and then to competition. Return to training and competition from minor injuries should be determined by:

1. no swelling or deformity
2. no pain through a range of motion
3. full range of motion
4. no continued bleeding

Head injuries and concussions are becoming more prevalent in many sports due to the speed and size of athletes in competitions. No athlete should return to competition or training after being struck heavily to the head unless a doctor has given permission. In almost all cases the athlete should not continue in a training or competition after a severe blow to the head.

TALENT IDENTIFICATION

Predicting Future Performance

Identifying talent is one of the most important jobs of the coach. Whether a coach or scout is selecting from a number of athletes trying out for a team or evaluating athletes for the future, he or she must be able to identify not only current skill, but also future potential.

A highly skilled athlete is usually easy to spot, as are the poorly skilled. The expertise in talent identification comes from being able to identify present and future potential in the middle group, which usually comprises more than half of the athletes observed.

Talent identification is directly associated with predicting the future performance of an athlete. Performance is generally thought of as a factor of three variables: ability, attitude, and opportunity, as shown in figure 2.6. Ability relates to talent, which is both inherent (inherited) and trainable.

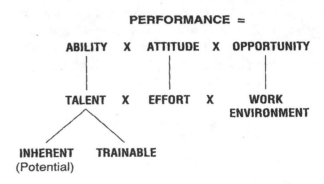

Figure 2.6: Predicting-performance equation

Talent

Heredity is very important in determining the potential to develop strength, speed (percentage of fast-twitch fibers), power, flexibility, cardiovascular endurance, and so on. Talent can also be developed through training, but the athlete must possess the physical attributes to be successful in the particular sport.

The former Eastern European countries selected athletes for their physical characteristics, and then selectively trained them for the sport they were most suited for, using the best coaches. These countries had established certain physical criteria for each sport and trained athletes selected on the basis of these criteria. Most coaches today also predetermine the physical characteristics they will look for in athletes for their sport. Coaches must always be aware that there are exceptions in physical traits, such as in sports where size is important, but a smaller, quicker player may also be successful.

Along with having the requisite physical characteristics, the athlete must be in good health. Awareness of a medical history of past illness and injuries is important when selecting athletes. A thorough medical examination, including vision testing, is essential to determine whether an athlete is able to undertake an intensive training program.

Physiological testing is quite common in the selection process in competitive sports today (see Part 3 for details). Measuring of strength, power, speed, and flexibility, along with aerobic and anaerobic endurance, can give a coach a profile of the athlete's physical suitability for a specific sport. Sport-specific tests, such as sprinting speed, and various skill tests are also used in the selection process. Talent is always the first and most important factor in the selection of athletes.

Character

The more experience a coach has, the more he or she realizes that the character of the athlete is a key component of individual and team success. Coaches, naturally, are looking for positive character traits, along with physical attributes and skill. Positive character traits include work ethic, self-motivation, competitiveness, ability to get along with others, coachability, and team orientation. Among the methods used to identify these traits in an athlete are observation, gathering of background information, and psychological assessment.

Observation of an athlete can be done during competition and training sessions. Basically, the observer, who is primarily looking at physical talent, also looks for evidence of the positive character traits noted above. This subjective evaluation can be augmented with discussion with others, including the athlete's current coach.

Background information includes a list of the teams and coaches for whom an athlete has played. Information about the athlete's character can be obtained from previous coaches, teachers, teammates, opponents, and others who have observed the athlete. It is important to gather a number of opinions, as some people may be biased for or against the athlete.

Assessment by a trained psychologist can be done via a written questionnaire or an interview. The AMI (Athletic Motivation Index), TAIS (Test of Attentional and Interpersonal Style), Catell 16 PF (personality factors), and MMI (Minnesota Multiphasic Index) are a few of the psychological profiles used.

The Sport Profile (Marshall & Chambers) has been used by a number of professional and amateur teams in North America to assess character. The Sport Profile is designed to provide a statistically validated, objective assessment of an athlete's character traits and personality. This gives coaches, recruiters, parents, and organizational management a comprehensive insight into an athlete's performance, beyond measurable skills and talent.

The profile includes ten attributes that are valued as useful yardsticks in measuring an athlete's potential for success in sport:

1. *Competitiveness* is the athlete's will to win and how hard he or she will strive for victory in competition. A strong competitive nature helps an athlete compete successfully.

2. *External versus internal motivation* describes the degree to which the athlete is motivated by external considerations such as the coach, the crowd, or peer group, and by internal considerations such as feelings about success and competence. Internally motivated athletes are less likely to need "pep talks" or coaxing.

3. *Motivation by challenge* looks at the relative importance of the factors challenge, recognition, and comfort. This scale will allow the coach to determine if the athlete is achieving his or her maximum potential and what motivational strategies might be required.

4. *Self-confidence* assesses the athlete's feelings of control and the degree of impact that he or she can have upon situations and circumstances. This helps the coach in understanding if the athlete will tend to be self-critical or blame performance on outside circumstances. It also provides the coach with some insight as to how much time or effort will be needed to address this issue with the athlete.

5. *Effort* provides a view of the potential of the athlete to work hard. This will give the coach insight into strategies to help the athlete work harder or more consistently in practices or competitions.

6. *Team orientation* is a way of looking at an athlete's relationship to a team environment. Those with a tendency to be dependent upon the team for structure will also be viewed as cooperative and loyal, while those who tend to be more independent will be viewed as more self-reliant and may seek more freedom from rules and regulations.

7. *Leadership* assesses whether the athlete has the right mix of independence, motivation, and people skills to be a team leader.

8. *Self-management* is a measure of the athlete's ability to manage his or her own athletic training program, to develop goals, to self-evaluate, and to reinforce his or her performance. Athletes with high self-management skills can be given more freedom of action by team management.

9. *Handling pressure* is a look at the athlete's performance in stressful situations. Some athletes enjoy pressure, and even thrive on it, while others may find that their performance is hindered by it.

10. *Toughmindedness* is a very important attribute which measures the ability to handle conflict, criticism, and tough situations. Toughmindedness is very important for success at higher levels of competition.

A typical athletic profile for a top athlete is shown in figure 2.7.

In conjunction with the Sport Profile, four types of athletes are described, as shown in the effort grid developed by Marshall in figure 2.8 (Chambers). This model is also applied to the business world.

The "Golden Eagles" are athletes who work hard and are highly talented. Coaches are fortunate to have these persons on their team as they lead by example and usually inspire others.

The "Effort Eagles" are those who have less talent but work hard all the time. Coaches usually like these individuals, and they make up a good portion of teams.

"Talent Trap" applies to those athletes who have talent but do not work hard. These athletes are usually problems for coaches. Marshall advises that these athletes must be prepared to meet a minimum standard of work ethic (the admission ticket) as established by the coach, or they should not be on the team. Coaches who allow these athletes to work less hard than the others and not meet the required standard are asking for problems. This lack of effort will usually cause dissension within a team.

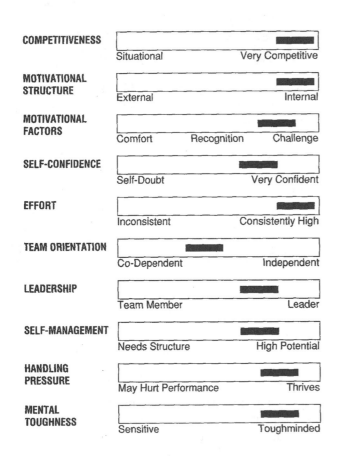

Figure 2.7: Athletic character profile for a top prospective athlete (Marshall & Chambers)

EFFORT

		GOOD	POOR
TALENT	**GOOD**	GOLDEN EAGLES	TALENT TRAP (Floater)
	POOR	EFFORT EAGLES	MIRACLE TRAP

ADMISSION TICKET

Figure 2.8: The effort grid

The "Miracle Trap" athlete is one who does not have talent and does not work hard. These athletes are very seldom selected for teams.

Coaches usually agree that the best type of athlete is the one who self-manages. The self-managed athlete is personally motivated to succeed and works hard to achieve his or her goals. This type of athlete prepares physically and mentally for competition, and works hard every day to achieve. Athletes can learn to self-manage, and coaches should help them do so and should reinforce this type of behavior. However, coaches should be spending their valuable time coaching instead of coaxing. For that reason, the character aspect of talent identification is important in the selection process.

Opportunity

Although talent and character are considered to be the key factors in the identification and development of an athlete, opportunity and an environment conducive to development are also necessary.

Some athletes develop later than others, and the classic example of a top athlete not being selected at an early age is basketball superstar Michael Jordan, who was not selected for a high school basketball team at age fourteen. Athletes need to be able to compete and develop their skills, and some potentially outstanding athletes may not be selected and, as a result, may not develop their skills.

Facilities also play a key role in the opportunity for an athlete to develop. Most athletes try to be involved in programs that have good training facilities. Poorer countries that lack playing fields, indoor gymnasiums and ice rinks, swimming pools, fitness facilities, and so on are at a disadvantage in the training of athletes, as is often evident at the national and international levels.

Climate is also an important factor. Nordic sports such as downhill and cross-country skiing, ice hockey, and figure skating are dominated by athletes from the colder countries such as Scandinavia, northern U.S., Canada, and Russia, while the warm-weather sports such as baseball, soccer, and field hockey are dominated by athletes from more temperate climates. The growing number of indoor facilities, such as tennis and ice arenas, and large indoor fieldhouses, are assisting athletes who train for warm-weather sports in the colder countries.

The availability of coaching specialists in the particular sport is also a key factor in the opportunity for the athlete to develop. Knowledgeable coaches with good leadership abilities are very important in the development of the athletes. Experienced coaches develop more athletes, and consequently athletes tend to gravitate to top coaches with the best programs. It is not uncommon for athletes to move to areas where the top coaches are available, especially in non-team sports such as gymnastics, swimming, and figure skating. The coaching an athlete has received is also a factor in the selection process.

The important point to remember in the identification and selection of athletes is that talent alone is not the determining factor in athletic success. The top athletes possess a high internal motivation and work ethic to succeed and must be in the proper situation to develop. Remember: Hard work beats talent unless talent works.

The Final Selection—Informing the Athletes

The task of informing the athletes who have made the team and those who have not is always a difficult one. Some coaches post lists of those athletes selected to play. It is recommended, however, that coaches inform the unsuccessful candidates personally, during a short interview. At this time the coach can point out the strengths and weaknesses of the athlete. The coach should emphasize the different ways the athlete can improve his or her skills, and should avoid becoming involved in a dispute with the athlete. In some cases, the coach may have to explain to the parents why the athlete was not selected. All such discussions are easier when the evaluation procedure has been as objective and thorough as possible, and should be held promptly and in a direct, honest, fair, compassionate, and positive manner.

TEAM BUILDING AND TEAM COHESION

Positive leadership and good character among team members are key factors in developing a team concept. Although selecting athletes with positive character and leadership qualities is essential, the coach also has a very important role to play in team building. The team concept can be applied to both individual and team sports. At a presentation by one of the most successful gymnastics coaches in North America, I was amazed to hear how much of his time was spent on developing team cohesion with his athletes, even though gymnastics is considered to be an individual sport.

It is important to realize that not all successful teams have ideal team cohesion. The Oakland As and the New York Yankee baseball teams of the 1970s had well-publicized player–manager feuds, yet still went on to win World Championships. Mikalachki distinguishes between groups that have a high level of task cohesion and those that have a high level of social cohesion. Teams with strong task cohesion can have less social cohesion and still be successful. Task cohesion focuses on getting the job done in the competition by cooperating and working with teammates, with less emphasis on extra-competition social relationships. The ideal situation, however, is for the team to have high levels of both task and social cohesion, and this is something the coach should strive for.

Team building and team cohesion develop a feeling of commitment and trust among the team members and improve communication within the group. They also help to clarify the team goals and promote acceptance of team rules.

Team building can be achieved through team meetings, practices, activities, travel, and extensive use of videos in game preparation. Through these various activities, individuals within the group get to know and understand one another better.

Here are some suggestions for improving team cohesion and building team concept:

1. Involve all team members in goal setting and encourage the team to take pride in achieving the goals.
2. Involve all team members in setting the team rules.
3. Treat all athletes fairly but with a firm hand.
4. Make it clear, to individuals and to the team, what roles different athletes have, and their relative importance to the team.

5. Try to communicate with each athlete daily.
6. Don't spend too much time with the best athletes or the problem athletes. Make each athlete feel important to the team.
7. Make decisions clearly, quickly, and fairly, and explain the decisions to the team and to the individual members.
8. Try to give all players a role in each competition. Make every athlete feel important.
9. Deal with problems immediately.
10. Rely on team leaders to assist in creating team cohesion and team building.
11. Stress the team approach in everything you do and say. Sell your message.
12. Use motivational videos, catch phrases, mottoes, music, posters, T-shirts with logos, and so on to reinforce the team-unity message.
13. Arrange for group activities outside of practice and competitions, including team get-togethers and parties.
14. Consider having the group perform some team-building tasks that encourage leadership, cooperation, group decision making, and so on. Examples of team-building tasks include:
    — *The Minefield:* Group members, who are blindfolded, follow instructions from a selected leader in order to complete the task of walking through a mock minefield.
    — *The Bucket:* Team members, lying on their backs with their feet raised, try to lower a bucket of water to the ground without spilling any.

For more details on these team-building tasks, refer to material by Rohnke, and Scannel and Newstrom.

Finally, Phil Jackson, former coach in the National Basketball Association, and coach of the NBA champion Chicago Bulls and Los Angeles Lakers, has some excellent suggestions for team building and developing team cohesion:

1. Formulate a vision for the team.
2. Create a team in which selflessness is the primary driving force.
3. Create a team identity.
4. Find a structure that will empower everybody on the team and allow the players to grow as individuals as they surrender themselves to group effort.
5. Try to keep everybody's mind focused on the same goal.
6. Constantly try to figure out ways to get the players to strengthen their commitment.
7. Humor can be effective.
8. Back off and just listen sometimes.
9. Before a vision can become reality, it must be owned by every member of the group.
10. At the core of the vision is to get the players to think more for themselves—be creative.
11. Open up the decision-making process to everybody.
12. Try to cultivate everybody's leadership abilities, to make the players and coaches feel they have a seat at the table.
13. Lead by pull instead of push.
14. Meet with the players privately to help keep in touch with who they are.
15. Learn to listen to the players—not just what they say, but also to their body language and their silence between words.
16. Do the unpredictable once in a while to keep the players from getting stale.
17. Be patient. There is no percentage to push the river or speed up the harvest.

HANDLING PROBLEMS

Dealing with problems is a large part of the coach's role. Whenever people are working together in an intense situation, such as in sport or business, problems among participants or with the leader are bound to arise. How the coach handles the problems will go a long way in determining the respect the athletes have for him or her. The athletes may also be involved in problem solving, with team leaders and captains playing an active role.

Problems on teams seem to arise in some or all of the following areas:

1. *Lateness.* Team guidelines should be set for dealing with lateness for practices, games, buses, team meetings, and so on. Penalties such as extra work after practice, fines (so much a minute of lateness), sitting out the next game, and, finally, removal from the team with repeated offenses are some of the problem-solving methods. The coach is in a vulnerable position if the athletes are allowed to be late for team activities. If guidelines are set, they should be enforced. The coach should make sure that he or she has all the facts for the reason of the lateness before acting. A car breaking down, sickness, and the like are legitimate reasons. A good communication system should be set up, such as phoning the coach or manager or another teammate if a lateness problem arises. It is a good practice to tell the other

athletes on the team why an athlete is late, and the penalty, if any, for the lateness. Some teams have the leaders or captains look after the discipline for these problems.

2. *Conduct detrimental to the team.* This can range from missing a curfew, drug- or alcohol-related problems, negative interaction with fans or media, or any action that is an embarrassment to the sport organization. It is important for the coach and the athletes to decide before the training begins what type of conduct is expected from the athletes. Once again, all the facts must be known before acting, but the coach and the team should have guidelines in place for what is expected from the athletes and the consequences of undesirable behavior. Consequences usually range from a reprimand to expulsion from the team, depending on the severity of the problem. Each year, it seems, some athletes miss major events because of curfew violations or are removed from the team for conduct detrimental to the organization. Some athletes may need professional help for extreme problems, such as drug use, and this should be considered as part of the solution in certain situations. Selecting athletes with good character goes a long way in solving problems before they happen.

3. *Work ethic.* Certain athletes do not work hard in practices or games. This can be even more of a problem when the top athletes do not have a good work ethic. The coach must act on this if he or she wants to retain or gain the respect of the athletes. Establishing a certain work level that is expected from the athletes early in the training is a possible solution to the problem. If the work level is not reached, then the coach must act. Solutions range from talking to the athlete one-on-one, stopping training and pointing out the problem, extra work for the athlete in question, or, ultimately, suspension from the team. The coach must act if there is a poor work ethic by an individual or a team. If not, the situation will get worse, and the coach will be seen as weak. Athletes should know what level of work ethic is expected. Once again, if your top athletes work the hardest at training, the other athletes will usually follow their example. However, if the star athletes do not work hard, problems usually arise with the overall work ethic of the team.

4. *Interpersonal problems among athletes or with the coach.* Very seldom does a group of people working together get along with few or no problems. Certainly, in the case of sport situations, where competition is intense and emotions are high, there will be some interpersonal problems. The coach should be alert to these problems, and the coach also can be assisted by the team leaders and/or captains. Problems should be dealt with as quickly as possible after they appear. Usually athletes have the common goal of performing well, and sometimes interpersonal problems can be tolerated because of this. Communication is, once again, the key with athlete–coach problems and should be looked after as quickly as possible.

Each year that a coach is involved with a group of athletes, new problems seem to arise. The coach should have a definite philosophy as to what he or she expects, and this philosophy will go a long way toward solving problems. The coach should discuss this philosophy with the athletes at the beginning of the training season. It may be in extreme situations that certain athletes, no matter how talented, are not meant to work for certain coaches or certain organizations. If this is the case, then it may be better for both parties to part ways. However, most problems can be solved through effective communication; selection of athletes of good character; guidelines for expected behavior; and quick, firm, but fair responses to problems. Remember professional and college hockey coach Bob Johnson's words: "If you don't want problems, don't get into coaching." The effectiveness of the coach in many ways is determined by how he or she deals with and solves the many problems which arise in the day-to-day running of a sport team.

PUBLICITY, PROMOTION, PUBLIC RELATIONS

The publicity the sport organization or team receives goes a long way in not only publicizing events, but also developing a name and tradition for the organization. Sport, and the reporting of it, is a part of our daily lives. The sports pages in the daily newspaper, and television and radio reporting, all inform the public about what is happening. Professional and college sport in the United States dominates the sports media, but each small town or suburb of a large city usually has some form of media to cover the sports scene. It is important for a good sport team or organization to have some form of publicity for the athletes. Not only does it keep the public informed about upcoming events, but, in many cases, such visibility in the community draws athletes to the organization.

Here are some methods of gaining publicity for your organization:

1. Send press releases to all members of the media to supply information about upcoming events. They should also present interesting items about the athletes, such as records broken and human-interest stories. Keep the items brief and to the point.
2. Issue a media guide that contains facts and statistics about each athlete, team and individual pictures, past history, statistics, prospects for the upcoming season, telephone and fax numbers for team contact for publicity, and so on.
3. Schedule a media day for before the season starts, inviting the media to interview players and coaches.
4. Provide press passes for all the media personnel.
5. The coach should be available at a certain time after games and practices for interviews. Establish a set time, such as ten minutes after games and twenty minutes after practices.
6. Posters with a clear, simple message about special events and upcoming matches or the home schedule should be placed in prominent places.
7. Pocket schedule cards are an excellent method for promoting the team to the public. A shorter version of the media guide, with the schedule and some player details, in brochure format, is another method.
8. Each home event should have a program outlining details of the game and visiting athletes, history and statistics of the team, prospects for the year, and so on. Local sponsors can advertise to help defray the costs of the program, and/or the program can be sold for a nominal fee.
9. Pep rallies and special events can be organized before matches to promote the sport.
10. Special announcements on the public-address system in schools, or a loudspeaker installed on a car, can be used to supply information to the public about upcoming events.
11. Regular reporting to the media of sport scores and game highlights is important for a good ongoing relationship. Reporting only wins and/or reporting sporadically is not recommended.
12. Use draws, special prizes, fun contests, and special pre-game, intermission and post-game entertainment to encourage people to come to games.
13. Encourage the athletes to take time for the media.

In any dealings with the media, the coach should be patient and courteous, although this sometimes can be difficult, especially in a losing situation when tough questions are asked. Encourage your athletes to do the same. Coaches and athletes usually don't win battles with the media. The media should also respect the coach's and athletes' time and privacy, and arrange specific times for interviews.

Remember, when the coach is speaking to the media, the words are usually going to be repeated in print, on television, or on radio. In many cases, only excerpts of what the coach says is going to be used. Remember that the athletes will read or listen to what the coach says. Don't speak to the media without thinking when you are angry or upset. Some coaches use the media to get a message across to their athletes. But be careful before you criticize one of your athletes in public. Know your athletes well enough to predict the outcome of this technique.

In speaking to the media about opposing athletes, teams, or coaches, praising, or saying nothing, is preferable to making inflammatory statements. Opposing coaches and athletes are known to post any such inflammatory comments in the print media in the dressing room to help motivate their team. Don't give them the opportunity.

Bear Bryant, the famous football coach at the University of Alabama, once said, "There are just three things I ever say to the media. If anything goes bad, then I did it. If anything goes semi-good, then we did it. If anything goes real good, then you [the athletes] did it. That's all it takes to get people to win football games for you." (Lyons)

FUNDRAISING

In today's tight financial climate, coaches and sport organizations are continually having to raise funds to augment their regular budget.

Here are some methods for raising additional funds:

1. Selling advertisements to be included in programs, brochures, schedule cards, and so on.
2. Selling advertisement for score clocks, boards of ice arenas, and walls of gymnasiums or any other playing facility.
3. Special fundraising events such as bingos, casino nights, roasts, special dinners, and auctions.
4. Selling chocolate bars, candies, cookies, and so on door to door.
5. Approaching equipment and sport-apparel companies for free products.
6. Approaching companies for sponsorship of the team or an athlete, or to give a special award.
7. Charging athletes a fee for participation.
8. Approaching a car dealership for use of vans for transportation, with their advertising on the vehicles.

9. Hosting a run, jog-a-thon, swim-a-thon, or a special sporting event such as a masters' or corporate track meet.
10. Setting up concession stands at special community or school events.
11. Selling T-shirts, caps, bumper stickers, mugs, and jackets.
12. Organizing alumni dinners, golf tournaments, and special alumni nights at games. Keep in touch with alumni with regular mailouts, and get alumni members to help raise funds for the team.
13. Organizing car washes, garage sales, pancake breakfasts, and so on.
14. Acting as ushers at games and special events. Cleaning facilities after games and special events.
15. Be innovative. Get ideas from athletes, parents, sponsors, and so on for other methods of raising funds.

PARENTS

Coaches should be very aware that the support of the parents of the athletes is very important in the successful operation of the organization.

In most cases, parents are supportive of the athletic endeavors of their children. In most sports involving younger children, the athletes would not be able to compete without financial assistance from their parents, which can range from a small participation fee, to hundreds of dollars for equipment, to thousands of dollars for training and coaching.

In many cases, parents are involved in the transportation of younger athletes to both training and competition and may devote many hours per week to this responsibility.

Parents may be only slightly involved in the sport organization, or they may be heavily involved, serving as executives, administrators, or coaches. Some parents become overly involved and may have an effect on the operation of a team and the role the coach plays. It is important to realize that the parents entrust their children to the coach and expect the coaching job to be done properly. Parents, on the other hand, should realize that the coach has a job to do and that they can help the organization in many ways but should support the coach and not interfere with his or her role.

With this in mind, it is very important for the coach to communicate with the parents. One of the best methods is to have a meeting with the parents before the training for the competitive season begins.

Here are some of the items to be included in this meeting:

1. State the objectives of the program. Outline the structure of the organization.
2. Discuss your coaching philosophy.
3. Introduce assistant coaches, administrators, support staff, and so on.
4. Introduce parents to one another.
5. Outline team rules, procedures, regulations, and so on.
6. Outline expenditures for which the parents are responsible (equipment, entry fees, and so on).
7. Discuss the medical procedure for the diagnosing and treatment of injuries.
8. Outline what is expected from the athletes and the parents.
9. Distribute the practice and competition schedule.
10. Outline areas where the parents can assist and be involved such as transportation, statistics, banquets, and social events.
11. Outline areas where the parents are not usually involved such as coaching decisions and practice planning.
12. Discuss behavior of parents at competitions and training.
13. Establish clear lines of communication between the coach and the parents. If a problem arises with their child, the parents should be contacted as soon as possible. Likewise, the parents should feel that they can come to the coach with problems related to their child.
14. Include a question-and-answer period.

If the coach communicates with the parents and involves them in a constructive manner, the parents can have a very positive effect on any sport organization. Remember, as a coach you are entrusted with the most important treasure parents have—their children.

LEGAL LIABILITY

Coaches must be aware of their responsibility in cases where sport or sport-related injuries lead to litigation against the coach and the sport organization. Some legal terms such as tort, omission, commission, negligence, and contributory negligence should be familiar to coaches.

A *tort* is a legal wrong resulting in a direct or indirect injury to another individual or to property. Torts can be committed through omission or commission, *omission* referring to a failure to perform a legal duty, and *commission* referring to an unlawful act such as assault. The coach's legal duties include not only those imposed by law but also to prevent injuries to others.

In many court cases, where someone is charged with *negligence*, the implication is that that person has not fulfilled his or her legal duty or has failed to act in a commonsense or prudent manner (Baley & Mathews). Negligence is the omission of something a reasonable person would do or the commission of something a reasonable or prudent person would not do (Black).

Athletes who participate voluntarily do accept that there is some risk involved in their sport. *Contributory negligence* is a factor where the injured party may have contributed to causing his or her injury.

Other areas for litigation involve defective or ineffective equipment, and violation of the rights of the individual.

Finally, there are four factors a coach should consider when dealing with the risk possibilities in the sport and the legal implications that can arise from this risk.

1. There is a risk inherent in most sports and they may be of a minor nature. Each sport has various levels of risk and the coach should be aware of the level in the particular sport.
2. The coach should take measures to reduce the risk in planning, supervising, and teaching the skills to the athlete.
3. If the risk is significant this risk should be transferred to others with contracts, waivers, and insurance.
4. If the risk is severe the coach should eliminate anything that may cause this risk in training or competition. (Coaching Association of Canada)

This is a complex topic area for coaches, and is very important. Here are some specific guidelines for coaches, which, if followed, can better prepare them against the possibility of a lawsuit if any injury occurs:

1. Provide safe playing facilities.
2. Allow only good-quality, properly fitted and maintained equipment. In some cases equipment must be certified as meeting a certain minimum standard.
3. Have a system (in writing) for the identifying, treatment, reporting, and recording of injuries. Consult a lawyer and/or your sport organization for advice on this.
4. Make sure participants have the proper health care and medical coverage.
5. Have a doctor and/or a paramedic at athletic contests if possible.
6. Plan a proper sequence of instruction. Move from

simple to more complex skills only when the athletes have mastered the previous one. In drills, match your athletes according to age, size, and skill level to prevent a mismatch, especially in body-contact sports.
7. Ensure that conditioning methods are up to date and based on sound scientific principles.
8. Supervise all activities.
9. Ensure that the facility, teaching formation, and drill activities do not present hazards for the participants.
10. Make sure that all activities follow the rules of the sport.
11. Ensure that all transportation for the team is with approved, insured carriers.
12. Keep up to date with the research on teaching methods, equipment, and so on.
13. Keep a written record of all practice and training plans.
14. Never jeopardize the safety of the athlete.
15. Treat the athlete with respect and fairness, regardless of race, religion, gender, age, and so on.

ASSISTANT COACHES

Very few head coaches work alone. In most cases at least one and as many as ten assistant coaches (football) may be involved in the coaching of a sports team. The success of a sports team can often be determined by the team of coaches and the ability of the head coach to manage successfully the work of his or her assistant coaches.

Selection

The selection of an assistant coach is a very important process. A poor decision at this stage can cause a head coach nothing but grief and may lead to the coaches parting ways and the team being divided.

Here are some qualities to look for in an assistant coach:

1. Similar philosophy as the head coach.
2. Teaching ability.
3. Knowledge of the sport.
4. Work ethic.
5. Athletic background.
6. Enthusiasm.
7. Ability to work and get along with others.
8. Organization.
9. Loyalty.
10. Ability to be flexible.
11. No behavioral, alcohol, or drug problems.
12. Ability to accept a role subordinate to that of the head coach.

13. Strengths in certain area to complement those of the head coach.
14. A personality that mixes well with that of the head coach, whether similar or opposite and complementary (quiet versus outgoing, etc.).

Management of Assistant Coaches

How the assistant coaches work with the head coach and with each other can be influenced by the head coach. The head coach must realize that assistant coaches need to feel they are an integral part of the coaching team and need to be given specific responsibilities in training and competitions. Assistant coaches should be part of the training and competition planning and be included in the decision-making process and feel they have importance. If they disagree with the head coach, they must be able to express their feelings, but never in front of the athletes. Any disagreements on fundamentals, strategy, and so on should be discussed privately, and a united opinion should always be presented to the athletes. The head coach is the final decision maker and the main spokesperson in dealing with the athletes, the media, and the public. The assistant coaches must feel comfortable with this line of authority and always support the head coach to the athletes, other coaches, media, parents, and so on. The ability to handle the assistant coaches effectively is an important aspect of becoming a successful head coach.

AWARDS

Most sports organizations have some type of award system. Some coaches are strong advocates of individual awards; others believe only in team awards. Awards generally should be motivators, and should be meaningful.

Here are some examples of awards:

1. Letters, sweaters, jackets, medals for team participation.
2. Naming a player of the week or month.
3. Decals, logos, stars, and so on for outstanding performance. This is common in football, where performance awards are placed on the helmets.
4. Awards for most valuable, most improved, best sportsmanship, best academic and athletic performance, hardest worker, best leadership, best rookie.
5. Forming all-star teams.

Most organizations have some type of awards night or banquet at the end of the season. At this occasion, athletes are recognized for their accomplishments and, in many cases, video or slide presentations of a review of the year are included. A relatively short speech from a prominent athlete, coach, or community leader can be part of the awards banquet. If possible, try to limit the awards banquet to two hours.

TEAM RULES

One of the most important roles a coach has is managing the athletes throughout the training and competitive season. Problems arise on all teams, and one of the measures of the coach is how he or she handles these problems. To aid the coach, most teams have some basic rules of conduct and operation. Rules range from very few unwritten ones to a long list of formal written ones. The philosophy of the coach will go a long way in determining how the rules are set up and, in most cases, the athletes are involved in formulating the rules.

Once rules have been established, their enforcement becomes a very important role of the coach or, in some cases, the captains of teams or a committee of athletes.

Before rules are set for a team, there must be agreement among the athletes and a general agreement between the coach and athletes that the rules are fair and enforceable, as are the penalties for breaking the rules. It should also be made clear that the rules apply to all athletes. Coaches should get all the facts before imposing punishment for breaking a rule, and punishments should be administered quickly and fairly.

Coaches should realize that every organization needs some code of conduct and rules of operation. If the athletes know what is expected of them, there will be fewer problems.

Here are some areas for discussion of team rules:

1. Being on time for practices and competition. Being at the training or competition site a certain amount of time before starting (e.g., 30 minutes).
2. Attendance at practices and games.
3. Behavior with officials.
4. Behavior and dress when traveling.
5. Curfews before competition.
6. Behavior during practice and games.
7. Language.
8. Use of alcohol, drugs, and so on.

Many coaches have four rules: (1) Be on time; (2) Work hard; (3) Treat your teammates and coaches with respect; (4) Conduct yourself personally in a manner that will never be detrimental to the team or the organization. Remember, if you have rules, you must enforce them. The coach will lose the respect of the athletes if rules are not enforced, especially if the coach allows exceptions. The more rules you have, however, the more time and effort is spent policing them.

SELECTING CAPTAINS

Does the coach select the captains or do the athletes vote for a captain? It is sometimes advisable to use a combination of the two methods, where the athletes vote for candidates for captain and the coaches make the final selection from among these candidates. It is important that both the athletes and the coaches respect the final decision of the captain or captains of the team.

Here are some of the suggested duties of a captain:

1. To discuss athletes' concerns and problems with the coach.
2. To be a leader in competition, practice, and the dressing room.
3. To assist in solving conflicts among players and between the coach and athletes.
4. To follow all team rules, and confront players who do not.
5. To help organize official and unofficial team functions.
6. To represent the athletes at team functions receiving team awards, thanking people, and so on.
7. To demonstrate sportsmanship, work hard, and support the coach and organization.

COACHING ADMINISTRATIVE TASKS

The coach has many functions to perform. As well as those tasks related to competitions and the training for them, the coach has many administrative tasks, most of which are common to all sports. These administrative tasks can be divided into three categories: (1) pre-season management; (2) in-season management; and (3) post-season management.

The pre-season administrative tasks relate specifically to the preparation for the competitive season, usually one month prior to the beginning of training. In-season tasks include all administrative goals that need to be accomplished during the competitive period. Post-season tasks include all things that must be done to complete the competitive season and prepare for the following season.

Pre-Season Management

Here is a checklist of areas that need to be addressed before the season begins:

- Meet with assistant coaches
- Meet with support staff
- Develop yearly training plan
- Training and competition facilities
- Equipment and supplies
- Meet with athletes
- Meet with parents
- Publicity
- Funding
- Team handbook
- Training camp
- Medicals
- Physical and skill testing
- Meet with media
- Awards
- Eligibility

Meeting with Assistant Coaches

Regular meetings may be held throughout the off-season with the coaching staff. One month before the training camp and selection process, the coaches should meet to plan for the upcoming season.

Here are some of the items to be discussed at these meetings:

1. Preview the organization and coaching philosophy and goals for the team and individuals.
2. Develop the yearly, monthly, and weekly training plan.
3. Plan for the upcoming training camp.
4. Have a clear list of responsibilities for each coach and to whom each is responsible.
5. Review schedule, practice times, travel, and accommodations.
6. Review contest-management details and organize for officials.
7. Plan for the first team meeting.
8. Review team rules.
9. Develop or review and update the team or organization handbook.
10. Review budget and possible limitations.
11. Review and update on new equipment, uniforms, and so on.
12. Evaluate and discuss each individual athlete coming to the training camp.
13. Review and update on the eligibility of each athlete, if applicable.

14. Communicate with each athlete through letters, telephone, and meetings. Responsibilities for this can be divided among the coaches.

Meeting with Support Staff

The support staff includes all persons connected with the team other than the coaches and management—that is, sport therapists (trainers), equipment managers, doctors, student or assistant managers, team statisticians, and so on.

The responsibilities of each position should be made clear and, in most cases, a written job description should be supplied.

The procedure, reporting, treatment, and follow-up for all injuries should be reviewed and discussed with the doctors, sport therapists, and coaches. Written job descriptions can also be of value to determine the interaction of all those responsible for injury treatment.

Meetings with Administrators and/or Finance Managers

The coach should meet with administrators and finance personnel to discuss budget, schedule, facilities, travel, publicity, equipment, eligibility, and so on. As well, any more general problems should be discussed. The coach may wish to update the administrators on any important items, and generally on the prospects for the upcoming season.

This type of meeting, which presents a good opportunity for liaison between the coach and administrators, should be held at regular intervals throughout the year.

Publicity

A press conference or a press release is important as the training camp approaches. Information on all the athletes can be developed as part of a media package. The announcement of dates and times of workouts, outstanding newcomers and returnees, and so on should also be part of the information given to the media. Coaches and some players should be available for media interviews in advance of the opening of training camp.

Facilities and Equipment

A doublecheck of the training times and the condition of the training facility should be done by the coaches at this time.

The equipment should be inspected to see if repair and cleaning has been finished. All new equipment and uniforms should have arrived at least three weeks prior to training camp, and a follow-up to the supplier should be done immediately if some items have not arrived.

Schedule, Transportation, Accommodation

All regular and exhibition contests or meets should be confirmed at this time. Letters should be sent confirming starting times, availability of practice facilities, and any other pertinent information regarding competition. Transportation and accommodation should also be confirmed at this time.

Funding

Sources of funding should be confirmed. Fundraising activities should be organized and under way. Shortfalls, if any, in the budget should be calculated, and methods devised to meet them.

Training Camp

Here are the details that should be addressed when organizing a training camp:

1. Facility, training times.
2. Initial meeting with athletes.
3. Medicals.
4. Physical testing.
5. Reporting of injuries.
6. Athletes' schedule.
7. Coaches' schedule.
8. Accommodation, meals.
9. Valuables.
10. Phone calls.
11. Rules.
12. Media.
13. Parents.
14. Letter informing athletes re: schedule, equipment, apparel.
15. Officials for team scrimmages, if applicable.
16. Organization and duties of the support staff.
17. Organization of evaluators.

Initial Meeting with Athletes

Here are some items that should be addressed in the initial meeting with the athletes:

1. Introduction of coaches and staff.
2. Basic philosophy and goals of the organization.
3. Background and successes of the organization.
4. Method of selection.
5. Eligibility.
6. Background information sheet (age, height, weight, addresses, telephone number, past athletic experience, statistics, awards, etc.).
7. Schedule of training camp.
8. Schedule of competitions and regular training times.

9. Introduction of athletes, if relatively small numbers.
10. General questions.

In-Season Management

Here is a checklist of areas that need to be addressed during the season:

- Planning the year
- Practice planning
- Development of drills
- Contest management
- Equipment
- Schedules, transportation
- Scouting
- Recruiting

Planning the Year

You should have a master plan for the entire year. The general areas of planning include the preparation, competitive, and transition periods throughout the year. (See the annual plan periodization, above, discussed earlier in Part 2 and again in more detail in Part 3.)

During the various training periods, give consideration to the development of technical (skill), tactical (team play, physical conditioning), and psychological (mental) training programs. Part 3 of this book deals with the technical, tactical, and physical preparation.

Include in your planning monthly, weekly, and daily practice programs for the different macrocycles (training periods). Important factors to consider are practice-to-game ratio and total amount of training time. See the discussion of planning the practice and designing effective drills, above, for more details on daily planning.

Contest Management

In some situations the coach has very little to do with contest management, whereas in others the coach may have the major responsibility. A well-run athletic competition reflects positively on the organization, the administrators, and the coach. An athletic contest can be organized into general preparation, game day, contest, and post-contest management. Consulting a coaching checklist for all these areas is the best method to make sure that no detail has been overlooked:

GENERAL PREPARATION

1. Facility
   — reserved, including warm-up and preparation time
   — inside facility cleaned, including playing surface and seating area, nets, goals
   — outside facility ready, including lines, playing surface, nets, goals
2. Game and minor officials
   — league or team responsibility
   — dates, game times, map, dressing room, parking, amount and method of payment
   — game and minor officials, such as scorekeepers, announcers, goal judges
3. Equipment
   — new or in excellent condition (depends on the sport: some sports such as gymnastics and track require large amounts of well-maintained equipment)
4. Tickets, ticket takers, ushers
   — printing of tickets
   — distribution, collection, and seating
5. Crowd control
   — usually at least one or two uniformed police or security for smaller crowds: large crowds require many security or police
6. Visiting team
   — letter of confirmation of dates, times, dressing-room, warm-up times, pre-game ceremonies, halftime ceremonies, map, uniform color, visitors' bench; supply of towels, soft drinks, and so on; medical care
   — met by designated person to show where to go and help with any problems
7. Publicity
   — press releases week of the contest
   — programs: visiting team names, numbers, additional information
   — posters, pocket-size schedules
8. Medical care
   — arrange for doctor, sports therapist
   — ambulance at game in some cases, e.g., football
9. Concessions
   — ordering food, drinks, and so on
   — staffing
10. Pre-game, intermission, and during-game activities
    — national anthem
    — bands, demonstrations, lucky draws, contests (e.g., shoot baskets, shoot at hole in board for hockey)
    — music during play stoppages
    — cheerleaders

GAME-DAY PREPARATIONS

1. Facility
   — playing surface cleaned and marked, and in good condition
   — seating prepared and cleaned
2. Equipment
   — cleaned and checked
   — loudspeaker, scoreboard in working order
   — lighting checked
3. Officials
   — designated dressing room
   — score sheets, game sheets, and so on for minor officials
4. Visiting team
   — someone to greet the team and show them dressing rooms, places to eat, game and warm-up facilities
   — provision of details such as benches, national anthem time, and so on
5. Team meeting
   — usually done the day of or the day before the contest
6. Media
   — media passes for entry to the contest
   — tickets and special seating
   — room for food and drink (provide free of charge if possible)
7. Special events and ceremonies
   — doublecheck times with participants in special events and ceremonies
8. Vendor, ushers, security
   — should have a special meeting time to be at their assigned areas, usually one hour before the contest begins
9. Medical personnel
   — should arrive at least forty-five minutes before the contest begins as injuries can occur during warm-up
10. Visiting fans
    — in some cases it is advisable to have a designated seating area

AWAY CONTESTS

1. Transportation
   — bus arrival time should be doublechecked two or three days before departure time
2. Itinerary
   — athletes should given an itinerary, showing departure times, game and warm-up times, hotel and telephone number (if overnight), meal times, departure time, and so on
3. Punctuality
   — athletes should be ready for departure fifteen minutes before designated time
4. Attire
   — appropriate attire should be decided upon

DURING THE CONTEST

The coach should focus only on coaching directly before and during the contest. All administrative duties should be delegated to other people. The coach must be prepared fully for both the tactical decisions and the handling of the athletes. The coach is responsible for appropriate behavior toward officials and other coaches, teams, and fans, both personal and from the athletes.

The coach should mentally prepare for all the types of decisions and options that can occur during a contest, including substitutes for injured athletes or those performing poorly, and change in strategy if winning or losing (team sports).

Assistant coaches, support personnel, team managers, and so on should all be assigned their specific roles during the contest, and the roles and line of decision making should be made clear.

POST-CONTEST

1. Visiting team
   — coaches usually shake hands and have a short conversation
   — keys, towels, and so on should be picked up by the home team personnel
   — medical personnel should check to see if there are any injuries to be attended to
   — home-team personnel should attend to any needs of the visiting team until they depart
   — in some cases, guarantees are paid directly to the visiting coach or manager
2. Officials
   — officials should be paid immediately after the contest
   — in some cases, officials may be rated on their game performance
   — officials should be supplied with towels and so on, and these should be picked up by the team manager
   — in some sports it is customary for the coach to thank the officials after a contest
3. Home team
   — some coaches hold team meetings to discuss the contest; others prefer to wait until the next training session to discuss the contest

— usually the head and assistant coaches meet to assess the performance of the athletes

4. Media
   — Time should be set aside for the coach to meet with the media. Scheduling this meeting time for about ten minutes after the game is finished allows the coach to have a few words with the team first. In some higher levels of competition, a formal press conference is held with both coaches in attendance.

   It is important for the coach to remember to be as patient as possible with the media. The coach should remember that the comments made are going to be heard or read by the public and the athletes, and careful thought should be given to what effects these comments will have. Win or lose, the coach should always be accommodating to the media.

5. Facility and equipment
   — appropriate arrangements should be made for the cleaning of the facility
   — equipment used in the contest should be stored and accounted for

6. Accounting
   — immediate accounting should be taken for all revenue from tickets, programs, concessions, and so on, and a financial statement should be prepared

7. Security
   — security must be involved in the post-contest crowd control for at least thirty minutes after the contest

8. Payment of ushers, security, and so on
   — the normal procedure is for all personnel involved in the running of the contest to be paid directly after the contest at designated time and place

Equipment

It is important that the coach and the support staff keep close control of equipment during the season. One person should have the responsibility for overseeing the use and care of the equipment. Equipment must be properly maintained, and each athlete must be responsible for all personal equipment. A record should be kept of all equipment issued, and broken equipment should be reported. Equipment should be properly marked, and a written record should be kept of equipment assigned to each athlete.

Schedules, Transportation

All home and away competition times and transportation should be doublechecked one week before competition by telephone or fax.

Recruiting, Scouting

Scouting for the upcoming competition should be done by the head or assistant coaches. Some scouting can be done with videotapes of games, but most is done by having someone observe. More than one observer and some type of sport-specific scouting form to be filled out are methods often used for scouting the opposition.

Recruiting is a very important part of coaching in some sports. Coaches usually recruit one year in advance. It is important for a sport organization to have criteria for selection which should be similar to the criteria discussed above, under "Talent Identification."

It is important to build a network of persons for recruiting.

The recruiting of athletes can be done by:

1. assistant coaches,
2. former athletes,
3. alumni,
4. parents, or
5. teachers.

It is important for the head coach to make all persons involved with recruiting familiar with league rules and regulations for recruiting.

It is helpful for recruiters to have a brochure or some written material on the organization to hand out. Recruiters should be honest with the athlete, and take care not to make promises or commitments that they cannot keep.

Post-Season Management

Here is a checklist of areas that need to be addressed at the end of the season:

- Evaluation—program, athletes, coaching
- Meetings with individual athletes
- Off-season training
- Team meeting
- Banquet, awards
- Equipment
- Facilities
- Budget
- Scheduling

When the competitive season concludes, an evaluation should take place of the various components, including the overall program, the athletes, and the coaching. The goals and objectives of the competitive season should be reviewed with the athletes, coaches, and administrators.

Program Evaluation

The athletes, coaches, and administrative personnel should all be involved in evaluating the overall program. All aspects, including facilities, equipment, travel, medical care, promotion, and publicity, should be evaluated, and suggestions should be solicited from all those involved.

Athlete Evaluation

The coaches should meet after the season is completed and evaluate the performance of each athlete. This can be done subjectively and objectively, and should be based on the ongoing evaluation undertaken during the competitive season. The goals and objectives of both the athlete and the coach should be reviewed. The coaches should meet with each athlete for this review, and should include positive suggestions for methods of improvement for the next competitive season. The coaches should encourage the athlete to evaluate his or her own performance for the season. Evaluation forms can be useful in this process.

Coaching Evaluation

Coaches can be evaluated by the administrators, fellow coaches, and the athletes, and in this way obtain valuable feedback and suggestions. Suggestions can be oral, or an evaluation form can be used.

Athletes may be reluctant to offer oral opinions on their coaches, especially if the comments may be viewed as negative. For this reason, it may be wise to use an evaluation form (see figure 2.9), where the athlete's comments are anonymous. In many cases, administrators will hold a meeting with the coach to discuss the performance of the team and evaluate the coaching.

In most cases, evaluations should be ongoing. Thus, the evaluations undertaken at the end of the competitive season should be a final report on cumulative appraisals throughout the competitive season. Areas such as training methods, design of practices, and handling of athletes should be evaluated at this time.

Sport: _____   Coaches: _____

Please answer all questions on the rating scale indicated.
Rating Scale

Not Applicable		Very Poor Inadequate Low		Extremely Good Excellent High	
0	1	2	3	4	5

Figure 2.9: Coach and program evaluation questionnaire

Athlete Information and Self-Evaluation

Rating

1. What percentage of practices did you attend during the season?
   5   greater than 80%
   4   greater than 50%
   3   less than 50%
   2   _____
   1   _____   _____
2. What *year of competition* are you in?
   5   5th year
   4   4th year
   3   3rd year
   2   2nd year
   1   1st year   _____
3. Rate your performance ability relative to teammates'   _____
4. Rate your personal performance (attitude, enthusiasm, practice/training habits)   _____

Evaluation of the Program

1. Rate the appropriateness of times, length, and number of practices   _____
2. Rate the organization and administration of travel, accommodations, and so on   _____
3. Rate the organization and administration of home games, including publicity and staff   _____
4. Rate the length of season and number of competitions for your sport   _____
5. Rate your satisfaction with the facilities and equipment related to your sport   _____
6. Rate your satisfaction with support services, including control-room staff, equipment personnel, and team manager   _____

7. Rate your satisfaction with medical and sport therapy services, including personnel, training room, injury treatment _____

8. Rate your knowledge of, and agreement with:

	Knowledge	Agreement
a) the philosophy of the program	_____	_____
b) the team rules	_____	_____
c) team goals and objectives	_____	_____

9. Everything considered, what is your rating of your sports program? _____

Comments on Program

_____
_____
_____
_____
_____
_____

Off-Season Training

1. Are you required to train in the off-season for the team?   Yes   No
2. Are you required to attend formal practices in the off-season?   Yes   No
3. Rate appropriateness of times, length, and number of practices   _____
4. What percentage of practices did you attend during the off-season?
   5   greater than 80%   _____
   4   greater than 50%   _____
   3   less than 50%   _____
5. Is enough attention given to off-season training in order to maintain competitiveness in the league competition?   Yes   No

Evaluation of the Coaches

1. Technical knowledge of the sport   _____
2. Organization and preparation for practices/competitions   _____
3. Effectiveness in teaching skills of the sport   _____
4. Ability to stimulate enthusiasm and develop team cohesiveness   _____
5. Ability to develop mutual team and individual goals and objectives   _____
6. Rate the coaches' concern for the athlete as an individual (personal, academic, athletic)   _____
7. Everything considered, overall rating of coaches   _____

Comments on Coaching

_____
_____
_____
_____
_____

In your opinion how has the organization assisted the team to achieve its objectives?

_____
_____
_____
_____
_____
_____
_____

Team Meeting

A final team meeting gives the coaches an opportunity to speak to all athletes and provide some thoughts on the season. Some of the topics which can be discussed at a final team meeting are:

1. Summary of the season—positive and negative.
2. Review of the goals and objectives.
3. Recognition of departing or graduating athletes.
4. Return of equipment and the policy for the use of equipment in the off-season (if applicable).
5. Recognition of departing coaches and staff.
6. Prospects for next season.
7. Changes in training, facility, schedule, and so on for next season.
8. Off-season training program.
9. Off-season social and special events, such as team get-togethers and sporting events such as golf tournaments and so on.
10. Review of the eligibility rules.
11. Off-season addresses, telephone numbers, and plans
12. Approximate dates for starting the competitive season and schedule highlights.

Meetings with Individual Athletes

The coach should meet with each athlete after the competitive season. Areas previously mentioned such as the evaluation of the athlete's season, the athlete evaluation of the program, and the off-season training program should be the main topics discussed plus any other related issues or problems. The coach should discuss the athlete's plans for the off-season and attempt to keep some contact with the athletes during this time. A follow up on the athlete's training program is also essential.

Off-Season Training

During the meeting with each athlete at the end of the competitive season, a detailed training program for the preparation period should be distributed. If possible, this program should be individualized. The important aspects of an off-season (preparation period) training program should be based on the following factors:

1. Physical testing as to present status.
2. An individualized program based on the strengths and weaknesses of the individual related to the specific physical attributes important in the sport.
3. Follow-up and control throughout the off-season if the athletes are working on their own. This can be done by personal visits or athletes sending in a training diary. The athletes may also undertake a supervised training program overseen by a specialist in training.
4. Physical testing done midway through the off-season or preparation period, and at the end of the off-season, is beneficial both as a progress check and as a motivational tool for the athlete. The testing can be elaborate and done in a fitness lab, or may be a simpler field test.

Banquet, Awards

An awards banquet is usually held at the finish of the season. As well as awards, a slide or video review of the highlights of the year and a prominent speaker are usually included. The speeches should be short, and a maximum of two hours is recommended for the banquet.

Equipment

RETURN OF EQUIPMENT

Equipment used by the athletes, especially in sports with expensive protective equipment, should be handed in immediately after the last competition. Items such as game jerseys should not be kept by the athlete unless authorized. A policy of giving game jerseys to graduating players has been effective.

INVENTORY, CLEANING, REPAIR

All equipment should be accounted for in an inventory immediately after the competitive season is completed. The condition of the equipment and whether there is a need for cleaning, repair, or replacement should be noted.

Equipment to be repaired should be looked after immediately by equipment managers or sent out to those who specialize in this area in order for a prompt return.

ORDERING NEW EQUIPMENT

Before ordering new equipment, the budget has to be generally set in this area. If the budget has not been decided for the next year, it is important to estimate the cost of all equipment. Purchase of large, expensive items of equipment in such sports as gymnastics and football may have to be planned over a two- or three-year period. Some suggestions for ordering new equipment are:

1. Order early.
2. Get two or three quotes on cost.
3. Order from reputable dealers.
4. Purchase from dealers who also offer service.
5. Order standardized, high-quality equipment—best price for best quality.
6. Establish set delivery time.

EQUIPMENT MANAGEMENT

Most athletic teams have tight budgets and, as one of the major expenditures in a budget is equipment, the efficient management of the equipment is essential. Procedures for receiving, marking, issuing, controlling, and storing are important to properly maintain the equipment and prevent theft and misuse. Each athlete should be accountable for all equipment issued to him or her. Equipment managers are essential in sports where large amounts of equipment are used, such as in football and ice hockey.

Facilities

The training and competition facility used by the team should be evaluated at the end of the competitive season. Improvements in the facility and training times should be evaluated and negotiated immediately at the end of one competitive season for the next season. If facilities are inadequate, negotiations for a move to different facilities should be considered.

Budget

As money for sports teams gets tighter, it is even more important that the coach becomes skilled at planning and implementing a budget. The budget, a careful estimate of expenditures and revenues, must be based on sound short- (one year) and long-term (three to five years) goals to properly develop a program within the constraints of limited funds. Large equipment items, renovations, new team uniforms, and so on must be planned for over a two- to three-year period.

The budget generally is composed of four sections: (1) statement of philosophy and goals; (2) an overview showing expenditures and revenues in broad categories; (3) an itemized list of expenses and projected receipts; and (4) supporting materials such as team schedules and catalogue prices.

The budget usually contains two types of expenditures: (1) capital expenses, which include large items such as weight machines, gymnastic equipment, and other equipment; and (2) general-expense items, such as uniforms, balls, trainers' supplies, travel, and maintenance of facilities and fields.

Budgets are usually of two types (1) traditional, based on the previous year, and (2) zero-base budgeting, which assumes that the sport club has no base budget and every item must be justified and prioritized with no reference to the past budget. In this second type of budgeting, which is becoming more common, all items must also be prioritized in terms of their importance.

In preparing the budget, it is important to conduct a complete inventory of equipment, supplies, and facilities as to their number and condition. Revenue can come from the following:

- budget from organization or school
- ticket revenues
- donations and fundraising
- athlete participation fee
- concession revenues
- advertisement sales
- program sales
- parking
- student athletic fees, in the school system.

Scheduling

The exhibition and league scheduling is done in the post season and the coach should attempt to have as much input as possible as to the degree of difficulty of opponent, schedule dates, and so on. Details on scheduling follow in the next section.

SCHEDULING

In many situations, the coach has the responsibility for setting up at least part of the schedule for his or her team. One coach in a league may be responsible for the complete schedule and this duty may be rotated each year.

If an administrator is responsible for constructing the schedule, the coach should have input.

Here are some guidelines to keep in mind when constructing a schedule:

1. Check the availability of the facility for the complete season. Factor in holidays, exam schedules in a school setting, special functions in the facility, whether the facility is shared, and events prior to or following the contest.
2. Some schools and clubs have a traditional day or days to play. Two choices of day should be submitted to the schedule maker.
3. In terms of the number of contests, leagues usually have a limit for the total number of competitions allowed, especially in school situations.
4. For away competitions, take into consideration travel time, both going and returning. In school situations, long trips on week days may not be feasible.
5. Consider traveling with another team of the same organization if budget restraints are a factor. Schedule two away games in the same area on successive days.
6. When planning an exhibition, non-conference contest, select opponents of comparable caliber to your athletes. A good rule is to schedule competitions with at least 10 to 15 percent of opponents who are above your team's caliber, the majority with teams of similar caliber, and 10 to 15 percent with weaker opponents. The exhibition schedule should be a part of what attracts athletes to your organization. Special trips or tours, at least one per season, add to the interest of a competitive season.
7. The climate and weather are factors in a schedule. In extreme heat, outside athletic contests should be scheduled in the evening or morning. Schedules in the fall should end before cold weather comes in northern climates. Alternative days should be added to a schedule if wet weather postpones games.
8. All scheduled contests should be confirmed in writing, and, in cases of exhibition or non-conference games, a contract with a guarantee may be involved.
9. All schedules should be prepared at least one year or one competitive season in advance. Once the base schedule is prepared, some alterations can be made.
10. When scheduling opponents, consider their strength or weakness. Depending on the caliber of your team, you may wish to start with easier opponents or schedule easier opponents between two difficult ones. Know the caliber of your athletes and remember that some success is important, as is challenging your athletes to improve against better opponents.

Types of Schedules

There are five basic types of schedules:

1. Round robin (double, triple, etc.).
2. Single elimination.
3. Single elimination with a consolation round.
4. Double elimination.
5. Challenge or ladder.

Round Robin

This common type of league schedule is used with team sports such as basketball, football, and baseball. A round-robin schedule allows each team or opponent to compete against the other competitors at least once. In a double round robin, each team or opponent faces the others twice, and in a triple round robin three times. With this type of schedule, the number of entries in a division or league must be smaller (six to eight is ideal), and availability of facilities and sufficient time to play are important. The round robin is a very fair method of determining the winner because all opponents play each other.

PROCEDURE

To determine the total number of games to be played in a round robin, use the formula $N(N-1)/2$, where N represents the total number of teams.

For an even number of entrants, assign each entrant a number and arrange them in a vertical column, as shown in figure 2.10. List the numbers down the first vertical column and up the second vertical column. Put a box around the team with number 1. The first-round pairings are listed horizontally. To determine the second round, rotate all the numbers counterclockwise, except the number 1 entrant with the box around it. Rotate again for the next round, until all opponents have played each other once. If there is an uneven number of entrants, a bye must be put in one of the positions of an opponent, usually the top left, as shown in figure 2.11.

Round 1	Round 2	Round 3	Round 4	Round 5
1 vs. 6	1 vs. 5	1 vs. 4	1 vs. 3	1 vs. 2
2 vs. 5	6 vs. 4	5 vs. 3	4 vs. 2	3 vs. 6
3 vs. 4	2 vs. 3	6 vs. 2	5 vs. 6	4 vs. 5

Figure 2.10: Round-robin tournament for an even number of entrants (six)

Round 1	Round 2	Round 3	Round 4	Round 5
bye - 5	bye - 4	bye - 3	bye - 2	bye - 1
1 vs. 4	5 vs. 3	4 vs. 2	3 vs. 1	2 vs. 5
2 vs. 3	1 vs. 2	5 vs. 1	4 vs. 5	3 vs. 4

Figure 2.11: Round-robin tournament for an uneven number of entrants (five)

The advantages of the round-robin format are that it is the fairest method of determining a winner, as every opponent plays everyone else, it is a method of ranking opponents, and it also includes more games and allows for a maximum use of facilities. Its disadvantage is that it takes a long time to complete, requiring more facility time, and the number of entries cannot be too large.

Single Elimination

The single-elimination tournament is quite common. This type of tournament determines a winner more quickly but eliminates half of the entries with each round. The NCAA tournament in United States college basketball post-season play is an example of a single-elimination tournament.

PROCEDURE

The number of entries in a single-elimination tournament is usually a multiple of two (i.e., 2, 4, 8, 16, 32, 64). If the number of entrants is not a multiple of two, byes must be added for a missing entrant. All byes must be in the first round, and the number of byes added must raise the total (byes plus entrants) to the next highest multiple of two (e.g., with fourteen entrants, you must add two byes to reach sixteen).

The position of the entrants can be chosen randomly or by drawing names. Another, more common method is by ranking or seeding the entrants. The top-seeded or -ranked opponents are put in different brackets, one in the upper bracket and one in the lower bracket, as shown in figure 2.12. This assures that the top-ranked opponents do not meet early in the tournament. If byes are included, the top-ranked entrants should receive them in the first round (see figure 2.13).

The formula for the number of games played in a single-elimination tournament is $N-1$, with N being the total number of teams (e.g., for 16 teams, $N-1$ is [16-1] = 15 games)

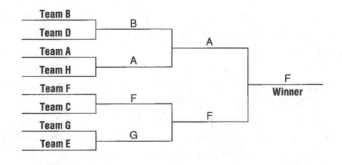

Figure 2.12: Single-elimination tournament for eight entrants (ranked)

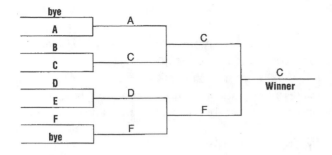

Figure 2.13: Single-elimination tournament with byes in the first round (six entrants)

The main advantage of a single-elimination tournament is that a winner is selected relatively quickly from among a large number of entrants. The tournament takes less time, with fewer bookings of facilities, and excitement is created with the "lose and you're out" situation. The disadvantages are that one loss eliminates the entrant, and some entrants get to play only once.

Single Elimination with a Consolation Round

When adequate time and facilities are available, having a consolation winner allows all entrants to play at least two games. In this type of tournament, all the losers in the first round move to a single-elimination tournament to determine a consolation-round winner. This means that every entrant plays at least two games, and losers of the first round have an added incentive.

PROCEDURE

There are two types of consolation/elimination tournaments. One has all losers in the first round, and those with byes in the first round who lose in the second round moving to a second single-elimination tournament, as shown in figure 2.14.

The second type of consolation tournament has the winner of the consolation play the winner of single-elimination tournament for the championship. This type of tournament is seldom used because the consolation winner usually has weaker teams to play against to get to the final.

The total number of games is N(N–1) for the original single-elimination round plus N(N–1) for the consolation elimination round.

The advantage of the consolation elimination tournament is that each entrant gets to play twice. This is especially important if entrants have traveled long distances to the tournament. Good entrants get to play longer if

upset in the first round, and more interest is created for the participants. The disadvantage of this type of tournament is that it takes more time and space to run when a large number of entrants is involved.

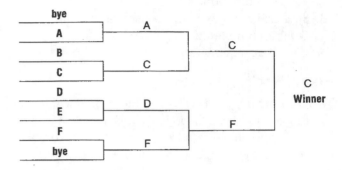

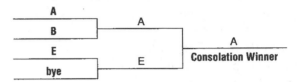

Figure 2.14: Single elimination with consolation elimination for losers in the first round and those with byes in the first round who lose in the second round (for six entrants)

Double-Elimination Tournament

The double-elimination tournament requires a much longer period of time to play than the single-elimination tournament as each team must be defeated twice before being eliminated from further competition.

A single-elimination bracket is carried out, as shown in figure 2.15, with the defeated entrants entering into a losers' bracket. The winners of both brackets play off for the championship.

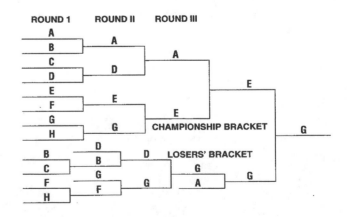

Figure 2.15: Double-elimination tournament (eight entrants)

The number of games to be played is determined by subtracting 1 from the number of entries and multiplying by 2 and adding 1 for the championship game (N–1) x 2 + 1. If byes are needed in the losers' bracket, they should not be matched to entrants who also had a bye in the original bracket. Entrants who have met in the earlier rounds should not be paired.

The advantage of this type of tournament is that a team must lose twice to be out of the competition for the championship. A top-ranked team can experience an upset and still have a chance to win, and perhaps the most deserving entrant can win. The disadvantage of this type of tournament is that more time and space are required and the excitement of "lose and you're out" is missing.

Challenge or Ladder Tournaments

This type of tournament is more informal and is usually used for singles and doubles competition in sports such as tennis, squash, badminton, table tennis, wrestling, handball, racquet ball, and archery.

PROCEDURE

The ladder tournament is the most common, with names of entrants put on cards and placed in slots or hung on hooks, as shown in figure 2.16. The entrants can be seeded or randomly placed. Once the ladder is set up, entrants can advance by defeating a competitor one or two places above on the ladder. If a challenger wins, he or she interchanges positions with the defeated person. After playing the contest, the two players cannot play again until they have played against another contestant. The players play in the order of the challenges, and usually a three-day limit is imposed to take the challenge or default.

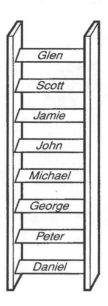

Figure 2.16: Ladder challenge tournament

The winner is the player on top of the ladder after a designated time period (e.g., two weeks, one month)

The advantages of this type of tournament is that it can be carried on without the coach, no one is eliminated, and a true champion can be chosen over a period of time. The disadvantage is that the players end up competing with the same people much of the time, and the excitement of the challenge is lost.

Part 3: Physical Preparation

Strength, power, speed, muscular endurance, the energy systems including cardiovascular endurance, agility, flexibility, and reaction time/movement time/response time are the most important physical factors in the development of an athlete. All these factors combined with, and developed in conjunction with, the physical skills of the sport allow the athlete to achieve his or her full potential. Mental (psychological) preparation, discussed in Part 4, is also a determining factor in athletic performance.

The modern coach should have an extensive knowledge of the latest techniques of physical conditioning. The majority of coaches do not have the luxury of employing a strength and conditioning coach, as most professional and some college teams do. Therefore, in many cases, the coach is the expert, and either directs the conditioning program or advises on the methodology. For this reason, it is imperative that every coach have the basic knowledge and principles of modern training methods. Part 3 provides some basic information on the training of the various physical factors that are important in the development of the athlete.

PERIODIZATION

Periodization, previously introduced in Part 2, is a systematic division of the training year into phases to allow the coach to develop the athletes to perform at their peak for the main competitions of the year.

The concept is not new, as most coaches have had some form of organized training program with pre-, main, and off-season periods. Even the Greek Olympians had some primitive form of a training program for developing certain aspects of their athletic skills.

The more sophisticated, modern theory of periodization was developed by the Soviet Matveyev in which he stated, "The training process can and must be aimed at achieving optimal form at the right moment." In addition to Matveyev, the former East German Harre and the Soviet Ozolin also contributed to the development and use of periodization as a standard tool for coaches in the Eastern Bloc countries in the former Communist regime.

Another key person in the introduction and development of periodization theory was Tudor Bompa of Romania. At the Eastern Bloc coaching institutes, Tudor wrote the book *Theory and Methodology of Training* and expanded and developed further the original periodization theory. His book was widely read and adopted by coaches in the English-speaking world. Today, most sports are using some form of the periodization model for their training program.

Nature of Periodization

The purpose of periodization is to develop an optimal state of preparation for each cycle or phase of the training program. Research and practical data suggest the development undergoes three phases: acquisition; retention and stabilization; and temporary loss of the optimal peak form (Cardinal).

The acquisition phase is included in a preparation period, which has two subphases: general and specific. Retention and stabilization are involved in a competitive phase, which has two subphases: pre-competition and main competition. The competitive phase may also include a tapering-off or unloading phase just before the final competition or commencement of a playoff in team sports. The temporary loss of optimal

	THE ANNUAL PLAN					
PHASES OF TRAINING	PREPARATORY		COMPETITIVE			TRANSITION
SUB-PHASES	GENERAL PREP	SPECIFIC PREP	PRE-COMPET.	COMPETITIVE	TAPER	TRANSITION
MACRO-CYCLES						
MICRO-CYCLES						

Figure 3.1: The three main phases of the annual plan and their subphases

sport preparation usually comes in the transition period, which immediately follows the final competition. The various training phases are illustrated in figures 3.1 and 3.2.

In the various phases, the longest period of training, called a "macrocycle," usually lasts for six weeks. Smaller training periods, called "microcycles," are made up of training units or lessons which usually last one week. The training unit is one training session directed toward achieving a training objective, for example, shooting in basketball.

The basic concept of periodization depends on the present state of training, which requires continuous analysis. Objective and subjective results of performance as well as physical, medical, and psychological testing can assist in the analysis of the training state. Competition cannot be used as the sole indicator, as the shifting of the training load in certain cycles can have a positive or negative effect on performance (Harre).

The planning of periodization should be based on the dates of competition, with the peak performance set for the final competition. However, training and competition must be planned so that preparation is maximized throughout the competitive period. Too many competitions, or too many easy or highly difficult competitions, can have a detrimental effect on the development of optimal performance. During the various cycles, the four areas of physical, technical, tactical, and psychological training should be addressed in a systematic, progressive manner.

Steps in Preparing the Plan

The coach must analyze the various performance factors in the physical, technical, tactical, and psychological areas, and rate their various importance in each phase, as illustrated in figure 3.3.

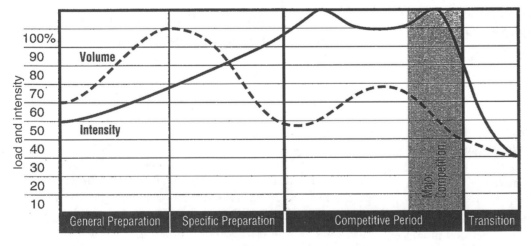

Figure 3.2: Volume and intensity of load in the annual plan

	PREPARATORY	COMPETITIVE	TRANSITION
PHYSICAL			
❑ Energy Systems			
• aerobic	1 2 3 4 5	1 2 3 4 5	1 2 3 4 5
• anaerobic alactic	1 2 3 4 5	1 2 3 4 5	1 2 3 4 5
• anaerobic lactic	1 2 3 4 5	1 2 3 4 5	1 2 3 4 5
❑ Strength	1 2 3 4 5	1 2 3 4 5	1 2 3 4 5
❑ Speed	1 2 3 4 5	1 2 3 4 5	1 2 3 4 5
❑ Power	1 2 3 4 5	1 2 3 4 5	1 2 3 4 5
❑ Flexibility	1 2 3 4 5	1 2 3 4 5	1 2 3 4 5
❑ Nutrition	1 2 3 4 5	1 2 3 4 5	1 2 3 4 5
❑	1 2 3 4 5	1 2 3 4 5	1 2 3 4 5
❑	1 2 3 4 5	1 2 3 4 5	1 2 3 4 5
❑	1 2 3 4 5	1 2 3 4 5	1 2 3 4 5
MENTAL			
❑ Emotional Control	1 2 3 4 5	1 2 3 4 5	1 2 3 4 5
❑ Attentional Control	1 2 3 4 5	1 2 3 4 5	1 2 3 4 5
❑ Strategies	1 2 3 4 5	1 2 3 4 5	1 2 3 4 5
(precompetition and competition)			
TECHNICAL			
❑	1 2 3 4 5	1 2 3 4 5	1 2 3 4 5
❑	1 2 3 4 5	1 2 3 4 5	1 2 3 4 5
❑	1 2 3 4 5	1 2 3 4 5	1 2 3 4 5
❑	1 2 3 4 5	1 2 3 4 5	1 2 3 4 5
❑	1 2 3 4 5	1 2 3 4 5	1 2 3 4 5
❑	1 2 3 4 5	1 2 3 4 5	1 2 3 4 5
TACTICAL			
❑	1 2 3 4 5	1 2 3 4 5	1 2 3 4 5
❑	1 2 3 4 5	1 2 3 4 5	1 2 3 4 5
❑	1 2 3 4 5	1 2 3 4 5	1 2 3 4 5
❑	1 2 3 4 5	1 2 3 4 5	1 2 3 4 5
❑	1 2 3 4 5	1 2 3 4 5	1 2 3 4 5
❑	1 2 3 4 5	1 2 3 4 5	1 2 3 4 5
LEGEND 1 = low priority 5 = high priority			

Figure 3.3: Priorities for the physical, mental, technical, and tactical in the training phases. Reprinted by permission from Coaching Association of Canada. *Level 3 Coach Assessment Workbook*, 1–3.

After this analysis has been completed, the following steps can be taken:

1. Fill in months and major training tasks.
2. Register competitions.
3. Identify periodization of training cycle.
4. Break down training cycle into macrocycles and identify types of macrocycles.
5. Measure and evaluate the essential factors in performance.
6. Sequence major training tasks throughout the training cycle and determine length of development.
7. Calculate percentage training time for physical, technical, and tactical factors/macrocycle.
8. Project the training load/macrocycle. (Cardinal)

Classification of Annual Plans

The type of annual plan depends on the number of competitions and the number of main competitions.

One main competition or a playoff structure after league play is classified as a monocycle, as illustrated in figure 3.4. In the monocycle, there is one preparation phase, with general and specific subphases, and one main competitive phase. The main competitive phase usually includes one tapering phase before the main competition. This tapering phase would include two shorter phases: an unloading phase, where volume and intensity are reduced; and a special preparation phase, which could include tactical alterations along with psychological preparation and relaxation techniques.

Some sports have two separate competition periods, such as track and field, with both an indoor and outdoor season. This type of periodization is classified as "bicycle" and includes two monocycles linked together, with a short unloading and preparation phase, as illustrated in figure 3.5.

The bicycle periodization would include the following:

- Preparation Phase I
- Competitive Phase I
- Transition Phase I (1 week)
- Preparation Phase II
- Competitive Phase II
- Transition Phase II

The volume of training is much higher in Preparatory I than in Preparatory II.

Periodization that must accommodate three important competitions per year, such as in gymnastics, is called "tricycle," with the most important competition following the last cycle (see figure 3.6). The tricycle would take the following format:

- Long Preparation Phase I
- Competitive Phase I
- Short Transition Phase I
- Preparation Phase II
- Competitive Phase II
- Transition Phase II
- Preparation Phase III
- Competitive Phase III
- Transition Phase III

In some situations, the short transition phases I and II can be combined with the normally shorter preparation phases II and III.

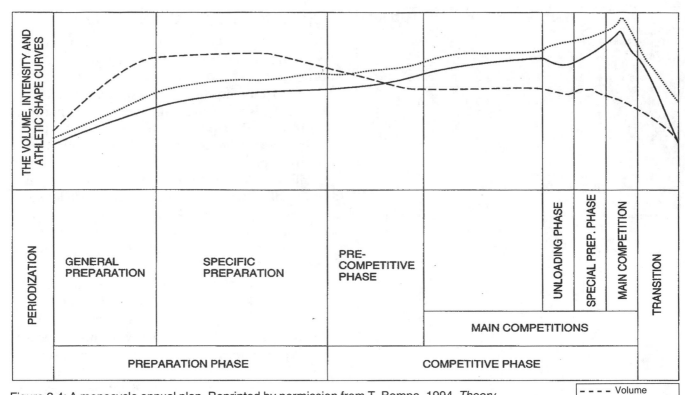

Figure 3.4: A monocycle annual plan. Reprinted by permission from T. Bompa, 1994, *Theory and Methodology of Training*. (Dubuque, IA: Kendall/Hunt), 171.

- - - - Volume
——— Intensity
········ Athletic Shape

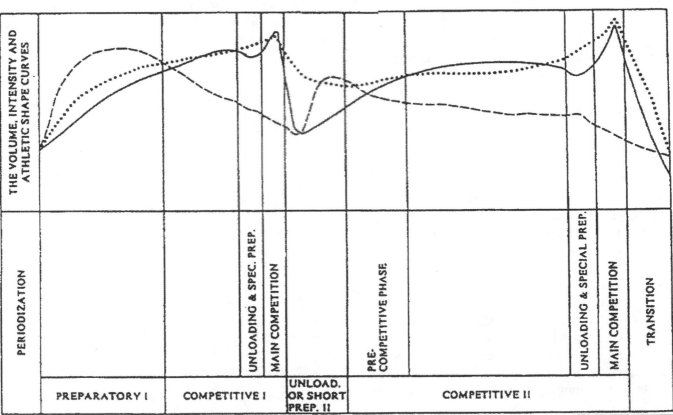

Figure 3.5: Bicycle annual plan. Reprinted by permission from T. Bompa, 1994, *Theory and Methodology of Training*. (Dubuque, IA: Kendall/Hunt), 172.

- - - - Volume
——— Intensity
········ Athletic Shape

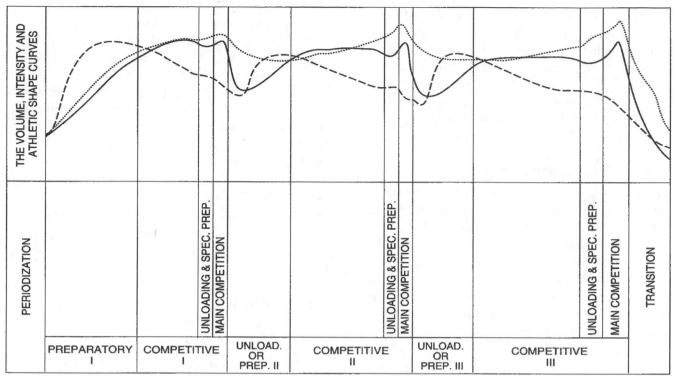

Figure 3.6: Tricycle annual plan. Reprinted by permission from T. Bompa, 1994, *Theory and Methodology of Training.* (Dubuque, IA: Kendall/Hunt), 173

Legend:
- - - - Volume
——— Intensity
········· Athletic Shape

Characteristics of the Various Phases

Preparation Phase

Preparation is the phase during which the foundation is built for the development of the athlete. The basis of the physical, technical, tactical, and psychological areas is developed during this phase, with an emphasis on high volume, which in the physical area should result in a greater resistance to fatigue.

The basic purposes of this phase are:

1. Acquire and improve general physical preparation.
2. Improve the physical factors required by the sport such as strength, speed, power, aerobic and anaerobic endurance, agility, and flexibility.
3. Develop psychological techniques.
4. Develop and/or improve technique.
5. Familiarize with the basic tactics to be employed in the following phase.
6. Improve athletes' theoretical knowledge regarding the theory and methodology of training specific to the sport.

The period usually lasts three to six months. For individual sports, the period is up to twice as long as the competitive phase, whereas in team sports the preparation period is shorter, usually lasting two to three months.

General Preparation Phase

The objective of this phase is the development of general physical preparation, improvement of basic technical skills, introduction of basic tactics, and a development and improvement of basic mental skills.

The prime concern in this phase, however, is the development of a high level of physical conditioning, on which the athlete can build in future phases. This stage is characterized by a gradual and progressive increase of volume at medium intensity. Each macrocycle in this phase should raise the number of training hours from one stage to the next, which allows the athlete to improve his or her general working capacity. Coupled with this high volume of work are the psychological aspect of drive, and determination to complete the program.

In endurance events, 70 to 80 percent of the total time should be spent on developing aerobic endurance; in strength events, the main objective should be maximum strength development. For team sports, only very basic technical and tactical skills should also be included.

In most cases, the time allocated to this phase should be one-third of the total time of the annual plan. No competitions are included in this phase.

Specific Preparation Phase

The objectives of the specific preparation phase are similar to those of the general phase, but the training is more specific. The volume remains high, but 70 to 80 percent of the exercises are sport-specific. Toward the end of this phase, volume starts to diminish by 20 to 30 percent, but intensity increases. This phase links up the various (physical) factors, such as strength and speed, and applies them to the technical skills of the sport. Mental preparation begins to deal with game-like situations, and tactical involvement is taken to a higher level, although actual competitions are only simulated. Physical, technical, and psychological evaluation may take place at the end of this phase.

Competitive Phase

In the competitive phase, the level of physical conditioning must be maintained for the base for further technical and competition-specific training. Ninety percent of the training in this phase is sport-specific, and the technical, tactical, and psychological training must be brought to the next level, with the ultimate objective being peaking for the best performance. In this phase, intensity increases, while total volume of work is lowered.

The objectives of this phase are:

1. Continuous improvement of physical abilities and psychological techniques in accordance with specifics of the sport.
2. The perfection and consolidation of technique.
3. Featuring and developing tactics and gaining competitive experience.
4. Maintaining general physical preparation.
5. Improving on the level of theoretical knowledge.

It should be noted that, although the intensity increases, and volume decreases for most sports, the volume may decrease only slightly from the preparation period for endurance sports. This period usually lasts from four to six months, depending on the sport.

Pre-competitive Subphase

This phase usually lasts from four to six weeks, especially in team sports, and consists of a higher-than-normal volume compared with the main competition period, but also includes unofficial, non-league, or exhibition contests that test all the elements of physical, technical, tactical, and psychological training developed in the preparation phase. Physical preparation, although not as high-volume as during the preparation period, still remains a major focus.

Main Competitive Phase

Specific sport-related exercises are included in this period for 90 percent of the time, with intensity levels reaching their highest levels two to three weeks prior to competition.

The weekly training (microcycles made up of various training units) should reach maximum intensity three to four times during the week. The stress levels should be varied (showing an undulating line if graphed), and hard/easy days should be well planned for regeneration. Competitions should build in order of importance and/or difficulty or alternate harder with lighter. Maintenance of the physical preparation should be highlighted with specific strength and endurance work.

Pre-competitive Subphase (Tapering)

Following an extensive competitive period, a tapering-off or unloading period of one to two weeks should precede the final competition, or, in team sports, the playoff period.

During this period, both volume and intensity are reduced, and not more than two intense training periods per week (microcycle) should be included. In the second week, any physical-conditioning maintenance programs, such as strength training, should be stopped.

In addition to the reduction of volume and intensity, additional tactical and psychology training, including relaxation techniques (already learned), may be included.

Transition Phase

This period of unloading and regeneration usually lasts three to four weeks, and not longer than five weeks. The first week is a detraining and evaluation period, and exercise should be moderate and non–sport-specific. The second week should be the resting period. The following two to three weeks are made up of active rest, fun, and exercising at a frequency of three to five times per week and at about half the competitive-phase volume.

The training and exercise environment should be changed if possible. It should be noted here that this phase is not a total rest period, since the gains made throughout the training year should not drop too far below the maintenance level. Athletes who follow this concept were found to be more physically and psychologically prepared for the beginning of the new preparatory phase.

The objectives of the various phases of the annual plan are summarized in table 3.1.

The objectives of the physical-performance factors in the phases of the annual plan are summarized in table 3.2.

It is generally believed that it takes six to eight years of systematic training to develop an elite athlete. After a number of years of specific training, basic conditioning in the general preparatory period usually cannot provide a training load that offers more than maintenance. It is for this reason that a quadrennial (four-year) plan must be developed that includes a higher degree of high-intensity sport-specific training (Balyi).

In addition, Portman contends that the number of hours devoted to training has increased many times, and there is a further need to refine the annual plan and the

Table 3.1: Objectives of periodized annual plan (Bacon)

Phase	General Objectives
Preparatory	
General	To develop basic technical skills and general fitness
Specific	To perfect technique and basic tactics and to develop sport-specific fitness
Competitive	
Pre-competitive	To make training competition specific and to raise intensity
Competitive	
Tapering	To maximize competitive performance and to regenerate in preparation for main competition
Transition	To allow active rest and maintenance of training gains

original theories of Matveyev. In the past twenty years, in the training of the elite athlete, volume and intensity have increased, in some cases, by as much as 50 and 100 percent, respectively.

Table 3.2: Objectives of the physical, technical, and tactical factors in the annual plan. Reprinted by permission from Coaching Association of Canada. *Level 3 Coach Assessment Workbook*, 1-8.

Perf. Factor \ Period Phase	Preparatory		Competitive			Transition
	General	Specific	Pre-Competitive	Main	Taper	
Development of Skill: • Techniques • Tactics • Strategies		• initiate the development of techniques	• emphasize the development of techniques • introduction of tactics and strategies	• continue the refinement of techniques for closed skill sports • emphasize the development of tactics and strategies for open skill sports (use of simulations)	• increase use of simulations with a reduction in practices and competitions	
Physical Preparation: • Aerobic • Anaerobic • Speed • Strength • Power • Flexibility • Nutrition	• aerobic base • train for general strength • train flexibility • initiate a nutritional education program	• continue to train aerobic base • train sport specific energy system • train sport-specific speed* • continue strength training* • train sport-specific power* • training flexibility *(if required by sport)	• train sport-specific energy system • continue to train speed • maintain strength • continue to train power • train flexibility	• maintain sport-specific energy systems • maintain speed • maintain strength • maintain power • maintain flexibility	• reduction of training volume and intensity • maintain flexibility	• maintain a level of fitness while avoiding staleness through a variety of recreational activities • maintain flexibility

The major adjustment the elite athlete must make occurs during the general preparatory period, which can be shortened, with more technical work added in the specific preparatory period.

It should be remembered that the periodization method, although based on some scientific research and practical experience, is still not an exact science, and coaches must continually evaluate and refine their training plan.

THE ENERGY SYSTEMS

Understanding how the athlete derives the energy to perform is essential to a coach who is responsible for the daily, weekly, monthly, and yearly training program. How much work, how much rest, and how to peak for competition is information the coach must have.

The energy an athlete uses to move the body is derived from the breakdown of a chemical compound named ATP (adenosine triphosphate). ATP is supplied in the body by chemical reactions classified as aerobic and anaerobic. Aerobic refers to the presence of oxygen and anaerobic means without oxygen. The anaerobic system is further divided into alactic and lactic which refers to the production of a byproduct lactic acid that causes fatigue. The alactic system means without lactic acid while the lactic system produces lactic acid.

These systems are summarized below:

Production of ATP
1. Anaerobic (without oxygen)
   a) Alactic System (without lactic acid)
   b) Lactic System (produces lactic acid)
2. Aerobic Oxygen System (with oxygen)

1. Anaerobic
   a) Alactic System (Also called the ATP-CP or Phosphagen Systems)
      1) This system supplies the ATP for all-out effort of up to ten seconds and contributes to up to thirty seconds.
      2) The ATP is stored in the muscle cell.
      3) The breakdown of ATP does not require oxygen.
      4) Creatine Phosphate (CP) is a chemical compound also present in the muscle cell which, with its breakdown, remakes (resynthesizes) ATP.
      5) The total stores of ATP and CP in the muscle are small so the system is limited. The energy however is rapidly available.
      6) One half of the ATP used can be restored in recovery in thirty seconds. Almost all is restored in approximately three minutes. (See page 123)
   b) Lactic Acid System (Also called Anaerobic Glycolysis)
      1) This system supplies the majority of ATP for activities requiring energy for longer than ten seconds and contributes up to three minutes. The system is predominant in intense exercise of thirty seconds to sixty seconds.
      2) Glycogen, which is stored in the muscle cell, is the immediate source used to generate ATP. Glycogen is the storage form of glucose (sugar). Some glycogen is also stored in the liver and can be converted to blood glucose to assist in the production of ATP.
      3) More ATP is supplied than the alactic system but the supply is also limited.
      4) A byproduct called lactic acid is produced, which, when it reaches a certain level is related to muscle fatigue and soreness. (See page 124)
      5) During recovery one half of the ATP is restored in approximately fifteen minutes and 95 percent in one hour.
      6) Light exercise aids in the removal of the lactic acid.
2. Aerobic
   a) The Oxygen System
      1) Used to supply energy in activities of a prolonged nature especially over three minutes.
      2) Capable of manufacturing large amounts of ATP by utilizing both carbohydrates (glycogen) and fats.
      3) No fatiguing byproducts such as lactic acid are formed.
      4) It takes several minutes for the oxygen we breathe to be assimilated into the blood and to be transported to the muscle cell. Therefore it takes several minutes before this system becomes the major producer of ATP.
      5) Carbohydrates contribute early in prolonged activity to manufacture ATP while fats contribute later. Carbohydrates can produce ATP more efficiently than fats.
      6) The supply of ATP in this system is unlimited and it is usually other factors such as lack of fluids or muscle soreness which causes the fatigue rather than a lack of ATP.

Interaction of the Energy Systems

Although the three energy systems all supply ATP, they act solely only in very-short-burst exercise lasting a few seconds (alactic system) or in longer endurance activities with a steady pace (oxygen system). From a few seconds to three minutes, there is an interaction of the energy systems to supply ATP, as shown in table 3.3.

Table 3.3: Relationship of performance time to energy systems supplying ATP

Performance Time	Major Energy System(s) Supplying ATP
Less than ten seconds	Alactic
Ten seconds to ninety seconds	Alactic and lactic
Ninety seconds to three minutes	Lactic acid and oxygen
More than three minutes	Oxygen

Note: For more detail on the physiology of the energy systems, see pages 123 to 130.

TRAINING THE ENERGY SYSTEMS

Before training the energy systems, the coach should have a thorough understanding of the energy demands of the sport. Research on the energy systems is quite extensive in some sports, whereas little work or analysis has been done in others. Where research is lacking, an analysis of the sport can be done by the coach by simply timing the low, medium, and high intensities during a competition. By analyzing the movement and duration of activity in the sport, the coach can make a fairly accurate measure of the energy systems used. Sports such as sprinting and quick gymnastics movements and long-distance running and swimming are obviously the two extremes of the anaerobic-alactic and the aerobic systems. Sports such as soccer, basketball, and ice hockey are more difficult to analyze because all three energy systems are used. However, by using a time–movement study, the coach can analyze the time spent in all-out, medium, and low effort during a competition, and can adjust the training program accordingly. The following guidelines will assist the coach in determining the energy systems used in his or her sport:

1. Alactic (ATP-CP) system—up to ten seconds and contributes up to thirty seconds.
2. Lactic (lactic acid or anaerobic glycolysis) system—thirty seconds to ninety seconds, and contributes up to three minutes.
3. Aerobic system—starts contributing after approximately 90 seconds and is the major contributor from three minutes on.

Remember that all three systems contribute somewhat to the supply of energy (ATP) in most sports and should be trained proportionate to their use in the sport.

Training the energy systems requires the manipulation of the variables of intensity, frequency, and duration, as well as the principle of specificity.

Intensity in training determines the measure of physical exertion. The more intense the training, the more extreme the body response. The intensity of training can be determined by the heart rate, Karvonon method, and the percentage of MVO_2.

The heart rate can be measured by placing the fingers on the wrist on the radial artery just below the thumb, or on the side of the throat, beside the windpipe, on the carotid artery. Heart rates can be taken at the completion of exercise for ten seconds and multiplied by six to determine beats per minute.

The training heart rate is determined as a percentage of the maximum heart rate. The maximum heart rate can be determined by the formula:

Max HR = 220 – age
or, for the highly trained,
Max HR = 210 – age

Another method for determining the training heart rate is the Karvonon method, using a percentage of what is called the "heart rate reserve" (HRR).

Heart Rate Reserve (HRR) =
Maximum Heart Rate (MHR) – Resting Heart Rate (RHR)
Example: MHR = 190
RHR = 70
HRR = 120
Training at 80% = (0.8 x 120) + 70
= 96 + 70
= 166 beats/min.

The rate of exercise can also be determined as a percentage of the measure of maximum oxygen uptake (MVO_2). This requires the testing of the MVO_2 (see section on physiological testing) for a real or predicted value. The predicted MVO_2 then is expressed as a training percentage of MVO_2. Training percentages usually start at 65–70 percent MVO_2 for untrained athletes, and 70–75 percent for trained athletes. Training adaptations usually occur at 75 percent plus. Having determined the percentage MVO_2 the athlete should be training at, the training heart rate can be determined using table 3.4, which are the guidelines for percentage MVO$_2$ training for a twenty-year-old.

Table 3.4: Percentage MVO$_2$ maximum-rated to percentage of maximum training heart rate for a twenty-year-old

Percentages MVO$_2$ Training Heart Rates

60% VO$_2$ max = 73% of heart rate max = 146 beats/min.
65% VO$_2$ max = 76% of heart rate max = 153 beats/min.
70% VO$_2$ max = 80% of heart rate max = 160 beats/min.
75% VO$_2$ max = 84% of heart rate max = 167 beats/min.
80% VO$_2$ max = 87% of heart rate max = 174 beats/min.
85% VO$_2$ max = 91% of heart rate max = 182 beats/min.

Note: The relation between percentage VO$_2$ max. and heart rate is altered for swimming.

Intensity of training can also be determined by monitoring breathing rates and a feeling of tiredness by the athlete.

Training heart rates vary from 70 to 95 percent maximum, depending on the energy system being trained. As the heart rates increase during exercise, a gradual transition for the supplying of energy occurs from the aerobic system to the anaerobic systems. Also, as the heart rate increases, a shifting from fats to carbohydrates as a fuel source occurs, as more fast-twitch fibers are recruited. High training heart rates (over 85 percent max.) mean the body is using predominately the anaerobic-lactic and alactic systems to supply the energy for muscle contraction.

The number of the training sessions or the frequency of energy-systems training should be at two to four times per week for eight weeks to produce a training effect. The duration of the training session will depend on the type of training, as continuous aerobic training can take much longer than intense, short-burst anaerobic training. These training variables are discussed below in the information on specific-anaerobic and aerobic training programs.

The intensity and duration of training must be gradually and continually increased to have a training effect. Specificity is a key concept in all training programs. The best method for training the energy systems is to train using the mode of the sport; that is, runners should run, swimmers should swim, ice-hockey players should skate, and so on. Using modes other than that used in the sport, such as a skater running, still has an application in the training of the energy systems and can be used when the sport mode is not available or when variety in training is desirable.

Training the Anaerobic Systems

Alactic (ATP-CP) System

The alactic system is usually trained with all-out bursts of speed, resistance (strength/power), and plyometrics (described later) movements lasting between five and ten seconds with a work-to-rest ratio of 1:6 or 1:10. The five- to ten-second bursts use the alactic system to supply the ATP without entering the lactate system. The rest periods of thirty to sixty seconds allow the ATP to be 50 to 75 percent restored for the next exercise burst. The total work volume should be sixty seconds for one set (a set being a number of repetitions), allowing three to ten minutes between sets, which facilitates the total restoration of the alactic system. The training should be related to the movements in the sport, and the intensity should be maximal. The frequency of training should be every other day, or three times per week, although elite athletes such as sprinters can work five or six times per week with this system. Noticeable improvement occurs in eight to twelve weeks. Progression occurs by adding sets, shortening the pause time, and/or increasing the intensity.

Maintenance of this system in the competitive period of training should be done two or three times per week. In detraining, the alactic system maintains 80 to 90 percent of the gains for the next six weeks without training, although some losses are evident in the first two weeks.

An example of an alactic workout using quick-burst acceleration sprinting would include:

- Duration—5 seconds
- Intensity—maximal or near maximal (95 percent)
- Repetitions—5 per set
- Rest between reps—30–50 seconds (1:6) to (1:10)
- Number of sets—3
- Rest between sets—3 minutes
- Total work time—75 seconds
- Total rest time—9 minutes
- Total workout time—10–12 minutes

Lactic System

The lactic system is a major supplier of ATP in intense exercise lasting from ten seconds to about two minutes, with peak output being at around thirty seconds. This system is usually preceded in the preparation period with the development of an aerobic training program, which acts as a base to build the lactic system. The aerobic base allows for a faster and more efficient recovery time between repetitions, sets, and training day.

The intensity of the training should be near maximal and, if possible, the exercises should be specific to the movements of the sport. The training intervals should range from fifteen to ninety seconds, with the optimal time being between thirty and sixty seconds. The rest intervals should range from a 1:6 or 1:5, to a 1:3 work-to-rest ratio. Recovery time between sets should range from ten to fifteen minutes, with light jogging and/or flexing/stretching being done in the rest intervals in order to help in the removal of lactic acid. The total workout should last between ten and twelve minutes. Training should be done three times per week on alternate days. Recovery of the glycogen stores from intermittent exercise of this intensity takes at least twenty-four hours.

A word of caution in the training of the lactic system: Younger and inexperienced athletes should reduce the intensity and duration of this type of training. Prepubescent athletes do not possess the capacity for any noticeable improvements in this system. Their total volume of training should be reduced to less than three minutes, the training intervals should be reduced to twenty-five seconds or less, and longer time should be given between sets.

Detraining effects occur more rapidly with the lactic system, compared with the alactic system, with 50 percent of the training gain lost within six weeks of stopping training. Maintenance of the system can be achieved with two or three workouts per week during the competition period.

An example of a lactic-system workout using the mode of running would include:

- Duration—30–40 seconds
- Intensity—near maximal (95 percent)
- Repetitions—5 per set
- Rest between reps—1:5 to 1:3—3 minutes to 1½ minutes
- Number of sets—2
- Rest between sets—5 minutes
- Total work time—5 minutes
- Total rest time—35 minutes (approx.)
- Total workout time—45 minutes (approx.)

Modes of training other than running could include swimming, cycling, stationary bike, skipping, and hill running.

Aerobic System

Aerobic training is important both as the main energy source for steady-state endurance sports lasting more than two or three minutes such as marathon running,

and as a means for improving recovery for intermittent anaerobic sports such as ice hockey, basketball, soccer, and football. The ability of this system to efficiently take in oxygen and deliver it to the working muscles is important in most sports, and therefore an aerobic-training base is an important part of most training programs in the general preparation period.

The aerobic system can be trained using two methods: continuous long-distance exercise and intermittent interval training (described on pages 62–64). Submaximal (75 percent MVO_2) continuous exercise improves the delivery rate of oxygenated blood from the heart to the muscles (central adaptations, i.e., cardiac output) and can be trained using a variety of modes, for example, running, swimming, cycling, on-ice skating, and in-line off-ice skating. Intermittent aerobic training trains both the central adaptations (cardiac output and oxygen delivery) and the peripheral adaptations (increasing the oxygen-extraction capabilities of the working muscles) and should, if possible, be sport-specific.

Continuous aerobic training should last a minimum of twenty to forty minutes with running, and should be done at least three times per week, on alternate days. Recovery of the glycogen stores takes longer with this type of exercise (usually forty-eight hours) as compared with intermittent exercise (approximately twenty-four hours). Improvement comes with increasing the intensity, duration, and/or frequency of the training. The intensity is usually 75–85 percent of the maximum heart rate or 75–80 percent MVO_2 max. As mentioned previously, several different modes of training can be used effectively to provide variety in training but still achieve improvements in the central adaptation.

Intermittent aerobic training, as mentioned, improves both the central adaptations and peripheral adaptations (oxygen extraction at the cellular level). This type of training allows for higher training intensities, and improves the anaerobic threshold (usually approximately 85 percent of maximum heart rate) and the point where lactic acid begins to build up and interferes with muscle contraction. Improved recovery times also result from intermittent exercise.

Intermittent aerobic training is of two types: training times of 2 to 5 minutes, with 2½ minutes being the most common with a 1:1 work-to-rest ratio, and shorter intervals of approximately 15–20 seconds repeated 20 to 30 times, working at a pace slightly above the anaerobic threshold.

Intermittent aerobic training should always be used after a continuous aerobic-training base has been established.

An example of intermittent aerobic training includes:

Intermittent—*Long Duration*
- Duration—2½ minutes
- Intensity—3–5 beats below maximum heart rate
- Repetitions—5
- Rest between reps—2½ minutes 1:1 work-to-rest ratio
- Number of sets—1
- Total work time—12½ minutes
- Total rest time—12½ minutes
- For improvement, build to two sets and a total of ten reps.

Intermittent—*Short Duration*
- Duration—15–20 seconds
- Intensity—maximal or near maximal
- Repetitions—20
- Rest—60 seconds (1:3 work-to-rest ratio)
- Sets—1 continuous
- Total work time—5 minutes
- Total rest time—20 minutes
- Total workout time—25 minutes

A comparison of the training of the three energy systems is shown in table 3.5.

Periodization of Aerobic Endurance

There are three phases of endurance training: aerobic endurance, development of the foundation of specific endurance, and specific endurance. Aerobic endurance is developed in the general preparatory phase using steady-state moderate- to medium-intensity work. The foundation of specific endurance is done in the specific preparatory period and is the transition from aerobic endurance to sport-specific endurance. During this period, uniform steady-state endurance training is alternated with long- and medium-interval training (Bompa). The volume of training is at its highest level in this phase. In specific-endurance development, the intensity often exceeds that of the event or race, and by alternating various types of intensities, good recovery is facilitated. The various phases of aerobic endurance training using periodization are shown in table 3.6.

PREPARATORY		COMPETITIVE		TRANSITION
GENERAL PREPARATORY	SPECIFIC PREPARATORY	PRE COMPETITIVE	MAIN COMPETITIVE	TRANSITION
ENDURANCE	AEROBIC ENDURANCE	DEVELOP THE FOUNDATION OF SPECIFIC ENDURANCE	SPECIFIC ENDURANCE	AEROBIC ENDURANCE

Table 3.6: The periodization of endurance. Reprinted by permission from Bompa, *Theory and Methodology of Training*. (Dubuque, IA: Kendall/Hunt), 178.

INTERVAL TRAINING

Interval training, periods of exercise interspersed with a period of rest, is used extensively in the training of the alactic and lactic anaerobic-energy systems. Interval training is also used, along with continuous exercise, in

ENERGY SYSTEMS AND TRAINING-PROGRAM VARIABLES

Training Program Variable	Energy System			
	Anaerobic Alactic	Anaerobic Lactic	Aerobic	
			Base	Power
Warm-up	Yes	Yes	Yes	Yes
Stages	Aerobic base first	Aerobic base first	Stage 1	Stage 2
Method	Intervals	Intervals	Continuous	Intervals
Activity	Sport related	Sport related	Alternatives	Sport related
Intensity	Max speed/effort	Near-max. effort/speed	60–70% VO_2 max	85–95% VO_2 max
Work Time	≥ 10 sec.	15 sec. –2 min.	20–60 min.	10 sec. –3 min.
Work/Pause	1:6 to 1:10 Ratio	1:5 or 1:6 to 1:3	—	1:2
Sets/Set	≥ 60 sec. Volume	≥3 min.	—	3–5 min.
Pause between Sets	3–10 min.	10–15 min.	—	10–15 min.
Total Work Volume	2–3 min. max	≥ 12 min.	15–60 min.	15–60 min.
Training Period	8–12 weeks	8–12 weeks	8–12 weeks	8–12 weeks
Frequency	Hard–easy (48 hrs)	Hard–easy	Daily	Hard–easy

Reprinted with permission from Coaching Association of Canada, Level 3 Theory, 6-85.

Table 3.5: A comparison of the training of the three energy systems

the development of the aerobic system.

The value of interval training is that the volume and intensity of exercise can be far greater than for continuous exercise using the same time period. Fatigue is delayed because there is more reliance on the alactic system, the lactic system is not completely exhausted, and time is allowed for recovery. The body also adapts and becomes more tolerant to lactic acid build-up, and thus a higher anaerobic threshold (point where lactic acid interferes with muscle contraction) is developed. As mentioned previously, intermittent exercise also develops the aerobic system and allows for 2½ times the intensity, as compared with continuous exercise, before lactic-acid levels are equal. Intermittent exercise also simulates the exercise-to-rest ratios, which are common in many sports such as basketball, football, soccer, volleyball, and ice and field hockey.

To apply interval training, it is important to determine the energy systems used in the specific sport. Exercise can be in the form of running, cycling, skating, swimming, and so on.

Some terms used in the discussion of interval training are:

- Work interval—high-intensity exercise
- Relief interval—time between high-intensity exercise bursts
- Repetitions—one exercise burst
- Set—a number of repetitions followed by a longer period of relief
- Intensity—rate at which the exercise is performed (involves time and distance)
- Frequency—the number of times per week the training is performed

Interval training involves the manipulation of certain variables to evoke an overload to improve the energy systems. The manipulation of these variables requires both science and art on the part of the coach. Programs can be too difficult or too easy, and in most cases have to be tailored to suit each athlete, although, in team sports especially, programs are developed for groups of similarly trained athletes.

The variables manipulated in interval training are:

1. Rate and distance
2. Repetitions and sets
3. Duration of the relief interval
4. Type of activity in the relief interval
5. Frequency of training

Rate and Distance

The rate of exercise is determined by heart rates and percentage of maximum oxygen uptake (discussed previously). Rate of exercise can also be determined by moving a certain distance in a certain time. Distances are usually determined as a percentage of the total distance covered in track or swimming, or as a percentage of playing time in some team sports. Distances usually range from 50 to 400 meters in most interval-training programs, depending on the predominant energy systems used. Times are usually slower than event times, with 85 to 95 percent of maximum being common. Swimmers usually use 1/4 running distances for the work intervals. Predicted times range from 0.5 to 2 seconds slower than event times, depending on the distances used.

Repetitions and Sets

Repetitions range from a low of two or three for longer distances to a high of ten for shorter distances. Sets also can range from one to a high of five or six. Total volume ranges from 1.5–3.0 miles (3–5 km) in running distances, and workout times usually range from thirty to ninety minutes, including rest and relief periods.

Duration of the Relief Period

The relief interval is in ratio to the work interval and can be varied. The alactic system uses a 1:6 or 1:5 work-to-rest ratio; for example, work for 5 seconds and rest for 30 or 25 seconds. The lactic system relief interval varies from the 1:6 or 1:5 to 1:3, and even 1:2, work-to-rest ratio, depending on training level.

Other methods use a recovery period when the heart rate returns to 140 beats per minute between repetitions and 120 beats per minute between sets. A guideline formula of 160 minus the age equalling the beats per minute can be used to determine when to resume exercise.

It is important to note that, if the athlete's pulse during relief does not go down to these guidelines, or the athlete feels he or she is not recovered fully, a further repetition should be delayed until this recovery point is reached. If the pulse rate remains above the normal recovery rate, the workout should be discontinued.

Activity during the Relief Period

The time between workout bursts is referred to as "the relief period." This is done to distinguish between relief and complete rest.

Light or mild exercise (60 percent MVO_2), consisting of jogging or rapid walking, causes the restoring of the alactic system to be partially blocked and allows the lactic acid to be more fully utilized in the next work burst.

Flexing, walking, and light jogging also help remove the lactic acid build-up. Therefore it is recommended that, when the training of the lactate system is predominant, light jogging, flexing, and stretching be performed during the relief interval.

Frequency of Training

It is recommended that alactic training be done three or four times per week, on alternate days. Lactate training should be done three times per week.

Aerobic training also is done on alternate days, although the elite endurance runners are known to train six days per week. Elite sprinters also vary their intensities between hard and easy and work out five or six days per week. The key to this type of training is to allow the athletes sufficient time to recover before starting the next workout.

Manipulating the various variables mentioned to effect a training change is an important role of both the coach and the athletes. Giving specific training programs to inexperienced athletes can be detrimental as the programs may be either too difficult or too easy. The training programs have to be monitored daily by the coach and changed according to the performance and feelings of the athlete. Special attention should be paid to beginning and inexperienced athletes. The first two weeks of their programs should be easier, to ensure that the essential orientation period is achieved.

Interval training had its origins in track and was adopted in swimming. Most sports now include this highly proven method as part of their training program.

OTHER METHODS OF TRAINING THE ENERGY SYSTEMS

There are a number of training methods, some of which incorporate interval-training principles, which can be used to train the energy systems. As variety of training is also important, the coach can use a number of different methods for training the energy systems.

Aerobic Methods

Training programs that focus on the aerobic system predominantly include continuous fast and slow running, and interval sprinting. Continuous running can be performed at a slower or faster pace, with the anaerobic threshold being stressed more in fast-pace continuous running.

Interval sprinting involves continuous sprints of 50 meters followed by a jog of 50–70 meters continuously for a distance of approximately 5,000 meters (3 miles).

Anaerobic Methods

Sprinting, acceleration sprints, hollow sprints, repetition running, stops and starts (shuttle runs), and hill running are all anaerobic training methods for both the alactic and the lactic systems. The intensity and duration of the exercise determine which of these two anaerobic systems is the predominant one being trained.

Sprint training involves a number of all-out sprints of 50–100 meters, with complete recovery between sprints. *Acceleration sprinting* involves increasing the running speed by jogging, striding, and sprinting in three equal segments of 50–100 meters.

Hollow sprints are two sprints with a period of jogging or walking between: for example, sprint 50 meters, jog 50 meters, sprint 50 meters, and walk 50 meters. This sequence is repeated several times around a track, or by estimating distances on a trail or road in a continuous fashion.

The exercise period and the relief period are both usually longer than in interval training with *repetition running*. The intensity level is high, and distances are usually half the event distance in track. The number of repetitions is also fewer than interval training because of the high intensity level over a longer period of time.

Stops and starts with a direction change, also called "shuttle running" or "line drills," have been used in team sports such as basketball, ice hockey, football, and volleyball for many years. The procedure involves starting on a line on the field, court, or ice; sprinting to another line; and continuing to change directions or move backwards and forwards, touching the various lines. This procedure usually lasts from thirty to sixty seconds.

Hill running, or running up and walking down hills, or running up and down hills and then resting, are good methods for achieving an anaerobic-power exercise. Running down hills has also been used in speed-training programs.

Combined Anaerobic and Aerobic Methods

A good method to combine the training of all three energy systems is Fartlek (trans: "speed play") training. Developed by the Swedes, it is an exercise system which uses the terrain of forests, trails, and hills of the countryside. It combines fast and slow running with periods of interval sprinting, repetition running, walking, hill running, and various other methods, while the athletes, usually in groups, make their way along a forest trail. This method is now used on golf courses or other suitable aesthetically pleasing terrains. It is meant to be a more informal, less precise, but more enjoyable type of energy-system training.

It is important that coaches keep variety in the workouts and use a number of different energy-system training methods, with special attention to the energy demands of the particular sport. With these general energy-system training methods, the coach can design, improvise, and apply the basic training concepts to the sport, varying the training methods to keep the interest and motivation of the athletes at a high level.

STRENGTH AND POWER TRAINING

Strength, power, and speed are components of most athletic movements and are interrelated. Strength, in simple terms, is the ability to apply a force. It can be further classified as absolute, relative, and maximal.

Absolute strength is defined as the maximum force an athlete can generate, irrespective of body weight and the time taken to develop this force. Body weight and strength are directly related to performance, and strength is applicable in sports such as football (linemen), and throwing the shotput.

Relative strength can be defined as the maximum force an athlete can generate per unit of body weight. This type of strength is important in sports where athletes have to displace their own weight, such as gymnastics, figure skating, and jumping, as well as weight-classification sports, such as wrestling and boxing. Quick-acceleration sports, such as soccer, ice hockey, and track and field, are also in this category.

Maximal strength is defined as the peak force the neuromuscular system is capable of producing in a single muscular contraction. Maximal strength applies to most sports where all-out short-duration effort is required.

The difference between strength and strength endurance or muscular endurance should be clearly understood. "Muscular or strength endurance" is defined as the ability to sustain or repeat a muscular contraction against a resistance. A swimmer's continuous arm and leg movements or a baseball pitcher's arm movement over several innings are examples of muscular endurance.

Power, important in sports of quick movement and large force, is a combination of strength and speed. Any sport that involves jumping, sprinting, throwing, striking, and changing direction requires power.

"Speed" can be defined as the maximum rate of contraction or moving the body as quickly as possible. Strength and power are key components of speed. The fiber type (fast or slow twitch) and the nervous-system involvement are also key components of speed. Fiber type is generally believed to be hereditary, and the amount of fast- and slow-twitch fiber in a muscle cannot be changed through training.

Agility is the ability to change directions quickly and is related to strength, power, and speed.

Types of Muscular Contraction

Skeletal muscles either contract or relax. When the muscles receive an impulse from the motor nerves, they contract, and when the impulse is stopped, the muscles relax.

The three types of muscle contraction are: isotonic, isometric, and isokinetic. Isotonic contractions are performed in three ways: concentric, eccentric, and plyometric.

Isotonic contractions are usually defined as those in which the muscle exerts a constant tension. Common free weights and various weight-training machines are usually referred to as isotonic, but this nomenclature is not exact. The tension exerted by the muscle throughout the range of motion is not constant but varies with the mechanical advantage of the joint involved with the movement, with highest tension being around 120 percent and lowest around 30 percent. The tension of muscle contraction is angle-related. The more accurate term to describe this movement is "dynamic constant resistance training."

Concentric contraction refers to contractions in which the muscle length shortens. This occurs when the muscle tension overcomes the resistance (the weight). The peak force in a concentric contraction occurs around an angle of 120° (Bompa). *Eccentric or negative contractions* are those in which the muscle lengthens. Muscle tension during an eccentric contraction is greater than during a concentric or isometric contraction. The risk of greater muscle soreness occurs with eccentric contraction, as compared with concentric and isometric contractions (Fleck & Schutt).

Isometric or static contractions occur when the muscle develops tension without changing its length. Thus, the muscle is unable to generate enough force against an object to cause movement. This type of resistance training is usually performed against an immovable object such as a wall, a barbell in a locked position, or an overloaded weight machine in which movement is not possible. Some strength programs combine isotonics and isometrics. The isometric contraction is done either before or at the end of an isotonic contraction.

An *isokinetic contraction* is performed at a constant speed in a full range of motion. There is no set resistance, as the resistance varies to keep the speed constant. A reaction force equals the force applied to the equipment, making it possible for the muscles to exert a continual maximal force throughout the range of motion. The Cybex machine is one common example of an isokinetic device.

Plyometrics refers to a concentric contraction immediately preceded by an eccentric contraction. One-leg and two-leg hopping and jumping from benches are examples of plyometric-type exercises.

Note: For more detail on the physiology of the muscular system, see pages 125 to 129.

Detraining and Strength Maintenance

Most athletes are involved in a strength program during the preparation or off-season period of their training program. The question often arises as to how much strength is lost when a strength program is completed and what type of maintenance program is necessary during an athlete's competitive season.

Studies have shown that strength gains can be maintained with one workout per week (Kraemer) and actually showed some improvement with one set of strength exercises once per week.

After training ceases, strength declines at a much slower rate that it increases. Strength gained rapidly appears to be lost rapidly, whereas strength gained over a longer period of time declines at a slower rate. Strength gained is lost at approximately one-third the rate at which it is gained.

It is therefore recommended that athletes strength-train at least once per week to maintain the strength gained during the preparation period. Although the intensity remains the same with the reps and sets, the volume is decreased.

COMPARISON OF ISOTONIC CONCENTRIC, ISOTONIC ECCENTRIC, ISOMETRICS, AND ISOKINETICS STRENGTH-TRAINING METHODS

Using the various research studies to compare different strength-development methods is difficult. Methods of testing, volume, intensity and duration of the exercise program, and the present development of strength of the participants are a few of the problems encountered in trying to analyze the various programs.

One conclusion is clear—all of the methods of isotonic concentric and eccentric, isometrics, isokinetics, and plyometrics have a place in a strength-development program.

Various studies have compared isotonic and isometric programs and the following conclusions can be made:

- Both isometrics and isotonics improve strength. Although many studies report appreciable gains using both methods, more studies report greater gains using isotonic exercises.
- Muscular endurance is developed more effectively with isotonic than isometric exercises.
- Isometric training develops strength at one point in a range of motion and not at other positions, and may be of benefit in sports which can have a static movement, such as wrestling and football. However, isotonic exercises produce a more uniform development of strength and have a better application to sport performance.
- Motivation is usually better with isotonics, as the athlete can see that more weight is being lifted or more repetitions are being performed.
- Isometrics have the advantage of being virtually cost-less and can be done anywhere in a smaller space.
- It is generally believed by many strength experts that isometrics should be an adjunct to a strength program, not the principal method of strength training.

Isotonic Concentric versus Isotonic Eccentric

Eccentric isotonic training is being included in many training programs as an adjunct to isotonic concentric training. Strength-training experts are intrigued by the fact that more tension can be developed in the muscle by an eccentric contraction (lowering the weight) compared with a concentric contraction (raising the weight). In the study illustrated in figure 3.9, eccentric contractions produced slightly better results than concentric methods.

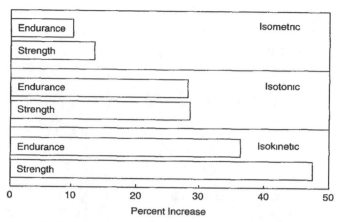

Figure 3.10: Comparison of isotonic, isometric, and isokinetic strength programs performed for eight weeks. Reprinted by permission from R. Bowers and E. Fox, *Sports Physiology.* (Dubuque, IA: Wm. C. Brown), 168.

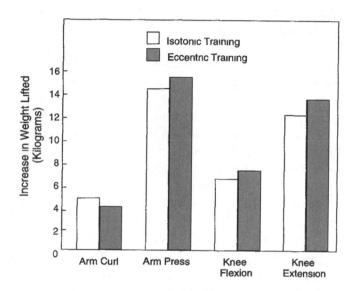

Figure 3.9: Comparison of strength gains following isotonic and eccentric strength-training programs. Reprinted by permission from R. Bowers and E. Fox, *Sport Physiology.* (Dubuque, IA: Wm. C. Brown), 165.

The major disadvantage of eccentric methods is the greater muscle soreness that they produce. For this reason the eccentric-contraction method is not the major part of a strength workout for most athletes.

Isotonic, Isometric, and Isokinetics

Some studies have compared the results of isotonic, isometric, and isokinetic exercises. Figure 3.10 illustrates one such study, which shows the superiority of isokinetic programs to the other two. It should be mentioned that, although isokinetic programs have been shown to be superior in both strength and muscular endurance, the availability and the cost of the equipment is a factor in their use. More research is needed in the comparison and effectiveness of various strength methods.

Free Weights versus Machines

Some athletes and nearly all world-class competitors in weight lifting use free weights as opposed to weight machines, while others use a combination of machines and free weights. A summary of the advantages and disadvantages of free weights versus machines is presented in table 3.6.

Table 3.6: Advantages and disadvantages of free weights and machines.

Free Weights

Advantages
1. More closely match the movement in the sport.
2. More effective in developing stabilizer and synergistic (helping) muscle groups.
3. Less expensive than machines.
4. Take up less space for individual use.
5. Strength and power can be achieved more efficiently.

Disadvantages
1. Can be dangerous without spotting. Also, collars can come off and weights fall off the bar.
2. Takes time to adjust weights. Collars must be removed.
3. In some exercises, it is difficult to isolate a muscle group.
4. For group use, they can take up too much space and time to change weights.

Machines

Advantages

1. Can more efficiently isolate a muscle group.
2. Generally safer, as weights are held in place with retaining pins.
3. More efficient for group use in terms of space utilization.
4. Easier to use, and faster workouts are possible. Minimal time is needed to change weights.

Disadvantages

1. Most machines work in predetermined path of movement, and consequently it is difficult to isolate stabilizer and synergistic muscle groups.
2. Because movement and range of motion in many cases is limited, the natural movement of the exercise has been removed. Some researchers believe this makes these exercises less effective due to the neurological aspect of strength and power development.
3. High-speed training in many cases is not possible.
4. Machines are usually more expensive.
5. A number of machines may have to be purchased to get the required number of body exercises needed.

PRINCIPLES OF STRENGTH-TRAINING PROGRAMS

Strength training is based on five principles: overload, progressive resistance, specificity, variety, and individualization.

Overload refers to exercising the muscles with a load that is greater than normally encountered. Thirty percent greater than normal is considered the minimal level for stimulation of the physiological responses that increases the strength in the muscle.

Progressive resistance is important in strength training as the overload which initially stimulates the physiological responses is no longer effective once the muscle adapts to this load. The training load must therefore be increased so that the muscle is extended to the fatigue level. Therefore, the resistance or the number of times the resistance is moved must be progressively increased to initiate further improvement in the strength of the muscle.

Specificity refers to the fact that strength development is specific to the muscle groups that are exercised and the movement patterns they produce. The specific muscle groups that are used in the sport should be trained, and the movement of the muscle group should, as closely as possible, simulate the movement used in the

sport. The direction and angle of the force and the plane of movement should be analyzed for each movement in the sport. The predominant energy system should be included in the time and intensity of the movement. In other words, a sprinter should be training with short-burst movement patterns in the exercises and the long-distance runner should be repeating the movement patterns over a long period of time.

Although the predominant strength-program exercises should attempt to simulate the sport movements, it is also important to develop all the muscle groups. The development of total body strength should be done in the general preparation phase of the periodized training, with the more specific strength exercises involving the sport movements being performed in the specific preparation period.

There are two main reasons in strength training that *variety* of the program is important. First, the rate of strength adaptation slows after two to three weeks and, second, boredom and monotony of the program can affect the motivation and the psychological well-being of the athlete. Athletes must strength-train for six to eight hours per week in the preparation period to be successful, and an innovative coach will design a program that keeps the motivation and interest level of the athlete high.

Variety in the strength program should be included at least every three weeks. It has been shown, as illustrated in figure 3.11, that the best improvements in training occur with a lessening of the volume and intensity of the load every three weeks. The type of contraction, especially between concentric and eccentric; the speed of contraction; and changing the exercises and changing

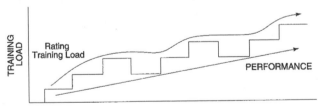

Figure 3.11: The curve of the training load with performance improving continuously. Reprinted by permission from T. Bompa, *Periodization of Strength*. (Toronto: Veritas), 54.

type of equipment (free weights, machines, isokinetic devices, etc.) are some of the methods used to provide variety in a strength program.

Individualization is an essential aspect of strength training. One of the biggest mistakes a coach can make is to apply one strength program for all athletes. Each athlete must be initially assessed on ability, level of performance, potential, and strength-training background before a program is initiated.

Another concept that summarizes the various aspects of training is the SAID principle (Specific Adaptation to Imposed Demands). This principle states that the training demands must be specific and, to obtain maximum results, must be gradually intensified over an extended period of time. This then incorporates the progressive resistance principle as well (O'Shea).

Other factors to consider for each athlete is his or her capacity for work, both psychologically and physiologically; ability to recover; the time available; and gender and anatomical structure.

The strength program for each athlete has to be well planned and should take into consideration an individual assessment of current status and planning for future needs in strength abilities for the specific sport.

DESIGNING A STRENGTH PROGRAM

The first step in designing a strength program is to analyze the movements in the sport and to determine the major and minor (assistive) muscle groups used. The duration and force of the muscle contraction, and the specific angles of push and pull, are also factors to be considered when analyzing the movement. Remember that both general muscle development and specificity are important.

The next step to consider is the current strength status and the relative strengths and weaknesses of the athlete. Factors such as age, skill level, height and weight, and previous background in strength training should be considered in designing the strength program. Combining different modalities, such as free weights and machines, and using concentric, eccentric, and isometric methods should also be considered.

The next step is to test the maximum strength of the athlete in each of the selected exercises to be used in the strength program. This procedure has the athletes perform each of the exercises and adjust the loading until only one repetition (1 RM) can be performed. However, caution should be exercised as injury can occur, and young athletes or those beginning a strength program should use only light weights. Whenever possible, universal-type machines should be used to test 1 RM, as they are better able to isolate the specific muscles to be tested.

After the movements of the sport and the athlete's strength have been analyzed, the exercises to be used in the strength program should be selected. The exercises for the program should be divided into prime movers, stabilizers, and specific exercises. It is also important to develop the core muscles of the body of the back and abdomen in any strength program.

After deciding on the exercises, or in conjunction with such decision making, the modality of performing the exercises will have to be selected. The decision about using free weights or machines, and concentric, eccentric, or isometric, and so on, will be made according to needs, availability of equipment, and the type and period of the program. Most strength programs use a variety of strength-training methods and modalities. The athlete should keep a training log, as shown in figure 3.12. Items such as exercises, sets, weights and repetitions, and days of the week should be included.

Name _____ Age _____

Week _____ Week _____
Day _____ Day _____
Weight _____ lb. Weight _____ lb

Exercise	Set 1 Weight	Set 1 Reps	Set 2 Weight	Set 2 Reps	Set 3 Weight	Set 3 Reps	Set 1 Weight	Set 1 Reps	Set 2 Weight	Set 2 Reps	Set 3 Weight	Set 3 Reps

Comments _____
_____
_____

Exercise   Modifications
_____   _____
_____   _____

Figure 3.12: Training log

69

The exercise program should be designed for the relevant segment of the periodization schedule (see pages 47–50). The volume of work will be greater for the general preparation period, and the exercises will be more sport-specific in the specific preparation period. During the competitive period, the number of exercises are reduced and the frequency is usually once or twice per week.

Selecting the Exercise

As mentioned previously, an analysis of the sport and the strengths and weaknesses of the athlete has to be performed before the selection of exercises for the strength program is made.

As well as categorizing exercises for major and minor muscle groups, exercises can be further categorized as body-part or structural (Fleck & Kraemer). Exercises which isolate specific muscle groups are designated as body-part exercises, and include, for example, biceps and leg curls and sit-ups. Structural exercises are ones that require the coordinated action of a number of muscle groups, and include, for example, squats, dead lifts, and power leans and snatches.

Order of Exercises

The traditional thinking in strength training is to exercise the large muscle groups first and then the smaller muscle groups. The rationale for this approach is that, by exercising the smaller muscle groups, they will fatigue and the athlete will not be able to provide a maximal stimulus to the larger prime-mover muscle groups later because of this fatigue factor. Bompa argues, however, that because strength-training exercises should mimic, as much as possible, the sport movement, a chain of muscle movement in a similar pattern should be the objective of the exercise. A volleyball player spiking the ball with a chain of movements involving both small and large muscle groups is an example of this theory. Working on the large muscle groups first is irrelevant for strength training in sports that use small muscle groups initially.

Recently eastern European literature has also challenged the large-muscles-first theory, and different types of pre-exhaustion methods have been used, with the small muscle groups being exercised first.

Exercises generally should be planned to alternate the limb/muscle groups in order to recover from fatigue, with a legs, arms, abdomen/legs, arms, back sequence. An alternation of agonist and antagonist muscles is often used as well.

Some strength programs challenge the method that alternates muscle groups, the pre-exhaustion use of agonist/antagonist muscles, by exercising the same muscle groups in succession. It should be noted that pre-exhaustion methods are for the more advanced athletes in strength training. It should be remembered that, in sport, the skills are performed with the prime movers together with the synergistic muscles, which assist directly in the performance of the skill. After establishing the order of exercises, there are two methods of executing the program. One method is to do each exercise with all the sets, and then move on to the next exercise (horizontal sequence). The other method is to perform all the exercises with one set for each muscle group, repeating this sequence until the desired number of sets is completed (vertical sequence). Bompa recommends the vertical sequence, as this method allows for a longer rest of the muscle groups between sets, and thus a better regeneration before the next set begins with the same muscle group. The theory here is that, with the horizontal method, local fatigue becomes so high that, instead of power or maximum strength, the outcome may be hypertrophy, which is more beneficial for body builders than for athletes.

Number of Repetitions (Load) and Speed of the Lifting (Rhythm)

The most important aspect of strength training is the resistance or load (McDonagh & Davies). Repetitions and speed of lifting or rhythm are directly related to load; that is, the higher the load, the lower the number of repetitions and the slower the speed of the movement.

There are two main methods of determining the load: using repetition maximums or a particular load which allows only a specific number of repetitions to be performed; and using a percentage of one maximum repetition (% 1 RM).

Once again, the needs of the sport are important, and what type of strength it requires. The continuum of strength ranges from maximum strength and power to muscular endurance. The strength program for a golfer is obviously going to be quite different from that for a football lineman.

There are many theories on the optimum number of repetitions—expressed as RMs (maximum reps)—for strength development. Fleck & Kraemer recommend RM loads of six or fewer for the greatest effect on maximal power and RMs of twenty and more for the most effective means of developing muscular endurance. The same authors later recommended ten RMs for strength/power, and fifteen RMs for muscular endurance.

Bompa recommends for the development of maximum strength that the load be 85–105 percent of maximum, and the number of reps be one to seven, for strength development, and for developing power, 50–80 percent of maximum, with five to ten RMs performed dynamically (quickly). For the development of muscular endurance of short duration, 10–30 RMs should be done, for medium duration 30–60, and for long duration 100–150. The important factor here is to analyze the sport for the type and duration of the strength used.

Table 3.7 (Charters) summarizes the continuum from maximum strength to maximum endurance. Poliquin has further contributed to strength guidelines for coaches by relating the percentage of maximum load to the number of repetitions, as illustrated in table 3.8.

Maximum Dynamic Strength		Strength and Endurance		Maximum Endurance	
% max	90+	% max	75–85	% max	65–75
Reps	2–4	Reps	4–10	Reps	12–20
Sets	6–8	Sets	4–5	Sets	3–4
Rest between Sets	3–5 min.	Rest	15–60 sec.	Rest	0–30 sec.

Table 3.7: Weight-training continuum for dynamic strength, strength and endurance, and maximum endurance

Maximum No. of Reps	% of Maximum Load	Coefficient (divide load by)
1	100.0	1
2	94.3	0.94
3	90.6	0.91
4	88.1	0.88
5	85.6	0.86
6	83.1	0.82
7	80.7	0.81
8	78.6	0.79
9	76.5	0.77
10	74.4	0.74

Table 3.8: Relating the percentage of maximum load to maximum number of repetitions for strength training

Number of Sets

A number of repetitions per exercise followed by a rest interval is called "a set." The number of sets is related to the type of strength being trained, the total number of exercises, and the number of repetitions per set. As the number of exercise repetitions increases, the number of sets decreases. If one is training for muscular endurance, the number of repetitions of the exercise is high, and therefore more than three or four sets would be difficult. On the other hand, if one is training with a lower number of repetitions per exercise, the number of sets can be increased to five or six. A general strength program usually has between three and four sets.

The training phase is also a factor in the number of sets performed in each training session. In the general preparation phase, the number of exercises is high and the number of sets is lower, whereas in the specific-competitive phase, the number of exercises is lower, and consequently the number of sets is higher. During the competitive phase, where strength maintenance is the prime objective, the number of exercises and sets is reduced for the one or two workouts per week, and more time is spent on technical and tactical work.

In general, the highly trained athlete should be able to perform between three and eight sets, depending on the state of training. Beginners should use only one or two sets per exercise each workout.

Rest Intervals between Sets

The rest interval determines the amount of restoration of the anaerobic energy systems (alactic and lactic acid) that is achieved and is of utmost importance in a well-designed strength program. The alactic system needs up to three minutes for complete restoration, and, if this is not allowed for, the energy depletion will begin in the lactic-system. When rest periods are reduced to thirty seconds and relatively heavy loads are used, lactate levels are at a high level, and early fatigue ensues. However, by shortening rest levels, a greater tolerance for lactic acid is developed for sports which use the lactic-system as the predominant energy source.

LOAD %	Rhythm of Performance	RI (minutes)	Applicability
>105 (eccentric)	Slow	4–5/7	Improve maximum strength and muscle tone
80–100	Slow to medium	3–5/7	Improve maximum strength and muscle tone
60–80	Slow to medium	2	Improve muscle hypertrophy
50–80	Fast	4–5	Improve power
30–50	Slow to medium	1–2	Improve muscular endurance

Table 3.9: Suggested rest intervals between sets for different loads. Reprinted with permission from T. Bompa, *Periodization of Strength*. (Toronto: Veritas), 67.

Table 3.9 summarizes rest-interval information, which should be useful in determining the rest intervals with the various strength programs. It is also believed that the central nervous system, including the motor nerve, the neuromuscular junction, and the contractible mechanism, recover with a rest interval of between four and five minutes.

Activity during Rest

Relaxation exercises such as shaking the arms and legs and light massage allow for faster recovery between sets. Walking, stretching, and light muscle contractions also aid in recovery from fatigue between sets, as they facilitate lactic-acid removal.

Rest Interval between Strength Workouts

It is generally believed that training three times per week, every other day, is the optimum method for efficient strength development. The level of conditioning, the training phase, and the energy source used are important factors in determining the rest days between strength training. Strength training can be performed on consecutive days using the split-routine method, which includes exercising different body parts each day or using different exercises for the same body part each day. One study even proposed four consecutive days of strength training followed by three successive days of rest (Hunter).

It is recommended that, when the same energy systems are being used in the technical and tactical training, the strength-training session should follow the technical/tactical training and be on the same day. The next type of this training should then follow forty-eight hours later to allow for full restoration of the glycogen stores.

Increasing the Resistance (Load)

As mentioned previously, overload and progressive resistance are the two key factors in strength development. The resistance in strength training must be gradually increased to initiate a stimulus to increase strength, taking into consideration that each individual has a different rate of increase, depending on the present and past state of training reactions of the body anatomically and physiologically, and improvements of the neuromuscular system.

Increasing the load or resistance is the basis of all athletic training. Training maintained at the same level throughout the year is referred to as "the standard load." Repetition of the standard load results in improvements

in the early part of a training period, but is followed by a plateau, and even detraining during the competitive phase. Not only will performance deteriorate, but expected improvements from year to year will not occur (Bompa).

The overload principle is the traditional approach, and this method suggests that the strength-training load should be increased throughout the training program. The overload principle involves brief maximum contractions, which result in high activation of the neuromuscular system, and submaximal contractions to exhaustion, which cause muscle hypertrophy. This is the common method of strength training and can cause extreme fatigue if carried out over a long period of time.

Guidelines for increasing the load for the weaker, less trained for the upper body are 2.5–5 pounds (1–2 kg) and lower body 5–10 pounds (2–4 kg). For the stronger, more trained for the upper body 2.5–5 pounds (2–4 kg) and lower body 10–15 pounds (4–7 kg) of increase are recommended.

The step method or linear periodization involves a three-week increase in the load, followed by a fourth week of reducing the load to the levels of the second week, as illustrated previously in figure 3.11. This fourth week allows the body to regenerate with lesser loads in order to take on a higher load in the next four-week cycle, as training performance usually improves following the regeneration phase. This microcycle (week) is not extreme, but rather a medium unloading phase.

Non-Linear versus Linear Periodization

Recently an alternative method called non-linear or undulating periodization has been shown in some research studies to be more effective, although other research suggests there is no difference (Fleck & Kremer). The undulating method supports the theory that the absence of neural fatigue caused always increasing intensities and the variety in the workouts shows this method has some merit. However, both linear and non-linear periodization methods have shown to be effective, and choice of which method should depend on the reaction of the individual being trained for a particular sport.

Examples of linear and non-linear periodization follows:

Linear Periodization

Microcycle 1: 3–5 sets, 10–12 RM
Microcycle 2: 4–5 sets, 8–10 RM
Microcycle 3: 3–4 sets, 4–6 RM
Microcycle 4: 3–5 sets, 1–3 RM
Active Rest

Non-linear Periodization

16 Weeks – 6 Day Rotation
Monday: 4 sets, 12–15 RM
Wednesday: 4 sets, 8–10 RM
Friday: 3–4 sets, 1–3 RM
Monday: 4–5 sets, 1–3 RM
Wednesday: Power Day
Friday: 2 sets, 12–15 RM
Active Rest after 16 weeks mesocycle is completed

Summary

As can be seen from the previous information there is not an exact method of determining reps, sets and loads in resistance training. The coach or strength and conditioning professional must adapt the training program and training goals to the specific sport and individual. Most programs based on sound principals of strength development produce results. More recently the following guidelines have been used.

Training Goal	Load (%/RM)	Repetitions	Sets	Rest Intervals Between Sets
Strength	≥ 85	≤ 6	2–6	2–5 mins
Power				
Single Effort Event	80–90	1–2	3–5	2–5 mins
Multiple Effort Event	75–85	3–5	3–5	2–5 mins
Hypertrophy	67–85	6–12	3–6	30 secs–1.5 mins
Muscular Endurance	≤ 67	≥ 12	2–3	≤ 30 secs

Adapted from tables 15.9, 15.11, 15.12 in *Essentials of Strength Training and Conditioning*, ed. Baechle, Earle and Wathen.

Warm-Up and Cool-Down for Strength Training

Every strength program should include a warm-up before beginning the strength exercises, and a cool-down after the exercises have been completed. The warm-up should consist of a general phase of between ten and twelve minutes, which should include a light jog, running on a treadmill or riding a stationary bike for five or six minutes, followed by five or six minutes of stretching. A specific phase lasting up to three to five minutes should follow, using some of the exercises to be performed in training with loads lighter than those used in regular training.

The cool-down follows the workout and consists of similar exercises included in the general warm-up such as stretching and light jogging or riding the stationary bike. The cool-down usually lasts five to ten minutes.

Proper Breathing

It is recommended that the lifter inhale just before and during lowering of a weight or resistance, and exhale when lifting. Some breath-holding may occur during the last repetition in a set or during a heavy lift. Breath-holding is not recommended as it causes the blood pressure to rise and reduces the blood flow to the heart. When the breath is released, blood flow is reduced to the brain, and dizziness and fainting can occur (Kraemer & Fleck).

Weight-Training Belt

The weight-training belt is designed to help support the lower back. The belt is not necessary but is merely an aid to counteract the lack of strong abdominal and lower-back musculature. The belt should be used only in exercises involving the lower back. However, strengthening the lower back and abdominal muscles is a better method than relying on the training belt.

Proper Technique and Spotting

It is very important in strength training that the exercise be done properly. The exercise should be demonstrated to the athlete with the proper spotting techniques, especially with free weights. Spotting is a procedure where another person is in a ready position to assist in the movement should the athlete need help in preventing an injury. Machines require less or no spotting, since the movement needs little balancing when done in one place.

Free weights require the lifter to balance the weights in all directions. A light resistance should be used when starting strength-program exercises, and the athlete should be given feedback as well as instruction in the technique. Special care should be given in the teaching of multiple joint exercises such as squats and cleans.

Training Log

The training log should record the number of sets, repetitions, and resistances for each exercise for each training session. Keeping this record enables the athlete to measure the progress in the strength-training program and determine the increases in repetitions and load. Short forms such as "75/6/2," meaning 75 percent 1 RM, 6 reps, for 2 sets, are commonly used in a training log. The training log is a good motivational tool to measure progress and to evaluate the success of the program.

PERIODIZATION OF STRENGTH/POWER TRAINING

The annual plan, as discussed previously, divides the training year into three main phases: preparatory or pre-season, competitive or in-season, and transition or off-season.

The periodization of strength training can be divided into five phases. (Bompa)

1. Anatomical adaptation
2. Maximum strength
3. Conversion to power
4. Maintenance
5. Transition

Anatomical Adaptation

The purpose of this first phase of strength/power development is to adapt tendons, ligaments, and muscle tissue to handle progressively increasing loads. The exercise program should be designed to strengthen not only the arms and legs, but also the core muscles of the body, which include the abdominals and lower back as well as the spinal-column musculature. These core exercises strengthen the trunk to support arm and leg movements and prepare the body for jumping, landing, and falling movements, which are a part of many sports. All muscle groups should be exercised, with special attention being paid to the balance between the agonist and the antagonist muscles, the balance between the two sides of the body, and strengthening the stabilizer muscles.

The duration of this phase should be eight to ten weeks for younger inexperienced athletes, and three to five weeks for athletes who have been strength-training for at least four years.

Maximum-Strength Phase

The objective of this phase is to develop the highest level of force possible. The body adapts the neuromuscular system to heavy loads and the recruitment of as many muscle fibers as possible in a given movement. The duration of this phase depends on the sport, but usually lasts from one to three months. This phase prepares the body for the development of power, as power is a product of maximum strength and speed. Heavier loads with a lower number of repetitions are used in this phase.

Power-Conversion Phase

The main purpose of this phase is to convert or transform gains in maximum strength into power and sport-specific movements. Lighter loads are employed with fast contractions, where the athlete is exposed to activities in which the nervous system is activated and the speed of the contraction is sport-specific. Weights and plyometrics are used in this phase, along with sport-specific movements using resistance with light weights, elastic tubing, medicine balls, and so on. This phase usually has a duration of four or five weeks, depending on the sport, with endurance sports taking longer.

Maintenance Phase and Plyometrics

This phase continues throughout the competitive season, stopping usually one to two weeks before the main competition or playoffs. Without this phase, strength and power gains can be lessened by a detraining effect.

Four to six exercises, performed one to two times per week, are usually sufficient to maintain the strength and power gained in the first three phases. The intensity of the training sessions should remain high, but the duration should be shorter, lasting between thirty and forty minutes.

Transition Phase

The main purpose of this phase is to remove fatigue and replenish the energy stores, relax, and maintain the fitness and strength levels acquired in the previous four phases (see table 3.10). Some strength work should be continued, as without it the detraining effect will cause a loss of muscle size and power. The workload is reduced by 50 to 60 percent in this phase. This phase lasts four to six weeks.

	Percentage of Maximum	Reps	Sets
Anatomical adaptation	50–70	10	2
Maximum strength	80–95	6	2
Power conversion	50–70	10	3
Maintenance	75–85	6	3

Table 3.10: Summary of the training phases

VARIOUS STRENGTH-TRAINING METHODS

Circuit Training

Circuit training was developed at Leeds University by Morgan & Adamson in 1959. The circuit-training program involves exercises at a number of stations, using different muscle groups at each station for a specific time period. The time period is usually thirty to sixty seconds of exercise, followed by sixty to ninety seconds of rest, which is included in the time it takes to change exercise stations and allows one to three minutes between circuits.

Circuit training can be used for general fitness and can include flexibility and cardiovascular-type exercises (skipping, running on the spot, and so on) as well as strength-development exercises and plyometrics. Apparatus for the stations can include barbells, dumbbells, wall pulleys, surgical tubing, strength machines, medicine balls, hurdles, benches and body-weight exercises. Circuits usually range from six to twelve stations, and alternate muscle groups in the station sequence. The individual usually goes through the circuit from one to three times, proceeding from each exercise station in a sequenced order. The load and number of repetitions or time is determined by finding the 1 RM for each exercise of each individual, or the general average for the group if the resistance is standard.

Circuit training is ideal for the anatomical-adaptation phase of strength training, and for team and group workouts as it allows a large number of individuals to work at one time.

An example of a typical circuit-training program using a number of repetitions at each station (the other method is using different levels of difficulty) is shown in table 3.11.

Exercise	Beginner	Repetitions Medium	Hard
1. Chin-ups	2	6	10
2. Sit-ups	10	20	30
3. Push-ups	10	15	25
4. Knee raises	5	10	15
5. Parallel-bar dips	1	3	5
6. Step-ups	10	20	30
7. Hip raises	10	15	20
8. Jumping jacks	20	35	50
9. Back extension	10	15	20
10. Leg raises	5	10	15
11. Bench jumps	10	15	20
12. Lateral leg raises	10	15	20

Table 3.11: Repetition circuit-training program with twelve stations and three levels of difficulty

Hypertrophy Method

The primary purpose of this method is to increase muscle mass, resulting in a larger cross-section of the muscle tissue. The hypertrophy method is also known as the body-building method, American system, repetition method, extensive strength loading, cross-section method, and repeated-efforts method. In the periodization model, the hypertrophy method is used between the anatomical-adaptation phase and the maximal-strength phase, and is used to develop overall muscle mass or mass of the prime movers. Poliquin uses this method, along with the maximal-weights method, to develop maximal strength.

The theory in this method is to fatigue the muscle fibers by repeating repetitions to exhaustion. The number of repetitions begins at six and ends at twelve, although some experts put the maximum number of repetitions at twenty. When the number of repetitions reaches the maximum, the load is increased and the repetitions are lowered. The tempo of the lifting is slow, and therefore the involvement of the nervous system is lessened and the recruitment of fast-twitch fibers is minimized. Loading parameters are outlined by Poliquin:

- Percentage of predicted max. load   70–82%
- No. of exercises/muscle group   1–3
- Sets of exercises   3–5
- Repetitions   6–12
- Tempo of execution   Moderate to slow
- Rest intervals   2–5 minutes

Split Routine

Using two or three exercises per muscle group, the total volume of work is divided so that strength training can be performed five or six times per week, with no muscle-group exercises on consecutive days. A typical program would have arms, legs, and abdomen exercised on Monday, Wednesday, and Friday, and chest, shoulders, and back exercised on Tuesday, Thursday, and Saturday.

Assisted (Forced) Repetitions

After performing a set of repetitions to exhaustion, two or three additional repetitions are performed with assistance of a partner.

Resistive Repetitions

The athlete performs a set of repetitions to exhaustion. A partner then assists the athlete to perform two or three more concentric repetitions, but provides resistance for the eccentric contraction to make it twice as long as the concentric contraction (two to four seconds concentric, six to eight seconds eccentric). *Note*: This is for advanced strength training only.

Super Set

There are two basic concepts for this type of training. The first method exercises the agonist muscle group and then immediately exercises the antagonist muscles of the same group without a rest. The second method exercises the same muscle group without a rest, using a different exercise.

Cheat System

The athlete performs a set of repetitions to exhaustion and then performs an additional two or three repetitions without going through the complete range of motion, or alters the motion with an assistive body swing to get the resistance moving.

Negative (Eccentric) Repetitions

Negative or eccentric type of contractions create a higher tension in a muscle as compared with concentric and isometric methods. Former East Germans claimed to have achieved a 10–35 percent greater strength gain using this method as compared with other methods (Hartman & Tunnemann). However the possibility of greater muscle soreness and slow movement with the exercises and thus less neural activation are two points against using this as the main mode of training.

Bompa recommends that, once the athlete reaches a strength-gain plateau, this method should be used.

Negative or eccentric contractions can also be performed at the end of a set by adding to the weight and partners assisting in the moving of the resistance in the concentric phase.

Poliquin outlines some guidelines for eccentric training:

- Percentage of predicted max. load   110–120%
- No. of sets   4–6
- No. of repetitions   4–6
- Rest intervals   3–5 minutes
- Tempo of execution   slow

Pyramid (Triangle) Method

The load increases progressively and the number of sets decreases, until a maximum of 1 RM is reached. A common progression is 85, 90, 95, 100 percent as shown in figure 3.13.

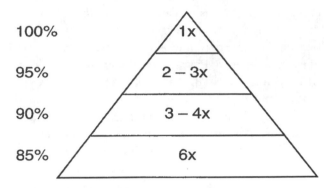

Figure 3.13 An example of the pyramid loading pattern. The number of repetitions (inside of the pyramid), refers to their number per training session.

Double (Triangle) Pyramid

Two pyramids are on top of one another peak to peak, as shown in figure 3.14. The number of repetitions decreases from the bottom up.

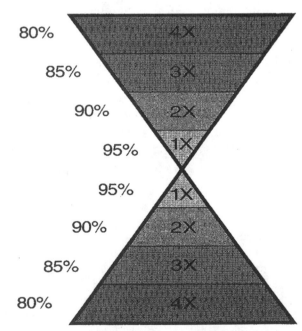

Figure 3.14: Double-pyramid loading pattern

Skewed (Triangle) Pyramid

The load is constantly increased except for the last set, which is lower, as illustrated in figure 3.15.

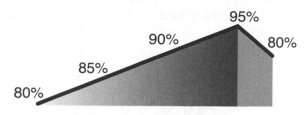

Figure 3.15: Skewed-pyramid loading pattern

Light-to-Heavy Method

DeLorme & Watkins developed a strength-development program that started with three sets of ten repetitions with 50 percent 1 RM, moved to 66 percent 1 RM in the next set, and concluded with a third set of 100 percent 1 RM. This system was popular in the 1930s and 1940s with Olympic lifters, and is still used today in some programs.

Heavy-to-Light Method

This system is a reverse of the DeLorme & Watkins method and begins after a warm-up, with the heaviest set being performed first and the resistance being decreased in successive sets. Research, although sparse, has tended to favor the heavy-to-light system over the light-to-heavy.

Wave-Like Loading

A set of exercises is followed by a five-minute rest; the resistance is increased, and the next set is performed with more speed.

Pre-exhaustion

A muscle is pre-fatigued with a single-joint exercise such as a biceps curl, and then followed with a two-joint exercise such as a clean and jerk.

Isometrics

Isometric-type exercises were developed in the 1950s by Hettinger & Muller, who reported strength gains of 5 percent per week, with one static contraction per day for five days per week.

This type of training proved to be joint-specific and is

used today as an adjunct to strength-training programs, especially in sports where a static contraction is involved, such as wrestling and football (linemen). The rate of force is not developed appreciably with the method.

Six to eight seconds with a maximum contraction is recommended, as shown in figure 3.16, although other percentages can be used. Most strength practitioners use a maximum contraction, as a percentage of maximum is difficult to determine. Three to five sets of one repetition are also recommended.

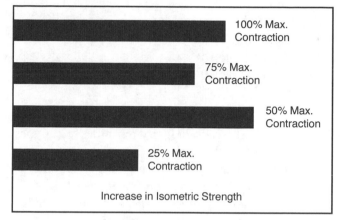

Figure 3.16: A comparison of different percentages of maximum tension with isometric exercises. Reprinted by permission from R. Bowers and E. Fox, *Sport Physiology.* (Dubuque, IA: Wm. C. Brown), 158.

Functional Isometrics

This method combines a concentric contraction finishing the movement by stopping the resistance at a certain angle, and an isometric contraction lasting six to eight seconds being performed against an immovable resistance. This method can increase the strength at a certain point in the range of motion and has been shown to cause significant increases in 1 RM bench-press strength, as compared with only dynamic concentric training alone (Jackson, et al.).

Ballistic Method

Applying a force quickly is a key factor in the conversion from the phases of maximal strength to power in the periodization model. If the force exceeds the resistance by a large amount, the resistance can be moved quickly and an explosive movement occurs. This is accomplished by moving lighter weights (50–70 percent 1 RM), medicine balls, rubber cords, and with surgical-tubing resistance. The quick recruitment of the fast-twitch muscle fibers and the coordination of the agonist and antagonist muscles allow this power-type movement to take place. Simulating the sport action is important in this type of resistance training.

Functional Overload

Weighted belts and vests, and ankle weights, have been used by athletes in training for quick power movements. Although it has not been scientifically proven, there is some concern that these extra weight belts could interfere with fine motor movements in certain sports. However, these methods have been used by some athletes in quick-sprint and jumping-type sports. More research is needed on the effects of these training devices.

Isokinetics

Isokinetics use especially designed machines (e.g., Cybex, Mini Gym) which allow the same speed throughout a range of movement and maintain constant resistance at various angles in both the concentric and the eccentric part of the contraction. The speed of contraction is important as slower speeds seem to increase strength only at that speed, while higher speeds of contraction provide benefits for strength at both high and low speeds (Sale).

To be beneficial in developing maximum strength, the load must be set near the maximum, and the athlete will be able to perform only three or four repetitions.

PLYOMETRICS

Plyometrics refers to a quick, powerful movement using a prestretch and is also called the stretch shortening cycle. The purpose is to increase the power of the subsequent movement using the elastic component of the muscle and tendon and the stretch reflex. Plyometrics are used in most training programs to increase power and speed and include hopping, depth jumps, medicine ball throws, etc.

Plyometrics can be used for the lower body, upper body and trunk. Lower body plyometrics allows athletes the ability to produce more force in the change of directions and jumping. Example of lower body plyometrics are standing jumps, multiple hops and jumps, bounding, box drills and depth jumps. Upper body plyometrics are used in throwing and all arm movement

sports such as baseball, golf, volleyball, tennis and track and field throws. Examples of upper body plyometrics are medicine ball throws and catches and push-ups. Trunk plyometrics involve trunk movements that must be shorter and quicker to allow stimulation and use of the stretch reflex. Exercises such as sitting medicine ball throws should be modified to decrease both range of motion and time to activate the plyometric aspect of the exercise.

Frequency

The number of plyometric training sessions per week ranges from one to three. Usually during a sport season one or two sessions per week are appropriate, allowing for forty-eight to seventy-two hours between sessions for recovery. In the off-season, a training program of three sessions per week may be appropriate.

Recovery

Recovery time between repetitions usually is five to ten seconds and two to three minutes between sets (1:5 to 1:10 work to rest ratio).

Volume

Volume is measured in number of repetitions and sets in a training session. Lower body plyometrics volume is measured by the number of foot touches or distance in bounding exercises. Foot touches may range from 80 to 100 for a beginner to 120 to 140 for an experienced athlete. Intensity increases from low to moderate volumes of intensity to high volumes of intensity. Most programs range from six to ten weeks in the off seasons and should be done at least once or twice a week in season.

Plyometrics should be preceded with a general warm-up and stretching, including low-intensity dynamic movements. For younger athletes, pre-adolescent, low-intensity plyometrics should be used, and only experienced, older athletes should be involved with depth jumps from boxes.

Guidelines to High-Intensity Plyometrics

Strength

Lower body—be able to squat 1.5 times body weight, 1 RM (repetition maximum)

Upper body—bench press body weight for 1 RM for 220 pounds (100 kg) plus person and 1.5 times for smaller athletes weighing less than 220 pounds —5 clasp push-ups in a row

Speed

Lower body—perform 5 repetitions of the squat with 60% body weight in 5 seconds

Generally athletes who weigh more than 220 pounds (100 kg) should not perform depth jumps of heights greater than 18 inches (45 cm). Boxes should range in height from 6 to 42 inches (15 to 107cm). Landing surfaces should have shock-absorbing surfaces such as grass fields, rubber mats, or suspended floors. The area should be at least 35 yards (32 m) for length and the ceiling should be 10 to 13 feet (3 to 4 m) to accommodate jumping from boxes.

Plyometrics are an important part of a strength/speed/power training program and can be improvised to simulate motions used in the particular sport, such as the shooting motion in ice hockey or the throwing motion in baseball for the upper body and change in direction of movement in sports such as football, soccer, and basketball.

Compatibility of Aerobic and Resistance Training

Combining resistance training and aerobic endurance training may interfere with strength and power gains, especially if the endurance training program is high in intensity, volume, and frequency.

There seems to be no adverse effect on aerobic training if it is combined with a resistance training program; in fact, benefits such as improvement in short-term exercise performance and reduction of muscle imbalance has been observed (Baechle and Earle).

WOMEN AND STRENGTH TRAINING

In the past, strength training was not as prevalent among women as it was for men. Old ideas that women would develop huge muscles from strength training, and the lack of intensive training in female sports, were probably the reasons for the very small amount of strength training being performed by women. However, this is not the case today, as women strength-train for the same sport and aesthetic reasons as do men.

Female and male muscle have the same physiological characteristics and are both responsive to training. In one study of strength training over a ten-week program, women increased their leg and bench press by 29.5 and 28.6 percent, respectively, while men increased theirs by 26 and 16.5 percent (Wilmore, & Costill).

Although similar strength gains are reported among men and women, less muscle hypertrophy occurred with women. The inability of women to develop large muscle bulk is normally attributed to the low testosterone-to-estrogen ratio. Males at rest have normally ten times the testosterone level of females (Wright). As one of the functions of testosterone is the development of muscle mass, the difference in gains between men and women can be attributed to this factor. Some women, however, do experience considerable hypertrophy with strength training, although the majority do not. It has been speculated that the testosterone-to-estrogen ratio is higher for the former group, which results in the greater muscle mass (Wilmore & Costill).

CHILDREN AND STRENGTH TRAINING

At what age should children start strength training? Is lifting weights harmful for children? These are only two of the questions asked by young athletes, parents, and coaches.

Common theory in the past was that children should not perform strength training, especially using weights, until post-puberty, between the ages of fifteen and seventeen. Early studies actually showed little or no gains among children undertaking a strength/resistance program (Vrijens). Recent studies, however, show that strength gains are indeed possible with younger children, although large changes in muscle mass are not evident (Blimkie; Ramsay, et al.; Sale; Sewall & Micheli;

Weltman, et al.). Without large-muscle hypertrophy, it would appear that the improvement of the neuromuscular system is the important factor in strength gains at earlier ages. Pre-pubescent children should not be using strength training for aesthetic reasons or for building bulk.

Concerns in the past about strength training for children has centered around injuries to the long bones and back. The vulnerable bone injuries to the end of the long bones, where growth occurs (epiphyseal plate), the site of the tendon insertion onto the bone (apophyseal insertion), and the cartilage on the surfaces of the joints (articular cartilage) are all areas of possible damage in the growing child. Separation of a portion of the articular cartilage from the joint surface (osteochondritis dissecans), common in little-league pitchers' elbows, damage to the patellar tendon where it inserts below the knee (Osgood-Schlatter's disease), and lower-back problems are all injuries that occur in growing children and are a concern if a strength program is undertaken.

The fear that strength programs are detrimental to bone growth appears to be unfounded. Any bone injuries that have occurred have been caused by lifting heavy maximal weights and the use of improper lifting techniques.

Some general guidelines for children using strength training are that the weights should be lifted with a minimum of six repetitions and that proper instruction and spotting be used. Children should *never* lift maximal or near-maximal weights. Here is the basic progression for the various age groups:

- *Under age 10*. Use basic exercises with no weights. Use body weight- and partner-resistant exercises.
- *Ages 10–12*. Increase the number of body and partner exercises. Introduce weight exercises with little or no resistance. Use only simple basic exercises.
- *Ages 13–15*. Increase resistance in basic weight exercise. Emphasize technique with repetitions high, and weight load low. Introduce advanced exercises with little or no resistance.
- *Age over 15*. Move to regular resistance programs. Emphasize technique. Add sport-specific and more advanced exercises in a natural progression.

STRENGTH-TRAINING EXERCISES

To develop a strength-training program, the coach should have a basic knowledge of the important muscle groups, as shown in figure 3.17 as well as the muscle groups used in each exercise.

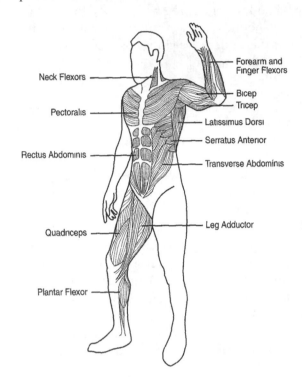

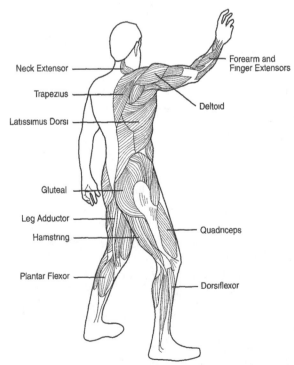

Figure 3.17: Muscles of upper and lower body

Upper Body

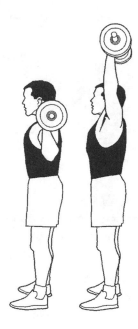

Military Press

With hands shoulder-width apart, grip the barbell. With your feet shoulder-width apart, rest the barbell on either the back of your shoulders or the front of your chest. Press the weight upward, fully extending your arms. Lower the weight slowly to the starting position. Repeat.

Muscles Strengthened

Triceps—back of upper arm
Anterior deltoid—front of shoulder area
Trapezius, rhomboids, serratus anterior—upper back

Incline Bench Press

Sit on the incline bench with the barbell at chest level, hands shoulder-width apart, knees bent, feet on the floor. Raise the weight to arm's length and lower slowly. Repeat.

Muscles Strengthened

Triceps—back of upper arm
Anterior deltoid—front of shoulder
Pectoralis major and minor—chest

Supine Bench Press

Lie on the bench on your back, with knees bent at right angles and feet flat on the floor. Hold the barbell flat on your chest, with hands slightly more than shoulder-width apart. Push arms upward until fully extended, then lower the barbell slowly to your chest. Repeat.

Muscles Strengthened

Triceps—back of upper arm
Anterior deltoid—front of shoulder
Pectoralis major and minor—chest

Biceps Curl

Hold the barbell with a wide or narrow grip. Keep the back straight, feet astride, and arms extended. Raise the bar to your chest, and then lower slowly to the starting position. Repeat.

Muscles Strengthened

Biceps brachii, brachialis—muscles in the front of upper arm and some muscles on the palm side of the forearm.

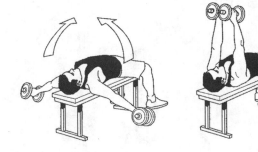

Lying Lateral Raise

Lie on the bench on your back, grasping the dumbbells with arms downward and outward. Raise the dumbbells slowly until they touch above your head. Lower slowly.

Muscles Strengthened
Pectoralis major and minor—chest muscles
Anterior deltoid—front shoulder area

Seated Triceps Extension

Hold the barbell above your head. Lower the weight behind your head, keeping the elbows close to your ears.

Muscles Strengthened
Triceps—muscles in the back of the upper arm

Lateral Pulldown

Kneel or sit with your hands holding the bar at the widest points. Pull the bar down behind or in front of your neck, then return the bar slowly to the starting position.

Muscles Strengthened
Latissimus dorsi—shoulder extensors
Trapezius, rhomboids—upper back
Biceps brachii, brachialis—elbow flexors
Finger flexors

Standing Lateral Raise

Hold the dumbbells with arms extended straight at your sides. Keeping your arms straight, raise the weights laterally to shoulder height. Lower slowly and repeat.

Muscles Strengthened
Deltoids—muscles which raise the arm to the side (abduction)

Chin-up (pull-up)

Grasp the bar with an overhand grip, hands shoulder-width apart. (The exercise can be varied with a wide or narrower grip, placed over the top of the bar.) Keeping the legs still, pull the body up. Lower the body until the arms are fully extended.

Muscles Strengthened

Posterior deltoid—upper shoulder area
Latissimus dorsi—shoulder extensors
Trapezius—upper back
Biceps brachii, brachialis—elbow flexors
Finger flexors

Good Morning Exercise

Stand with feet shoulder-width apart, the barbell resting horizontally across the shoulder blades. Bend at the waist until the upper body is parallel to the ground. Keep your back straight at all times.

Muscles Strengthened

Gluteals—buttock
Hamstrings—muscles on the back of the legs
Spinal erectors—muscles of the back

Dips

Start with the arms and body straight, then lower your body, keeping your elbows close to your body. Repeat.

Muscles Strengthened

Triceps—back of upper arm
Pectoralis major and minor—chest area
Anterior deltoid—front shoulder area
Trapezius, serrates anterior, rhomboids—upper back

Upright Row

Using a narrow grip, grasp the barbell and raise it until even with the shoulders. Hold, then return to the starting position.

Muscles Strengthened

Deltoid—shoulder area
Trapezius, rhomboids—upper back
Biceps brachii, brachialis—elbow flexors
Finger flexors

Abdominals and Back

Bent-Over Rowing

Keep the feet astride and the arms extended downward. Grasp the middle of the bar, with hands 8 inches (20 cm) apart. With head raised and eyes looking forward, pull the bar up to your chest and then lower it. Repeat.

Muscles Strengthened

Trapezius, rhomboids—upper back
Latissimus dorsi—shoulder extensors
Posterior deltoid—back of shoulder area
Biceps brachii, brachialis—elbow flexors
Finger flexors

Prone Hyperextension

Lie on the bench with the trunk extended. Place the hands behind the head and lower the trunk toward the floor. Raise the body in a straight line. A light weight may be placed behind the head.

Muscles Strengthened

Spinal erectors—lower back (lumbar region)

Bent Knee Sit-ups

Lie on your back with knees bent and feet flat on the floor. Clasp your hands behind your head and raise your upper body toward your knees. During the movement, rotate your trunk and touch left elbow to right knee. Lower your trunk to the floor slowly and repeat, touching right elbow to left knee. Repeat sequence.

Muscles Strengthened

Abdominals—stomach area

Shrug

Using a shoulder-width grip with the barbell, with arms locked, raise the shoulders as high as possible. Do not bend your knees. Repeat. This movement is a shoulder exercise only.

Muscles Strengthened

Trapezius—muscles which connect the shoulder and shoulder blade to the spine.

Crunches

Lying on your back, sit up slowly, raising bent knees and chest at the same time. Lower slowly. Repeat.

Muscles Strengthened
Abdominals—stomach area

Lower Body

Lateral Side Step, and Front Step

Stand with one foot on a box 16 to 18 inches (40 to 45 cm) high, with the thigh parallel to the floor. Keeping your back straight and head and chest up, raise and lower your leg. Repeat. A front step-up can be done in a similar way.

Muscles Strengthened
Gluteals—buttock
Quadriceps—front of thigh
Hamstrings—back of thigh
Gastrocnemius, soleus—calf area, back of the lower leg
Spinal erectors—lower back

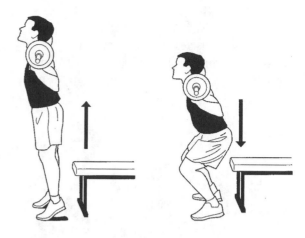

Half Squat

With your feet shoulder-width apart and your head up, place the barbell on the shoulders. Bend slowly to the half-squat position. As the movement is completed, push up onto your toes. Repeat.

  Note: Younger, inexperienced athletes should do the half squat. More advanced athletes may do a full squat as long as the weight used is not excessive.

Muscles Strengthened
Gluteals—buttock
Quadriceps—front of thigh
Hamstrings—back of thigh
Spinal erectors—lower back
Upper back and shoulder girdle

Leg Thrust

Lie on your back, knees bent. Extend the knees slowly, pushing the weight with the buttocks kept on the platform. After the knees are fully extended, lower the weight slowly to the standing position.

Muscles Strengthened
Gluteals—muscles of the buttock
Quadriceps—muscles in the front of the thigh
Hamstrings—muscles in the back of the thigh
Gastrocnemius, soleus—calf (muscles in the back of the lower leg)

Reverse Leg Press
Stand to one side of the machine and push back with one leg, using a motion similar to skating.

Muscles Strengthened
Gluteals—muscles of the buttock
Quadriceps—muscles of the front of the thigh
Hamstrings—muscles of the back of the thigh
Gastrocnemius, soleus—calf (muscles of the back of the lower leg)

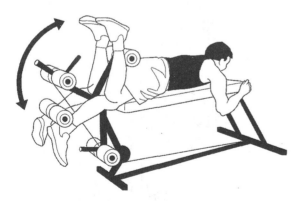

Hamstring Curl
Lie face down on the bench and place your feet under the roller pads, just above the ankle joint. Grasp the handles to keep your body from moving. Curl your legs by bringing your heels to your buttocks. Pause and slowly lower the resistance. Repeat.

Muscles Strengthened
Hamstrings—back of upper leg
Gluteals—buttock

Heel Raise
Standing with your toes on a block about 2 inches (5 cm) high, rest the barbell on your shoulders. Slowly raise up onto your toes, hold, and return to the starting position. Repeat.

Muscles Strengthened
Gastrocnemius, soleus—calf area, back of lower leg

Upper and Lower Body

Cleans
Use a palms-down grip, grasp the barbell on the floor, bending your knees and keeping your back straight. Lift the weight in one motion to the shoulders. Use only the arms to lower the weight slowly.

Muscles Strengthened
Gluteals—buttocks
Quadriceps—front of the thigh
Hamstrings—back of the thigh
Spinal erectors—lower back
Trapezius, rhomboids—upper back
Deltoids—shoulder area

extended. After gaining control and balance, stand up by extending the hips and knees to a fully erect position and stabilize the bar overhead.

Note: This is an advanced move and caution should be used when learning the progression for this exercise.

Muscles Involved

Gluteus maximus, semimembranosus, semitindinosus, biceps femoris, vastus lateralis, vastius intermedius, vastus medialis, rectus fermoris, soleus, deltoids, gastrocnemius, trepezias

Dead Lift

Stand over the bar with your hands 2 feet (60 cm) apart. Making sure that your back is straight, your head is up, and your knees are bent, lift the weight until your body is completely upright. Repeat.

Muscles Strengthened

Gluteals—buttocks
Spinal erectors—lower back
Quadriceps—front of thigh
Hamstrings—back of thigh
Trapezius, rhomboids—upper back
Deltoids—shoulder area

Snatch

Start the movement similar to the clean. After the lower body has fully extended, pull the body under the bar and rotate the hands around and under the bar.

Simultaneously flex the hips and knees to do a quarter squat position. Once the body is under the bar over and slightly behind the head with elbows fully

Lunge

Place the barbell on the shoulders with a wide, shoulder-width grip. Keeping the back arched and the head and chest up, step forward until your back knee touches or almost touches the floor. The step forward should be long enough to feel the stretch in the rear leg.

Muscles Strengthened
Gluteals—buttock
Hamstrings—back of upper leg
Spinal erectors—lower back
Gastrocnemius, soleus—calf, back of lower leg
Wrist and lower arms

Wrist Rolls

Stand with the arms extended at shoulder height. Slowly wind the rope until the weight is raised to the handle. Then slowly lower the weight.

Muscles Strengthened
Clockwise rotation: wrist flexors—palm side of forearm
Counter-clockwise rotation: wrist extensors—back of forearm

Forearms and Wrists

Wrist Curl

Sit and rest the forearms on the bench, with the wrists extended over the end. Hold the bar, with the palms facing upward. Let the bar roll to the end of the fingers. Roll the fingers up and grab the bar with the palms of the hands. Flex the wrists as far as possible.

Muscles Strengthened
Flexors of wrist and fingers—palm side of forearm

Reverse Wrist Curl (not shown)

Same as wrist curl except the bar is gripped with the palms facing down.

Muscles Strengthened
Extensors of the wrist and fingers—back side of forearm

Forearm Twist

With your elbows bent at right angles, use the wrist to rotate the weight, alternating right and left.

Muscles Strengthened
Wrist flexors—palm side of forearm
Wrist extensors—back of forearm

Plyometrics

Lower Body Muscle Groups

Continuous Standing Long Jump

Standing with your feet parallel and shoulder-width apart, swing your arms backward, bending your knees and hips, then swing your arms forward, in an explosive upward and forward movement. In midair, pull your knees up to your body. Land, extending your legs forward and bending your knees, to absorb the shock. Continue moving forward with a succession of standing long jumps.

Alternate Leg Bound

Start with one foot slightly ahead of the other. Push off with the back leg, driving the knee up to the chest. Extend outward with the driving foot and gain as much height as possible. Use a double arm swing. Alternate landing and taking off with each leg.

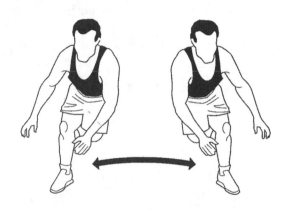

Single Leg Hops

From a standing position, drive one leg up and forward to gain distance. Land on the same foot and continue with the same leg while holding the other leg in a stationary position. Pull your arms in to the sides before landing and swing them upward and forward during takeoff. Repeat with the other leg.

Side Steps

Starting with your knees bent, step to the side as far as possible, then stride back. Repeat. A slide board can also be used for this exercise.

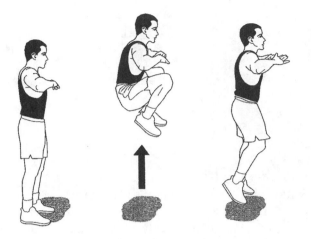

Knee Tuck Jump

Assume a comfortable stance and place the hands palms down at chest height. Begin by bending the knees to a quarter-squat level, and then drive the knees upward toward the chest and attempt to touch them to the palms of the hands. Tuck the feet under the body. Upon landing, repeat the procedure.

Side Jumps over the Bench

Stand on one side of a bench or a series of parallel benches, swing your arms, and jump over the bench(es), moving forward. Land and jump again, moving down the length of the bench(es).

Stride Steps

With your knees bent, take one stride step forward and to the side. Absorb the impact with the ball of the foot, then stride forward with the other leg. Repeat. This exercise is similar to the side steps, except the movement is forward and to the side.

Stair Bounding

This exercise is similar to the stride steps except stairs are used. Bound sideways up one or two steps of the stairs each time. This exercise can be varied by bounding straight up the stairs with one or two feet.

Depth Jump

Begin by standing at the edge of the box (25–45 inches/62–112 cm, in height) with the knees slightly bent and the arms relaxed at the sides. Drop (do not jump) from the box to the ground (usually grass or a mat). Land with both knees bent and feet together. Immediately upon landing, initiate the jumping phase by swinging both arms upward and extending the body as high as possible.

Upper Body Muscle Groups

Bar Twist

Place the bar on the shoulders and hold it securely with both hands, keeping feet slightly more than shoulder-width apart. Twist the body in one direction and, when it is fully rotated, twist the body in the other direction.

Medicine-Ball Rotation

Grasp the medicine ball and rotate right and left, using quick, explosive movements.

SPEED TRAINING

Athletes with a higher percentage of fast-twitch fibers are genetically more predisposed to be successful in sports which require speed (see pages 126–29 for more details on fiber types). This potential for speed of movement can be developed by a carefully designed training program and good coaching technique.

Speed is the ability to move the body quickly and is directly related to strength, power, reaction/movement time, and technique. Strength and conversion to power have been discussed previously, and the various methods described, including resistance-weight programs and plyometrics, are known to improve power and speed.

Other methods include running drills using accelerated arm action, high knee action, skipping stepovers (carrioca), and running in sand. Resistive training using rubber cords, ropes, chutes, sled pull, uphill running, and assistive training such as being pulled by pulleys and rubber cords, downhill running, and overspeed training (pedaling or running as fast as possible) on stationary bikes and treadmills are also methods used to improve running speed.

Reaction time, the response time to a stimulus, and movement time, the time from the start of the movement to the end of the movement, are also trained to improve speed. Reaction and movement-type drills are common in most sports and should be practiced at high speeds.

Technique is also a factor in the development of speed. In running, the start, the length of the stride, the frequency of the stride, and arm action are all factors which can be improved through practice of the correct technique. Stride frequency is the most influential factor in determining maximum velocity. Being supervised by a knowledgeable coach with an ability to detect errors is very important in the development of good technique.

Reducing negative factors such as air or water resistance through aerodynamics is also a factor in some sports such as downhill skiing and cycling races, where equipment and wearing apparel are aerodynamically designed to have less air resistance.

PERIODIZATION OF SPEED TRAINING

Speed training depends on the sport and the level of performance of the athlete. Aerobic and anaerobic endurance are considered the base for speed training, which is done during the general preparatory period. Steady-state, interval, repetition training, and fartlek (speed play) are all used to build the anaerobic base. In the specific preparatory period, training becomes specific and relates directly to the sport. During the competitive period, specific sport-related drills are utilized to develop speed. Figure 3.18 summarizes the periodization of speed.

	Preparatory		Competitive		Transition
	General Preparatory	Specific Preparatory	Pre-Competitive Competitions	Main Competitions	Transition
Speed	Aerobic and Anaerobic endurance	Develop the foundations of speed	Specific speed, agility and reaction time		

Figure 3.18 The periodization of speed training. Reprinted by permission from Bompa, *Theory and Methodology of Training.* (Dubuque, IA: Kendall/Hunt), 178.

AGILITY AND QUICKNESS

The ability to change directions quickly is a key component of many sports, especially team sports such as soccer, football, volleyball, basketball, rugby, and ice and field hockey.

Agility is a combination of strength, speed, power, reaction and movement time, and coordination. In order to improve agility, all of the above factors must be developed using the various methods discussed previously.

As coaches have known for years, the best method for improving agility is to practice sport-specific movement patterns over and over again at high speeds. Agility drills should be incorporated into most practices, and they should simulate the movements used in the sport. Sports other than the one being trained for, such as tennis, squash, handball, and racquet ball, can be used to assist in the development of agility.

Non-sport specific drills are used in many sports to improve agility and quickness. Specific exercises using stopping and starting, change of direction, and other quick movements can augment a training program both during the competitive season and in the non-competitive season. Drills can be incorporated in circuit training as one or more of the exercise stations or can be done solely as an agility training session.

Agility and Quickness Exercises

1. Stepovers (Carioca)
   Move laterally, alternately crossing one leg in front and one leg behind.

1   2   3   4

2. Shake and Bake (Fast Feet)
   Short, knees low, running on the spot. Fast movements moving forward.

3. Stride Crossovers
   Tape a line on the floor. Stand with feet on either side. Touch right toe to left calf. Alternate.

4. Forward Crossovers
   Stand with one foot forward and one foot behind. Switch feet back and forth.

5. Lateral Crossovers
   Stand with feet apart. Jump and cross over feet. Land with ankles crossed. Repeat.

6. Backward Crossovers
   Moving left, right leg crosses behind left leg.

7. Box Jumps (Single Four)
   Using one or both feet, jump from square to square inside a box that is 2 feet (60 cm) square, taped to the floor as shown.

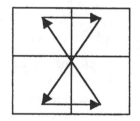

8. Box Jumps (Double Four)
   Same as single four, but perform the jumps on both feet, in all possible directions.

9. Slalom
   Use a line on a gymnasium floor or tape a 10-foot (3 m) line. With feet together, jump in slalom zigzag fashion across the line while moving forward. Move forward and then backward.

10. Slalom Jump and Sprint
    Use a tape or line on a gym floor, or on a field (approx. 10 feet/3 m). Jump in slalom skiing fashion (zigzag), and at the end of the line, sprint forward for 10 to 15 yards (9 to 14 m).

11. Skipping
    Skip fast for 30 seconds, then rest for 30 seconds.

12. Squat Thrusts (Burpees)
    Stand, squat, thrust legs backward. Pull knees into a squat position again. Stand up. Repeat.

13. Side Hops (18-inch/46-cm bench)
    Side to side with both feet together.

14. Single Hops (18-inch/46-cm bench)
    Take off and land on a different foot diagonally and across.

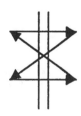

15. Step Hopping
    Hop up stairs on one foot and then use both feet. Hop up one step at a time and then two steps at a time.

16. Split-Leg Shuffle
    Stand with feet together. Jump and land in a wider stance. Jump again and land with feet together. Repeat.

17. Crossovers
    Similar to drill No. 1 except there is no lateral movement. Jump in the air and land with legs crossed. Jump in the air again and cross legs the other way.

18. Hop the Box

Stand in the middle of a taped box on the floor with four quadrants. Hop in and out from the center to the eight points, returning to the center each time.

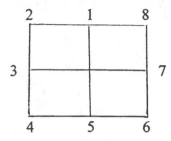

19. Forward Lunges

Fall forward with one bent leg forward and the back leg fully extended. Push the front leg and return to the starting position. Repeat with the other leg forward.

20. Depth Jumps

Jump off a 16-inch (40 cm) box, landing on one or both legs, and then jump high in the air, fully extending the legs.

21. Depth Jumps—Side Movement

Same as drill No. 17 except on landing take one side step right or left and then sprint forward.

22. Single and Double Leg Hops

From a standing position, drive one leg up and forward to gain distance. Land on the same foot or alternate foot. Pull arms to the side before landing and swing them upward and forward during take-off. Repeat. Vary this by landing on both legs.

23. Side Steps (Slide Board)

Using a slide board, step to the side as far as possible and then stride back.

24. Shuttle Run

Run 10 feet (3 m) and touch the line, run 10 feet (3 m) back and touch the line. Rest for 30 seconds. Repeat.

FLEXIBILITY

Flexibility can be defined as the full range of movement about a joint. Joints are points where two or more bones connect, and the connections are performed by ligaments assisted by muscles. The muscles are attached to the bones by tendons, which are the strong ends of the muscle. The relatively stationary point of attachment is called "the origin" of the muscle, and the end of the muscle that moves is called "the insertion." It is the contraction of the muscle which causes movement and creates tension in the muscle, and the consequent release of tension causes relaxation of the muscle.

The physiology relating to flexibility or stretching involves the stretch reflex and the muscle spindles, the Golgi tendon organs, and the sliding filament theory, discussed in the physiology section on pages 126 and 128.

The stretch reflex is operated by the nervous system and is initiated whenever a muscle is stretched. Stretching a muscle lengthens both the muscle fibers and the muscle spindles. This stretching results in the firing of the stretch reflex, which helps prevent injury to the muscle from overstretching. The inverse myotatic reflex is associated with the Golgi tendon organs, which cause an involuntary muscle relaxation when the muscle contraction or stretch on a tendon exceeds a certain point. The excessive tension is removed and the muscle can be stretched farther without causing injury.

Flexibility or range of motion is limited by:

1. the muscle and its surrounding sheath of fascia;
2. the collagenous and elastic connective tissue;
3. tendons in extreme joint movement;
4. joint capsule and ligaments; and
5. bone structure.

All athletes should perform a flexibility program daily to prevent injuries, alleviate muscle soreness, and allow for greater range of motion in their sport. The type and number of flexibility exercises should be sport-specific, as some sports such as gymnastics and wrestling require a high amount of flexibility, while other sports require a moderate amount. The value of some extreme flexibility exercises such as back bridges and deep knee bends has been questioned as they can cause overstretching of the ligaments.

The objectives of a flexibility stretching program should be to reduce the resistance by stretching and lengthening the connective tissue surrounding the joint and by lowering the muscle tension.

Methods of Stretching

Static Slow Stretch

Static stretch involves the athlete going through the range of motion slowly to the farthest point and holding this position for twenty to thirty seconds. This is repeated five or six times. Going through the movement slowly allows adequate time to reset the sensitivity of the stretch reflex, and a semi-permanent change in length of the muscle fibers and connective tissue can be gained. If the stretch is held long enough, muscular relaxation with the firing of Golgi tendon organs can be achieved. This is also the safest method of flexibility training.

Ballistic Stretching

This type of stretching involves a fast, strong, bouncing, rebounding, bobbing range of movement. This type of movement can cause muscle soreness and injury and is a controversial method and not recommended.

Ballistic flexibility initiates the stretch reflex, and therefore increases muscular tension, making it more difficult to stretch the connective tissue.

Dynamic Stretch

Dynamic stretch is a functionally based stretching exercise that uses sport-specific movements to prepare for activity. Dynamic stretching varies from ballistic stretching as it avoids bouncing, is performed in a more controlled manner and the range of motion is smaller and is less likely to cause the negative effects of ballistic stretching. It also goes through a range of motion that is sport specific, which the slow stretch does not and is increasingly used as the preferred method during warm-up for a specific sport. In addition the dynamic stretch helps in the temperature-related benefits of a warm-up unlike that of the slow stretch.

Proprioceptive Neuromuscular Facilitation (PNF)

Originally used as a physiotherapy procedure in rehabilitation, PNF is now accepted as an excellent method for developing flexibility. In this exercise, which uses a partner, the muscle is actively stretched to its end point, and then maximal isometric contraction, for five or six seconds, is performed against the partner's resistance. The muscle is then relaxed and stretched again to a new end point, and another isometric contraction follows. This procedure is usually repeated three times with each exercise (Holt).

Generally,

1. flexibility stretching training should be done daily and included in both the warm-up and cool-down;
2. stretching should progress from major joints to sport-specific stretching;
3. flexibility is also developed by playing or practicing the sport;
4. dynamic stretching should be used in the warm-up of a training session, static stretching should be used at the end of a training session in the cool-down;
5. significant increases in flexibility can be achieved in twelve weeks. Flexibility can be maintained with two sessions per week. Flexibility is lost at a slower rate than it is gained;
6. children are most flexible in their early years, become less flexible up to adolescence, and then increase in flexibility until early adulthood. Generally, females tend to be more flexible than males.

FLEXIBILITY EXERCISES

Neck Stretches

Head Tilt
Tilt the head to the right, bringing the right ear toward the right shoulder. Repeat to the other side.

Head Rotation
Rotate your head to the right, trying to look over your right shoulder. Repeat on the other side.

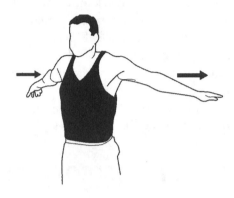

Side Stretch
Standing with your left arm above your head, slide your right arm down the right side of the body until the stretch is felt on the left side of the body. Repeat on the other side.

Shoulder Stretch
Keeping your arms straight at shoulder level, try to touch your palms together behind your back. Repeat with both palms facing upward.

Back Stretch
Lying on the back, bring the bent knees toward the chest. Grasp both knees with the hands and draw closer to the chest until the stretch is felt in the lower back.

Cross-Chest Triceps Stretch
Place your right hand on your left shoulder and, with your left hand, push your right elbow toward your left shoulder. Repeat on the other side.

Lower-Limb Stretches

Inner-Thigh Stretch
Sit with heels together and drawn toward the buttocks, knees apart. Push slowly on knees with elbows until a stretch is felt in the groin.

Lunge
Keep the head and the chest up and bring the knee to the floor. Push the hip forward. Repeat with the other leg.

Side Groin Stretch
Extend your right leg to the side, keeping your left leg straight. Place your right hand on your right hip. Bend your left knee and move toward your left leg. Repeat on the other side.

Hurdler's Stretch
Extend your left leg straight forward and your right leg back in a bent position. Grasp your left foot with one hand and bring your forehead slowly down to your knee. Repeat with your right leg forward and your left leg back. Then extend both legs forward, grasp both toes, and bring your forehead down to the knees.

Lying Hamstring Stretch
Lie on the back with both knees bent, feet flat on the floor. Grasp the knees with both hands. Pull the knees toward the head, slowly. Raise the knees again and repeat.

Quad Stretch

Stand with one hand on the wall. Hold one leg at the ankle and pull the foot toward the buttocks. Move the leg back until the stretch is felt in the front of the thigh and hip. Repeat with the other leg.

Calf Stretch

Place both hands on a wall at shoulder height. Place one foot ahead of the other, both feet flat on the floor. Bend the front knee with the back leg out straight. Lean the body forward until the stretch is felt in the lower leg. Keep the back straight and the feet flat on the floor. Repeat with the other leg.

Flexibility Exercises Not *Recommended*

The following flexibility exercises are *not* recommended, for the reasons given:

- Deep Knee Bend (with or without weights)
  - puts extra stress on the lateral ligaments of the knee
  - pinches and damages cartilage
  - compresses the knee cap

- Straight Leg Standing Floor Touch
  - forces knees to hyperextend
  - places more pressure on the lumber (lower) vertebrae

- Inverted (Leaning back) Hurdler's Stretch—single or double leg
  - overstretches medial (inside) ligaments of the knee
  - crushes the meniscus
  - twists and compresses the knee cap
- Standing Upper Body Twist (with or without weights)
  - can strain the ligaments of the knee
  - momentum can cause overstretching and consequent tissue damage

- Wrestlers' Bridge
  - squeezes spinal discs
  - pinches the nerve fibers
- Inverted Hang
  - raises blood pressure
  - may rupture blood vessels, especially in the eyes

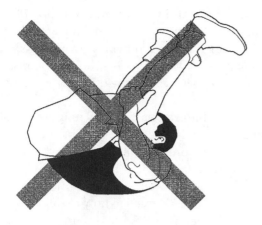

- Plow
  — places excessive strain on the lower back and excessive pressure on the discs
  — can interfere with breathing

OVERTRAINING

Directly related to recovery time and work-to-rest ratios is the state of overtraining. The coach is responsible for planning and implementing the training program and must provide the overload to provide a training stimulus for improvement. However, a poorly designed program that fails to allow the athlete to recover between work bouts can produce a state of overtraining or exhaustion which interferes with the athlete's recovering in order to undertake further intense training and conditioning improvement. In addition to not allowing proper recovery time between work bouts and training days, causes of overtraining include either an excessively high volume of training or an excessive amount of high-intensity training. Both these types of overtraining are usually the result of an abrupt increase in intensity or volume of training, or both. Medical signs include low glycogen and haemoglobin levels, as well as elevated blood lactate levels.

Other factors which can contribute to overtraining are a lack of sleep; poor diet; smoking; excessive alcohol consumption; personal, work, and family problems; and illness.

Signs a coach can look for in the athlete which could be caused by overtraining are: poor performance; loss of motivation; personality change, usually temperamental and/or depressed; loss of appetite; loss of body weight; chronic muscle soreness; slow healing of minor cuts and bruises; and general tiredness.

When overtraining occurs, the training program must be reduced by cutting back the volume and eliminating high-intensity work. In extreme cases, the athlete should move to light alternative exercises done outside the normal training environment, or take at least one to two weeks off before resuming training.

Other methods for the treatment of overtraining include proper diet; physiotherapy, including methods such as massage and various heat modalities; and a change to a warmer climate if the athlete is living in a climate that has small amounts of sunshine in the winter months.

Staleness, a term related to chronic fatigue and poor performance, can, in many cases, be related to over-training.

RECOVERY FROM MUSCLE SORENESS AND FATIGUE

When to work, how hard to work, when and how to recover: these are issues that coaches continually try to resolve when designing training programs. Recovery from competitions and hard training can be categorized into: restoration of the energy stores, recovery from muscle soreness, recovery of the central nervous system, and psychological recovery. Some mention should also be made of recovery from injuries.

Methods of recovery include rest, diet, light exercise, massage and other modalities such as sauna and hydrotherapy, and relief of psychological stress.

Restoration of the energy stores is critical in the recovery period after hard training and competitions. As mentioned previously, it takes twenty-four hours after intermittent exercise and forty-eight hours after continuous endurance exercise (lasting two or three hours) to restore the glycogen stores. Diet is important, and it is recommended that foods high in carbohydrates be ingested in this time period .

It has also been determined that foods and fluids taken soon after a hard workout or competition have an effect on recovery. It is recommended that carbohydrate-rich foods and fluids should be ingested within one to four hours after the competition or training. This intake should consist of one gram of carbohydrates per kilogram of body weight within the first two hours, repeated two hours later (Clark). This carbohydrate can come in a snack form, from fruit juices, bananas, muffins, bread, rolls, and so on, or from a high-carbohydrate meal, such as pasta. Consuming carbohydrates within two hours of the competition or workout is especially important in sports where another competition takes place within twenty-four hours.

Along with the glycogen stores, it is also very important to replace fluids and electrolytes (such as sodium and potassium). Plain water can help replace fluids, and electrolytes can be replaced by drinking fruit juices. Sport drinks such as Gatorade contain electrolytes, although fruit juices contain more sodium and potassium.

Rest and sleep are essential in recovery from stressful exercise. Repair of damaged tissue as well as some restoration of the energy stores takes place during this time period. An athlete should get eight to ten hours' sleep per day, and the total amount of sleep can be attained through naps lasting fifteen to thirty minutes as well as continuous sleep. Relaxation techniques, as well as taking a warm bath or shower, can assist in ensuring a restful sleep.

There is increasing evidence that a limiting factor to performance is the recovery of the central nervous system from intense physical exercise (Bompa). The central nervous system has two basic processes: excitation and inhibition. "Excitation" is the favorable process, and "inhibition" the restraining process. When the central nervous system is fatigued by intense exercise over a long period of time, such as a hard, explosive training workout or an intense competition, the nerve cells are in a state of inhibition, which causes muscle contraction to be slower and weaker. For recovery of the central nervous system, it is recommended that a high-intensity training day be followed by a low-intensity workout the next day, or a day of complete rest.

Massage and other modalities are used for general recovery and specific recovery from muscle soreness (Francis & Patterson). Muscle soreness is usually caused by tissue damage, such as microscopic tearing of muscle fibers, overstretching of the connective tissue surrounding the muscle fibers and tendons, and local muscular spasms (Bowers, Foss, & Fox). Massage, the systematic manipulation of the soft tissues for therapeutic purposes, is becoming a more frequently used method for general recovery, and recovery from muscle soreness (Cinique; Yessis). Massage is believed to increase circulation, stretch muscle adhesions, promote the removal of lactic acid, and remove excessive swelling. It should be noted here that massage is not used in the initial stages of extreme muscle soreness or acute tissue injury to the muscles, but after swelling and pain have subsided.

Other forms of relief from muscle soreness and general recovery include heat therapy, in the form of saunas, steam baths, and heat packs. Also used are cold baths, contrast baths, and hydrotherapy (whirlpools). Sports therapists and physiotherapists should be consulted on the use of massage and the other above-mentioned modalities.

Light aerobic exercise and stretching are useful in the recovery period between exercise bouts and after strenuous training or competition. Research on this subject has shown that lactic acid is removed from the blood more rapidly if light exercise is performed during the recovery period as opposed to only resting.

Track athletes use a form of running called "tempo training" to recovery on days after intense workouts (Francis & Patterson). Tempo work is running at 60–80 percent maximum heart rate with long recovery periods between work intervals. The implications for the coach and athlete is that light exercise should be performed at the end of training workouts and competitions, and light exercise and tempo work should be performed the day after intense training or competitions, rather than rest only.

Relief of psychological stress in recovery is also very important. Various relaxation techniques (discussed in Part 4) as well as a break and/or a change from the training regime are important methods of relieving psychological stress in the recovery period. Psychological stress may also come from the lifestyle of the athlete, and factors such as personal relationships, problems, and the relative happiness of the individual have an effect on recovery.

Recovery from injury is both physiological and psychological. The athlete should return to competition after an injury only when there is full range of motion, at least equal strength if a limb or joint is involved, little or no pain, and a psychological readiness to return. Coaches should always work with a doctor and/or a sports therapist to make the final decision about when an athlete can resume training and competition.

Generally, the coach plays a major role in recovery. The training program should be designed to include proper rest and recovery periods. It is important for coaches to understand the concepts of recovery, to design programs that do not overstress athletes, include adequate recovery time, and to be familiar with positive recovery techniques.

DETRAINING

What happens when athletes stop training? With the periodization method of training, the year is carefully planned, and, even in the transition period, after the competitive season is over, exercise and training are not stopped completely but form a part of the maintenance and regeneration period.

Strength and Power

Research has shown that the levels of strength and power are reduced following cessation of training, but that these changes are relatively small. It appears that little or no loss in strength occurs following a six-week cessation of training, and approximately 50 percent of the strength gained will be retained for up to a year after training has been stopped. However, it has been shown that maintenance programs once every seven to ten days can maintain the strength and power gained originally and are highly recommended.

Muscular Endurance

The endurance factor in the muscle is affected more by a cessation of training. Some oxidative enzymes such as SDH (succinate dehydrogenase) decline as much as 60 percent after two weeks of inactivity, whereas there is no change in muscle glycolytic enzymes such as PFK and phosphorylase (Wilmore & Costill). This may partially explain why endurance events are affected more by detraining than sprint, power-type movements.

Speed, Agility, Flexibility

Speed and agility are affected less by detraining than other factors such as strength and muscular endurance. Technique is important in both speed and agility, and small losses can be reversed quickly. Speed and agility require a high level of nerve-cell adaptation, and loss of either speed or agility may initially be related to the susceptibility of the nervous system to detraining.

Flexibility is lost at one-third the rate at which it is gained. It is recommended that a maintenance program of two to three times per week should be included in a year-round program. Flexibility exercises, if possible lasting ten minutes per day, should be part of the athletes' daily regime throughout the year.

Cardiovascular Endurance

Cardiovascular endurance (MVO_2) is diminished in training largely as a result of a reduction in blood volume and a consequent reduction in the stroke volume of the heart (the amount of blood pumped by the heart per beat). Studies have shown a drop of 6 percent in the MVO_2 after two to four weeks of inactivity (Coyle, et al.) and even greater declines of 15 percent after a three-month cessation for male and female track athletes.

It appears that maintenance of cardiovascular endurance is more difficult when regular training is stopped in comparison with strength, power, and speed and agility. Studies conducted show that the cardiovascular-endurance training must be performed three times per week, as anything less will result in declines of MVO_2 values.

WARM-UP AND COOL-DOWN

Warm-up is an important aspect for all athletes before training and competitions. A well-designed warm-up:
- increases muscle temperature and blood flow
- improves rate of force development and reaction time
- improves in muscle strength and power
- causes faster muscle contraction and relaxation of both agonist and antagonist muscles
- improves oxygen delivery

There does not seem to be any clear evidence that stretching prevents injury. Static stretching appears to be more useful following training or competition as it has been shown to decrease force production, running speed, reaction and movement time, and strength endurance. PNF and ballistic stretching have also been shown to have a detrimental effect to subsequent performance (Jefferys).

The warm-up should consist of 2 components:
1. General
2. Specific

The general warm-up should consist of five to ten minutes of slow activity such as jogging. The purpose is to increase the heart rate, blood flow, and muscle temperature.

The specific warm-up should include ten to twelve minutes of dynamic stretching followed by sport-specific movements. The dynamic stretching drills should also be related to the movements in the sport.

It is important that the warm-up should progress gradually and increase muscle and core temperatures and replicate the movements in the sport without causing fatigue or lowering energy stores. Warm-ups vary from sport to sport and are important to prepare the athlete both physically and mentally for the training or competition to follow.

TRAINING AND COMPETING IN EXTREME HEAT (HEAT STRESS)

Coaches must be very aware of the danger posed by training and competing in extreme heat and humidity (see figure 3.19). Sports such as track and field, football, and soccer are very prone to these types of conditions in the summer months.

The coach has a number of responsibilities when training in the high heat and humidity. The first is to acclimatize the athletes to training and competing in a heat-stressful situation. It is recommended that, at least four to eight days prior to starting regular training in the high heat and humidity, an acclimatization period take place. Light workouts, with athletes dressed in shorts and T-shirts, should start out lasting only ten to fifteen minutes, and another ten to fifteen minutes should be added each day to allow the athletes to adjust to the heat and humidity. If the training progressively increases in intensity as well as volume, by the time the regular training sessions begin the athletes should be acclimatized. If regular team workouts can not be held, the athletes should follow this program on their own before team workouts begin.

The second responsibility of the coach is to decide whether training should take place in extreme conditions at all. Training should be either canceled or changed to early morning or evening in extreme conditions of high heat (over 90°F /33°C, and relative humidity of 90–100 percent).

The third responsibility of the coach is to allow time for frequent drinking of water (every ten to fifteen minutes) and to ensure that the athletes drink water before and after training. The athletes should drink 14–20 ounces (400–600 ml) of cool water (50°F/10°C) before training and competition, and 3–6 ounces (100–200 ml) at the water breaks. Each athlete should have his or her own squirt-type water bottle. Salt and salt tablets are not recommended as they inhibit the body's ability to absorb the water.

The fourth responsibility of the coach is to ensure that the athletes are wearing the proper clothing. The clothing should be loose fitting and minimal to allow evaporation. Athletes in sports such as football, where padding covers over 50 percent of the body, are particularly susceptible. On days with extreme heat and humidity, football players should have a light workout without the total padding. Also rubber suits should not be worn while the athlete is training as they prevent evaporation from taking place.

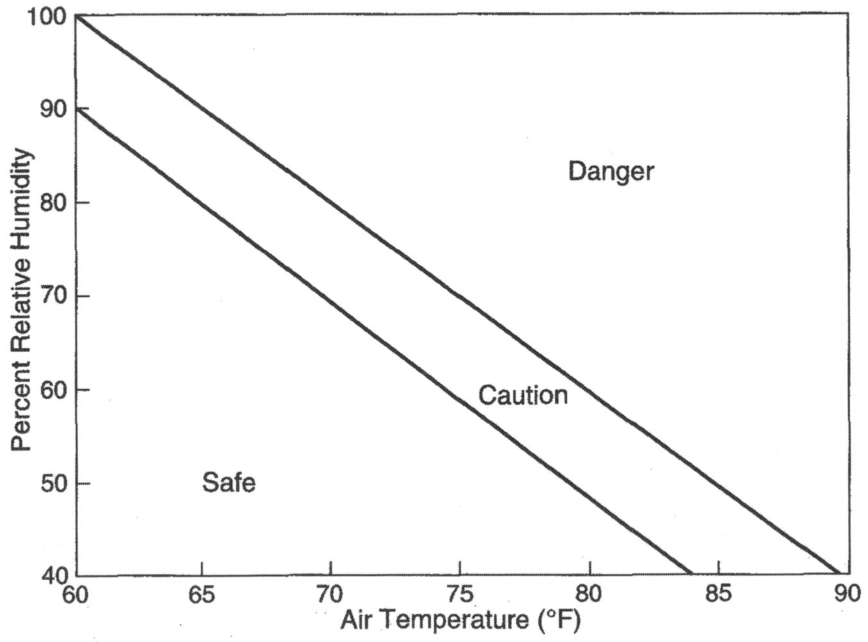

Indoor sports can cause heat stress as well, as many sporting arenas are quite hot and humid. Special attention must be paid to the dehydration problem in these environments.

There are three types of heat disorders that coaches and athletes should be knowledgeable about: heat cramps, heat exhaustion, and heat stroke.

Heat cramps are characterized by fatigue, heavy sweating, and muscle cramps. Coaches should remove the athletes from the training and allow them to rest and drink fluids before returning. In some cases, training should not be resumed until the next day.

Heat exhaustion is the next stage of heat illness; symptoms include

Figure 3.19: Football weather guide for the prevention of heat illness (adapted from Fox and Bowers)

cool skin, nausea, dizziness, and an elevated pulse rate. Athletes showing these signs should be removed from the training or competition, placed in a cool place out of the sun, and not allowed to return to training until the next day.

Heat stroke is the final and most serious stage of heat illness. The symptoms are hot, dry skin, confusion, headache, nausea, and an elevated body temperature. The athlete should be immediately removed from training or competition and placed in a cool environment. Clothing should be removed, and cool cloths and water applied to the skin. The individual should be transported to hospital immediately and the hospital advised of the heat-stroke conditions.

Some deaths have been attributed to heat illness, especially in the sport of football, and it is imperative that the coach be very aware of the dangers and not force athletes to compete and train in conditions conducive to heat illness.

PERFORMANCE AT ALTITUDE

It has been known for some time that physical performance is affected by altitude, especially at 4,000–5,000 feet (1,300–1,600 m) or over (Bowers, Foss, & Fox). This effect is due to a decrease in the partial pressure of oxygen, and a consequent reduction in the driving force for oxygen uptake in the lungs called "hypoxia." Other factors that have an influence on performance at altitude are a decrease in air density, a decrease in the force or pull of gravity, and a decrease in air dryness and air temperature (Blimkie).

Oxygen uptake (MVO_2) declines the higher the altitude, and therefore there is a decline of performance in events lasting longer than two minutes.

Events lasting less than two minutes are affected less, as the aerobic system contributes less to the energy requirements, and lower air resistance can actually aid jumping, throwing, and lifting events.

Acclimatization by arriving and training at least one week before competition, especially in aerobic events, will assist athletes to perform optimally. Acclimatization allows resting heart rates to return to near normal, but the exercise heart rate will remain above normal. Ventilation rates actually increase, and the MVO_2 which is lowered by altitude increases but does not reach the levels attained at lower altitudes or sea level. Performance in endurance events improves but will remain lower than at sea level. Performance in short events should not be affected adversely by the altitude factor, especially after a period of acclimatization. Training programs may have to be reduced from normal levels for the first few days but should reach normal training-intensity levels by the end of a week of acclimatization.

The effectiveness of training at altitude to improve performances at lower land levels has not been proved conclusively (Blimkie). Returning to lower land levels also requires four to eight days of training for best performances.

The taking of oxygen during rest periods at altitude has not been shown to aid in recovery, but may have a positive psychological effect for some athletes.

JET LAG

Many athletes, especially elite amateurs and most professionals, travel extensively to meets, games, and tournaments, often by airplane and across several time zones. The body operates on a regular rhythm, and jet lag can affect sleep, heart rate, metabolic rate, and blood pressure, as well as strength, power, and reaction time. It is important that athletes do all they can to alleviate jet lag, which is a form of extreme fatigue, sluggishness, decreased reaction time, and disorientation associated with extended air travel.

Jet lag is caused by lack of sleep, irregular and sometimes unfamiliar meals, dehydration, and a disruption of the biological clock. Muscle stiffness and constipation can also be associated with jet lag.

In most cases, crossing one or two time zones (one hour difference for each time zone) may have little effect on the athlete. However, crossing three to six times zones has a noticeable effect, and crossing more than six can have a considerable effect on athletes' performance.

Here are some guidelines for adjusting to jet lag:

1. Drink fluids on the plane to prevent dehydration. Avoid alcohol, as it adds to dehydration.
2. Be well rested before the trip begins.
3. Shift the hours of sleeping and eating to adjust to the time of the country. Adjust one hour per day before the trip begins; for example, for a six-hour time-zone difference, start adjusting six days before the flight.
4. If possible, make eastbound flights during the day, leaving early in the day in order to not miss a night of sleep.
5. If possible, make westbound flights later in the day in order to arrive near the normal sleeping time of the country.

6. Eat light meals.
7. Every one or two hours, stretch and walk around the plane, if permissible.
8. Wear comfortable clothing.
9. Take regular naps as often as possible. Use a blindfold to facilitate sleep.
10. Go on the time zone of the place you are arriving at and sleep at the normal night hours. This may mean staying up without sleep for long periods. This is why napping or sleeping on the plane is important.
11. If possible, allow one day per time zone on arrival before competing. Schedule a light practice session on the first day of arrival.

GROWTH CHARACTERISTICS AND TRAINING IMPLICATIONS

It is essential for anyone involved in children's sport to incorporate periodization training of children and youth. The periodization of training can be divided into two main phases namely:
1. Generalized 6–14 years
2. Specialized 15 years plus

The generalized phase can then be divided into
1. Initiation 6–10 years (pre-puberty)
2. Athletic Formation 11–14 years (puberty)

The specialized phase can be divided into
1. Specialization 15–18 years (post-puberty and adolescence)
2. High Performance 19 years plus (maturity)

In sports that involve children, special attention should be paid to growth characteristics to determine what systematic training method, if any, should be used at various growth stages. An understanding of both growth and maturation is essential. Growth refers to changes in body size such as height and weight, while maturation is the genetically determined process where the various parts of the body (organs, and cardio and circulatory systems) gradually reach their full development.

A thorough understanding of the growth stages that boys and girls go through will better equip the coach with the knowledge to train and assist in the development of the young athlete. Improper training at various age groups can lead to serious developmental problems, injuries, and high dropout rates in sport.

Over the past decade, outstanding performances have been achieved in a variety of sports. Several sport scientists and coaches claim that those athletes who were exposed as children and youths to a well-organized and systematic training program usually accomplish the best performances. Coaches who are impatient and pressure children to achieve quick results usually fail because the athletes quite often quit before attaining athletic maturation. We are more likely to produce healthy and outstanding athletes by employing correct principles of training, and by dividing the training of children and youth into systematic stages with clearly defined objectives.

Athletes, regardless of their high-performance potential, should participate in a generalized phase and a specialized phase of training. Within the generalized phase, athletes are gradually introduced to a sport-specific training (initiation) and their athletic talents are progressively formed (athletic formation). The primary purpose of the generalized phase is to build the foundation upon which complex physical abilities can be effectively developed, resulting in a smooth transition to the specialized phase.

There are two stages within the specialized phase, namely, specialization and high performance. During the specialization stage, athletes choose which sport or event to participate in and which position in the chosen sport or event they would like to play. Once athletes have specialized, the intensity and volume of training can increase progressively, resulting in high performance.

Although periodization outlines ages associated with each stage, it is important to understand that this model can shift considerably depending on the sport. For example, in sports such as women's gymnastics and diving, the age at each stage may be reduced by two to four years. It is also critical to understand that the rate at which children and youth grow and develop is highly varied, and the individual maturation differences of each athlete must be considered. The training and competitive program must, therefore, be adjusted accordingly. Familiarity with some of the physical, mental, and social characteristics of athletes in the initiation, athletic information, and specialization stages of development will allow better establishment of training guidelines that will enhance athlete development, ultimately resulting in high performance.

Growth characteristics presented here will be divided into the categories of physical, mental, and psychosocial, along with suggested guidelines for training.

Initiation Stage 6 to 10 Years

Children in this stage of development should participate in low-intensity training programs. Most young children are not capable of coping with the physical and psychological demands of high-intensity organized competitions. Training programs for these young athletes must focus on overall athletic development and not sport-specific performance. The following guidelines will help you design training programs that are suitable for young athletes.

General Training Guidelines for 6 to 10 Years

- Emphasize overall motor development. Introduce children to specific drills and exercises that will help them learn skills that are fundamental for their chosen sport and other sports. Basic motor skills should include running, sprinting, jumping, catching, throwing, batting, balancing, and rolling. It is also important to encourage children to learn the skills of activities such as cycling, swimming, and skiing.
- Provide every child with enough time to adequately develop skills, and equal playing times for games and activities.
- Positively reinforce children who are committed and self-disciplined. Reinforce improvements in skill development.
- Encourage children to develop flexibility, coordination, and balance.
- Encourage children to develop various physical abilities in low-intensity environments. For example, swimming is a good environment for developing the cardiorespiratory system while minimizing the stresses on joints, ligaments, and connective tissues.
- Select a suitable number of repetitions for each skill, and encourage children to perform each technique correctly.
- Modify the equipment and playing environment to a suitable level. For example, children who do not have the strength to shoot a normal-sized puck in ice hockey using the correct technique should use a smaller and lighter puck.
- Design drills, games, and activities so that children are provided with opportunities for maximum active participation.
- Promote experiential learning by providing children with opportunities to design their drills, games, and activities. Encourage them to be creative and use their imagination.

- Simplify the rules so that children understand the game. If they cannot understand the rules of the game, they may not develop feelings of self-control, which will likely affect their self-esteem and desire to continue participating.
- Children should participate in games that introduce them to basic tactics and strategies of their sport. During the game the young athletes could be introduced to situations that demonstrate the importance of teamwork and position play.
- Encourage children to participate in drills that develop concentration and attention control. This will certainly help them prepare for greater demands of training and competition that take place in the later stages of development.
- Emphasize the importance of ethics and fair play.
- Provide opportunities for boys and girls to participate together.
- Make sure that sports are fun for all children.
- Parents should find time for children to play. Children who don't play don't develop imagination.

Development Stage 11 to 14 Years (Beginning of Puberty)

The first phase of puberty begins around the ages of eleven to twelve for girls and thirteen to fourteen for boys, and lasts for about two years. The activity for growth and sexual hormones starts increasing one to two years before puberty. The increase in the secretion of testosterone during puberty contributes to the increase in muscle mass in both boys and girls.

It is appropriate to moderately increase the intensity of training during the next stage of development. Although the majority of athletes are still quite vulnerable to injuries and emotional damage, their bodies and capacities are rapidly growing and developing. It is, however, important to understand the variances in performance may be the result of differences in growth and development. Some athletes may be experiencing a rapid growth spurt, which can explain why they lack coordination during particular drills. As a result, the emphasis should still be on the development of skills and physical abilities. The following guidelines will help in designing training programs that are appropriate for athletes between eleven and fourteen years of age.

CHARACTERISTICS OF ATHLETES' DEVELOPMENT DURING ADOLESCENCE

Physical

- Following the growth spurt, adolescents continue to grow slowly. In some cases they will reach adult capacity in size. As a result, the awkwardness that was characteristic during early adolescence gradually corrects itself and, consequently, there is improvement in complex coordination.
- The bone ossification process nears completion toward the end of adolescence.
- The cardiorespiratory system is approaching, and in some cases reaches, maturity. Adolescents are capable of training the anaerobic lactic acid system.
- Females generally have less muscular strength than their male counterparts, but muscle mass occurs in both sexes.

Mental

- The brain has reached full size, although it continues to mature neurologically. Complex and abstract thinking abilities are improving.
- Adolescents are analytical. They often develop strong opinions.
- Mental capacities such as cognitive thinking, memory, divergent thinking, convergent thinking, and evaluation become highly functional.

Social-Psychological

- The adolescent is searching for a stable self-image, which is still based primarily on success and failures.
- Adolescents have a better understanding of their emotions and, generally, are relatively better at identifying and coping with training stress.
- Adolescents need to be recognized and accepted by their peers.
- Decision-making and leadership skills are becoming more developed.
- Adolescents continually seek independence.
- Relationships with the opposite sex become increasingly important.

General Training Guidelines for 11 to 14 Years

- Athletes should participate in a variety of exercises in their sport that will help them improve their general athletic skills and prepare them for competition in their sport. The volume and intensity of training should be progressively increased.
- Design drills that introduce athletes to fundamental tactics and strategies, and reinforce skill development.

- Athletes should be refining and automating the basic skills they learned during the prior stage of development (six to ten years), and learning skills that are a little more complex.
- Place emphasis on coordination and balance.
- Emphasize ethics and fair play during training sessions and games.
- Provide all children with opportunities to participate at a challenging level.
- Avoid placing young athletes in potentially humiliating situations.
- Introduce the athletes to exercises that develop general strength. The foundation for future strength and power gains should begin at this stage of development. Place emphasis on developing the core sections of the body, in particular the hips, lower back, and abdomen, as well as muscles in the extremities—shoulders joints, arms, and legs. The equipment needs are minimal since most exercises should involve light body weight and light equipment such as medicine balls, rubber (surgical) tubing, wall pulleys, and dumbbells. Low-resistance, high-repetition weight training will also enhance general strength development.
- Continue the development of aerobic capacity. A solid endurance base will enable athletes to cope more effectively with the demands of training and competition during the specialization stage of development.
- Introduce athletes to moderate anaerobic training. This will help them adapt to high-intensity anaerobic training that takes on greater importance, in most sports, during the specialization stage of development. Athletes should not compete in events that place excessive stress on the anaerobic alactic acid energy system. They are usually better suited for short sprints that involve the anaerobic alactic energy system. Also, endurance training of longer distances at slower speeds, such as 880–1,650-yard (800–1,500 m) runs, is more suitable for this age than training that challenges the lactic acid system.
- To improve concentration and attention control, introduce athletes to more complex drills.
- Encourage athletes to develop strategies for self-regulation and visualization. Formalized mental training should be introduced.
- Introduce athletes to a variety of fun competitive situations that allow them to experience the application of various techniques and tactics. While young athletes like to compete, it is important to

de-emphasize winning. Structure competitions to reinforce skill development.

- Provide time for play and socializing with peers.

SPECIALIZATION STAGE: ADOLESCENCE 14 TO 18 YEARS

For girls, adolescence begins around age thirteen to fourteen; while for boys it begins around age fourteen or fifteen, and usually ends between the ages of twenty to twenty-five. It is characterized by a slowing of the growth process, and can vary from individual to individual.

The majority of athletes in this stage of development are capable of tolerating greater training and competition demands. The most significant changes in training take place during this stage. Athletes who have been participating in a well-rounded program, with a great emphasis placed on total development, will now start performing more exercises and drills aimed specifically at high-performance development. Closely monitor the volume and intensity of training to ensure the athletes improve dramatically with very few, if any, injuries. The following guidelines will help in designing training programs that are suitable for players specializing in hockey.

GENERAL TRAINING GUIDELINES FOR THE SPECIALIZATION STAGE

- Closely monitor the development of athletes during this stage. They will be developing strategies for coping with the increased physical and psychological demands of training and competition. They are also quite vulnerable to experience physical and psychological difficulties from overtraining.
- Athletes should be progressively improving the dominant general physical abilities such as power, anaerobic capacity, specific coordination, and flexibility.
- The volume of training for specific exercises and drills must increase to facilitate a performance improvement. The body must adapt to specific training load increments to prepare effectively for competition; therefore, now is the time to stress specificity.
- Increase intensity of training more rapidly than volume, although volume must still be increased progressively. Athletes should be prepared to perform a particular skill, exercise, or drill with the appropriate rhythm and speed. Training should closely simulate the actions that take place during a game. Although fatigue is a normal outcome of high-

intensity training, it is important that athletes do not reach the state of exhaustion.

- Involve athletes in the decision-making process whenever possible.
- Basic motor skill training must still be emphasized, particularly during the pre-season. It is more important, however, to emphasize sport-specific efficiency, that is, to utilize training methods and techniques that will develop a high level of sport-specific efficiency, particularly during the season.
- Encourage players to become familiar with some of the theoretical aspects of training.
- The development of strength should start to reflect the specific needs of the sport. Place emphasis on exercising the muscles that are primarily used when performing technical skills (prime movers). Athletes who are weight training can start performing exercises that require fewer repetitions and a heavier weight. Maximum strength training, where fewer than four repetitions of an exercise are performed, should be avoided, particularly for athletes who are still growing.
- Make developments of the aerobic capacity a high priority for all players.
- Progressively increase the volume and intensity of anaerobic training. Players are capable of coping with lactic acid accumulation.
- Improve and perfect the techniques of the sport. Select specific exercises that will ensure the skills are being performed with correct biomechanics and physiological efficiency. Difficult technical skills should be performed frequently during training sessions, incorporated into specific tactical drills, and applied in games.
- Improve individual and team tactics. Incorporate game-specific drills into tactical training sessions. Select drills that are interesting, challenging, and stimulating and require quick decisions, fast actions, prolonged concentration, and a high level of motivation from the players. They should demonstrate initiative, self-control, competitive vigor, and ethics and fair play in game situations.
- Increase the number of competitions progressively so that by the end of this stage the players are competing frequently. It is also important to set objectives for games that focus on the development of specific skills, tactics, and physical abilities. Although winning becomes increasingly important, it should not be overemphasized.
- Athletes should practice mental training. Drills and exercises that develop concentration, attention

control, positive thinking, self-regulation, visualization, and motivation should be structured to specifically enhance sport-specific performance.

- Toward the end of this stage of athletic development, the athletes should have no major technical problems, and the coach can move from a technical teaching to a coaching (training) role.

HIGH PERFORMANCE 19 YEARS AND OLDER

A well-designed training plan based on sound principles of long-term development will lead to high performance. Good results that were achieved during various stages of development will increase after athletes have reached athletic maturation.

The primary objective during this stage of development is to achieve the highest possible performance. Winning is unquestionably the most important objective; however, it is extremely important to ensure that winning takes place within the rules and regulations of ice hockey. The values of ethics and fair play must be constantly reinforced. Athletes should be discouraged from taking illegal performance-enhancing drugs, such as steroids, to achieve international-caliber results. The following guidelines will help in designing a training program that will facilitate high-performance results.

GENERAL TRAINING GUIDELINES FOR HIGH PERFORMANCE

- Progressively increase the volume and intensity of training for the specific physical abilities and capacities, relative to the current physical and psychological state of individual athletes. Training should consist primarily of exercises that lead to adapting to the needs of hockey. Maintain basic motor development, especially during the pre-season.
- Specific exercises and drills in training sessions should stimulate the rhythm and speed required in competition.
- Specific technical skills and tactics should be perfected and mastered.
- Sport-specific mental training strategies should be perfected.
- Base training programs on sound scientific principles.

SPECIFIC TRAINING IMPLICATIONS

The power of the alactic system is low before puberty in both boys and girls. The production of energy (ATP) is limited because of the smaller muscle mass in children,

although adults and children possess approximately the same amount of ATP and CP in the resting muscle.

Anaerobic alactic system training can be performed at any age, provided the training loads are not excessive. This means that the total number of repetitions and sets must be lower than for more mature players, recovery time must be longer, and work times should not exceed eight to ten seconds in duration.

ANAEROBIC LACTATE

The production of energy from the lactic system is relatively low before puberty but increases appreciably during puberty. The activity of enzymes such as LDH (lactate dehydrogenase) and PFK (phosphofructo-kinase) is increased during this phase. Although the capacity of this system is improved during puberty, it is still well below adult levels. The development of the anaerobic system appears to be directly related to the increased production during puberty of testosterone levels in boys and estrogen levels in girls.

PHYSIOLOGICAL TESTING

How do we determine the present status or improvements shown during and after training of the physiological factors that are important in athletic performance such as the energy systems, strength power, speed, and agility? The physiological testing can be done either in a sports science laboratory by specially trained personnel or in field tests administered by the coach and/or assistants.

Physiological testing can provide the athlete and the coach with useful information such as present strengths and weaknesses relative to the specific sport; improvement after training programs; and the present status of the relative health of the athlete. The tests also are a motivational tool for training in the preparation period, as the athletes know that their training improvements can and will be measured.

The coach and the athlete should realize that results of physiological testing alone cannot predict athletic success, nor should they ever be used as the sole criterion in selecting athletes. The author's experience in professional sport can illustrate this point. A professional ice-hockey team tested all players physiologically before the training camp began. The athlete that scored the highest on the various tests did not even make the second team. However, notably, the next three highest scores belonged to the three best players on the team. The point here is that physiological testing is only one aspect of evaluation, and there are many other components that determine the success of an athlete.

An effective testing program should test variables that relate to the sport; be valid (measures what it claims to measure) and reliable (results are consistent); be as sport-specific as possible (swimmers swim, runners run); and should be administrated properly.

Laboratory Test versus Field Tests

The coach must decide whether laboratory tests or field tests are more appropriate for the team. A laboratory test is one in which the environment is controlled, and the testing is normally performed in a sports science laboratory, and by some fitness-testing organizations, although some equipment is portable.

The field test is usually performed by the coach or assistant in a simulated sports situation in the facility where the training takes place. For example, measurement of an ice-hockey player's anaerobic power on the ice while skating is a field test, whereas testing the player's anaerobic power on a bicycle ergometer is a laboratory test.

The advantages of field tests are they are more sport-specific and related to performance, relatively inexpensive, simpler to score and administer, and can be done in the regular training facilities. Norms may be available, but, if not, team-specific norms can be developed.

Laboratory tests are more reliable, valid, and precise than field tests. They are very specific in terms of the factor measured but are not as sport-specific as field tests. One of the biggest problems for amateur organizations is that the equipment is expensive and trained personnel are needed to administer the tests. Thus, the cost may be prohibitive.

A third type of tests could be classified as lab-like tests. These modified lab tests are not usually as accurate as the highly controlled laboratory tests but can be administrated with minimal training by coaches and their assistants and in most cases involve minimal cost.

Measuring Aerobic Power (MVO$_2$)

Field Test

The Cooper twelve-minute run and the half-mile run are the most common field tests to measure aerobic power.

TWELVE-MINUTE RUN

Aerobic fitness is assessed by the distance covered in twelve minutes around a 400-meter track.

Method

The athletes work in pairs, with one athlete taking the test and the other recording the total distance covered. A whistle is blown at the end of the twelve minutes, and the number of laps covered (to the nearest lap) is recorded. Include a warm-up before starting.

Equipment

A stopwatch, recording sheets, pens, clipboards, use of a 400-meter track.

Table 3.14: Twelve-Minute Run Scores

Percentile	Distance Covered, Age 18<		Distance Covered, Age 19>	
	Laps	Miles	Laps	Miles
90	7¾	1.93	8	2.00
80	7½	1.88	7¾	1.93
70	7¼	1.81	7¾	1.93
60	7	1.75	7½	1.88
50	6¾	1.69	7¼	1.81
40	6½	1.63	7	1.75
30	6¼	1.56	6¾	1.69
20	6¼	1.56	6¾	1.69
10	6	1.50	6½	1.63

HALF-MILE, OR 1,500-M, RUN

In this test of aerobic fitness, the athlete runs the half-mile distance in the best time possible.

Method

The athletes work in pairs, with one performing the run and the other recording the time called out by the timer as the athlete completes the distance.

Equipment

A stopwatch, pens, recording sheets, clipboards, a measured half-mile or 1,500-m distance.

Table 3.15: Half-mile (1,500 m) run scores (in minutes)

Percentile	Age				
	12	13/14	15/16	17/18	19>
90	5:45	5:25	5:10	4:45	4:25
80	5:50	5:30	5:15	4:50	4:30
70	5:55	5:35	5:20	4:55	4:35
60	6:00	5:40	5:25	5:00	4:40
50	6:05	5:45	5:30	5:05	4:45
40	6:10	5:50	5:35	5:10	4:50
30	6:15	5:55	5:40	5:15	4:55
20	6:20	6:00	5:45	5:20	5:00
10	6:25	6:05	5:50	5:25	5:05

Table 3.16: Aerobic fitness rating for males and females as estimated from running a half-mile (1,500 m)

Aerobic Fitness (ml/kg/min.)

	Low	Average	High	Very High
Males	Under 45	45–55	45–65	Over 65
Females	Under 40	40–50	50–60	Over 60

Laboratory Test

Aerobic capacity is measured by an open-circuit metabolic unit. The maximum oxygen an athlete can consume (MVO_2) is calculated along with other measurements such as blood pressure and electrocardiogram activity. The treadmill is the most common apparatus for determining MVO_2, with a variety of tests including Balke, Bruce, Naughton, and Ellestad being used. The treadmill allows the application of precise exercise intensities, using walking and running at increasing intensities without a rest period between stages.

The bicycle ergometer is also quite popular for increasing the exercise intensity and measuring MVO_2. The bicycle ergometer should include indicators of frictional resistance and revolutions per minute. Oxygen consumption is either measured directly or estimated during bicycle geometry, using a predictive equation.

The Forest Service Step Test is a lab-like test that uses recovery heart rates after bench-stepping for five minutes to the count of a metronome. The recovery heart rates then give a predicted MVO_2 value, obtained by referring to a table.

Maximum oxygen uptake is usually measured in ml/kg/min. or in some cases in liters/min.

Measuring Anaerobic Power (Alactic)

The short-burst anaerobic alactic system can be measured with quick power bursts of under ten seconds.

Field Test

50-METER SPRINT

Method
The athlete sprints 50 meters, from a standing start. Time is recorded to nearest tenth of a second.

Equipment
Two or more stopwatches, clipboards, pens, recording sheet, 50-meter straight track, four pylons to indicate start and finish line.

Table 3.17: 50-meter scores (seconds)

Percentile	Age 12	13/14	15/16	17/18	19>
90	7.5	7.0	6.5	6.3	6.0
80	7.6	7.1	6.7	6.4	6.1
70	7.8	7.2	6.8	6.5	6.2
60	7.9	7.3	6.9	6.6	6.3
50	8.0	7.4	7.0	6.7	6.4
40	8.1	7.6	7.1	6.8	6.5
30	8.2	7.8	7.2	6.9	6.6
20	8.3	7.9	7.3	7.0	6.7
10	8.4	8.0	7.4	7.1	6.8

Laboratory Tests

The Margaria–Staircase Test is used for measuring lower-body anaerobic power. The test involves the athlete running up a series of stairs as quickly as possible, stepping on every third stair. A timing device on the third and ninth step activates to measure the elapsed time between these two points.

The Wingate Anaerobic Test requires the athlete to pedal on a stationary bike at a maximum rate against a high constant resistance; and the highest five-second output is measured.

Muscle biopsies, where a small amount of muscle tissue is analyzed for the amount of enzymes, ATP, and CP, is also a laboratory procedure for measuring alactic power. This procedure now must be performed by a medical doctor.

Measuring Anaerobic Lactic Power

Anaerobic lactic power can be measured with intense exercise lasting from thirty to ninety seconds. The power aspect of the lactic system is usually measured with all-out activity in approximately thirty to forty seconds, while capacity is usually measured with all-out exercise in approximately ninety seconds.

Field Test

400-METER RUN

Method
The athlete runs 400 meters as fast as possible from a standing start. Time is measured to the nearest tenth of a second.

Equipment
Two to four stopwatches (to test two to four athletes at one time), clipboard, pens, recording sheets, 400-meter track.

			Age		
Percentile	12	13/14	15/16	17/18	19>
90	65	60	57	54	52
80	68	63	59	56	54
70	70	65	61	58	56
60	72	68	63	60	58
50	74	70	65	62	60
40	76	71	67	64	62
30	78	72	69	66	64
20	80	74	71	68	66
10	82	76	73	70	68

Table 3.18: 400-meter run times (seconds)

Laboratory Tests

The Wingate Anaerobic Test is also used to test the anaerobic lactate system. The total work accomplished in thirty seconds is used instead of the peak power in five seconds with the alactic power test.

Measuring Strength and Muscular Endurance

Strength is the ability to exert or apply a force, and muscular endurance is the ability to sustain repeated muscular contractions.

Measuring strength and muscular endurance is usually related to specific muscle groups such as arms and legs, and in some cases strength can vary in the different muscle groups. It is important, therefore, to measure strength and muscular endurance in the major muscle groups used in the specific sport.

Strength Field Tests

MAXIMUM ONE REPETITION (1 RM)

Method
For a given weight, a number of trials are given to determine the maximum weight which can be lifted just once (1 RM). Exercises such as bench press, standing press, curl, and leg press are the most common maximum-strength tests. The exercises being used should be included in the training program, and extreme caution should be used if the athlete has had no experience with the designated lift or lifts.

Equipment
Designated barbells or weight machines used in the specific exercise, two spotters, recording sheets, pens, weight room or gymnasium.

Table 3.19: Optimum strength values for 1 RM

Body Weight	Bench Press		Standing Press		Curl		Leg Press	
lb	Male	Female	Male	Female	Male	Female	Male	Female
80	80	56	53	37	40	28	160	112
100	100	70	67	47	50	35	200	140
120	120	84	80	56	60	42	240	168
140	140	98	93	65	70	49	280	196
160	160	112	107	75	80	56	320	224
180	180	126	120	84	90	63	360	252
200	200	140	133	93	100	70	400	280
220	220	154	147	103	110	77	440	308
240	240	168	160	112	120	84	480	336

CHIN-UPS OR PULL-UPS (UPPER BODY)

Method
With palms of the hands facing the body, the athlete pulls the chin above the bar. The athlete must keep the legs straight, with no motion of raising the knees or kicking the legs. The maximum number of chins is performed, with only complete chin-ups counted.

Equipment
Wooden or metal bar 1½ inch (3.75 cm) in diameter and higher than the athlete, pens, clipboard, recording sheet.

Table 3.20: Strength ratings estimated from number of pull-ups

		Number of Pull-ups	
Age	Low	Average	High
9–10	0	1	6
11	0	2	6
12	0	2	7
13	1	3	8
14	2	4	10
15	3	6	12
16	4	7	12
17+	4	7	13

FLEXED ARM HANG (FEMALES)

Method
This test is specifically for females and is similar to the chin-up test, except the female athlete does one pull-up with the elbows flexed and the chin above the bar, and then holds the position for as long as possible. This held position is timed until the chin touches the bar or is tilted backward to avoid the bar, or goes below the bar.

Equipment

Stopwatches, clipboard, pens, recording paper, 1½ inch (3.75 cm) metal or wood bar approximately the height of the athlete.

Table 3.21: Strength ratings for females in the flexed-arm hang

	Hang Time in Seconds		
Age	Low	Average	High
9–10	3	9	30
11	3	10	30
12	3	9	26
13	3	8	25
14	3	9	28
15	4	9	27
16	3	7	23
17+	3	8	26

Laboratory Tests

No one test is accepted as standard for measuring total body strength. There is a high degree of specificity of major muscle groups, and a high level of strength in one muscle group does not always correlate to high levels of strength in other muscle groups. Total body strength seems to be best represented by strength tests in three areas: upper body, lower body, and trunk. Devices to measure strength include spring-type, pressure, and electrical devices. In the past, spring-type dynamometers, specifically the cable tensiometer, have been most commonly used. The pressure and electrical devices coupled with microcomputers are becoming more prevalent, being able to provide detailed analyses of strength and power curves throughout a full range of motion.

Measuring Leg Power

Field Test

VERTICAL JUMP

Method

A piece of cardboard or blackboard marked off in inches or centimeters is mounted on the wall. The athlete stands beside the wall sideways, with heels on the floor, and reaches as high as possible and touches the board with the outstretched fingers of one hand. The height is recorded. The athlete then crouches and jumps as high as possible, touching the board with one hand. Three trials are used, with the best score being recorded. Chalk may be used on the fingertips. The score is the difference between the standing reach height and the jump and reach height.

Table 3.22: Vertical jump scores (centimeters)

	Age						
Percentile	12	13	14	15	16	College	Pro
90	43.0	50.0	53.0	58.0	63.5	70.0	70.0
80	41.0	48.0	48.0	56.0	61.0	67.0	68.0
70	40.0	47.0	46.0	53.0	58.0	64.0	65.0
60	38.0	46.0	43.0	51.0	56.0	63.0	63.0
50	36.0	41.0	43.0	48.0	53.0	60.0	60.0
40	31.0	39.0	41.0	48.0	50.0	58.0	58.0
30	30.0	38.0	40.0	46.0	48.0	55.0	56.0
20	25.0	36.0	36.0	43.0	45.0	52.0	54.0
10	23.0	33.0	30.0	41.0	43.0	48.0	52.0

Measuring Muscular Endurance

Field Tests

PUSH-UPS

Method

The body is in the prone position, with the hands beneath the shoulders and the toes pointed. The arms are straightened with full extension, and then flexed until the nose touches the floor, with the back kept straight. The maximum number is done in succession. Only whole push-ups, with the arms fully extended, are counted. The athletes work in pairs, with one counting and the other performing the push-up.

Equipment

Mats, clipboards, pens, scoring sheet.

Table 3.23: Muscular-endurance ratings from the number of push-ups

Age and Sex	Low	Average	High
Under 14			
Males	Under 15	15–30	Over 30
Females	Under 10	10–20	Over 20
Over 14			
Males	Under 20	20–40	Over 40
Females	Under 10	10–30	Over 30

SIT-UPS

Method

The athlete assumes a lying position with the hands placed behind the neck. The knees are bent at 90 degrees. The heels are on the floor, the ankles held by a partner. The athlete sits up and touches the elbows to the knees, then returns the upper body to the floor. Each time the elbows touch the knees counts as one sit-up. The number of sit-ups recorded in one minute is the score.

Equipment

Stopwatch, mats, clipboards, pens, recording sheet.

Table 3.24: Muscular-endurance ratings from the number of sit-ups

Age and Sex	Low	Average	High
Under 14			
Males	Under 15	15–30	Over 30
Females	Under 10	10–20	Over 20
Over 14			
Males	Under 30	30–50	Over 50
Females	Under 25	25–45	Over 45

Measuring Flexibility

Field Test

Method

A common test measures the flexibility of the trunk and hamstrings. The athlete sits with the legs flat and toes upward. After the athlete has pre-stretched a couple of times, the athlete reaches forward with one hand on top of the other and reaches as far forward as possible toward the toes.

The distance between the toes and the outstretched hands is measured by a ruler (in inches) with the number 6 at the toes.

Equipment

12- or 18-inch ruler, mats, recording sheet, pens, clipboards.

Table 3.25: Flexibility ratings (in inches)

	Low	Average	High
Males	< 3	2 to +2	3+
Females	< 1	2 to 4	5+

Laboratory Test

Trunk flexion is tested with the Wells–Dillan sit-and-reach apparatus, or by a protractor device called a "goniometer" or a more accurate device called the "height on flexiometer."

Measuring Body Fat and Lean Body Weight

When assessing body composition, the total body weight is divided into lean body weight and fat weight. "Lean weight" refers to the total body weight after the body fat is removed, and consists of the weight of the muscle, skin, bone, organs, and all other non-fat tissue. Lean weight is determined in the laboratory, using Archimedes' principle and an underwater weighing technique to determine the density of the body.

Body fat can be determined in the field by using skinfold calipers. Measurements are taken, with folds of the skin being held firmly between the thumb and the index finger. The calipers are placed as closely as possible to the thumb and the index finger. Measurements are usually taken at triceps, biceps, sub-scapula (below the shoulder blade), and abdomen.

Table 3.26: Classification of body fat from skinfold thicknesses for male and female athletes

Male Athletes

		Skinfold Thickness (mm)		
Classification	Body Fat	Triceps	Scapular	Abdomen	Sum
Lean	<7%	<7	<8	<10	<25
Acceptable	7–15%	7–13	8–15	10–20	25–48
Overfat	>15%	>13	>15	>20	>48

Female Athletes

		Skinfold Thickness (mm)		
Classification	Body Fat	Triceps	Scapular	Abdomen	Sum
Lean	<12%	<9	<7	<7	<23
Acceptable	12–25%	9–17	7–14	7–15	23–46
Overfat	>25%	>17	>14	>15	>46

For more detailed information on physiological laboratory and field testing, refer to J. MacDougall, H. Wenger, & H. Green's *Physiological Testing of the High-Performance Athlete* (see bibliography).

NUTRITION

Most athletes and coaches know that a well-balanced diet is essential when training, but what the exact nutritional requirements are for this diet is not clear to them.

Athletes' Diet

The average person consumes between 1,200 and 1,500 calories per day from food. An athlete who trains daily, however, may require between 2,000 and 5,000 calories per day, depending on the training intensity, age, body size, and so on.

An optimal athlete's diet would include approximately 60–65 percent carbohydrates, 25 percent fats, and 15 percent protein.

The carbohydrates, fats, and proteins are supplied by the four basic food groups:

1. Milk and cheese
2. Meat and fish
3. Fruits and vegetables
4. Breads and cereals

Also essential for the well-balanced diet are vitamins, minerals, and water.

The carbohydrates in the diet, which are broken down to simple sugars, primarily glucose, are stored in the muscle and liver as glycogen and are the key to the supplying of energy for athletic performance. The major problem for today's athlete is to have a 60–65 percent carbohydrate diet and limit the amount of fat to 25 percent along with 15 percent protein. High-carbohydrate diets produce more stored glycogen and have an effect on performance, especially in endurance events lasting more than one hour that deplete these glycogen stores. In short-burst power events, the glycogen stores are usually not fully depleted. Today's so-called junk food (hamburgers, hot dogs, french fries, and so on) contains high fat levels, and it is important for the athlete to limit intake of these foods and concentrate on those rich in carbohydrates.

Although the common prescription of three meals per day may be suitable for the average person, the athlete, who may need twice as many calories, can eat five or six meals per day as well as planned nutritional snacks.

As well as the daily meals, the athlete must eat a well-planned pre- and post-competition meal, along with some additional fluid and nutrition during the event.

Carbohydrates

Carbohydrates are made up of carbon, hydrogen, and oxygen, and are commonly known as starches and sugars. Carbohydrates, the main source of energy in intense exercise, supply the cells with glucose and glycogen, which are then converted to energy. Carbohydrates are found in three groups that vary in complexity and size of the molecules: simple sugars or monosaccharides; disaccharides, which are two linked monosaccharides; and polysaccharides, or complex carbohydrates.

Monosaccharides, or simple sugars, are often listed on the labels of foods as glucose, fructose, or dextrose. Disaccharides are made by linking two monosaccharides such as fructose and glucose, which forms common table sugar. Other simple sugars such as maltose and lactose are also formed by the joining of two monosaccharides.

Polysaccharides can be of two types: starch and fiber. This complex carbohydrate is formed by a large number of simple sugar groups. These types of starches are found in grains and cereals and in vegetables such as potatoes and corn.

Most food products contain mixtures of all three types of carbohydrates, and it is important for the athlete and coach to read and understand the labels on food products to ascertain the carbohydrate value.

For the carbohydrates to be used as fuel for energy, they must be broken down to simple sugars by digestive enzymes before leaving the stomach to enter the small intestine to be absorbed by the blood. Only glucose can be used directly by the cells, and the remaining simple sugars are carried by the blood to the liver, where they are converted to glucose. When glucose enters the cell, some is used directly while the rest is stored as glycogen for future use. Any excess glucose that remains after the glycogen stores are filled is stored as fat.

Glycogen stored in one muscle cell cannot be used by another. The liver has the only cells in the body which can convert glycogen back to glucose, which can, in turn, be re-released into the blood stream.

Insulin is important for the carrying of glucose to the cells and is released by the pancreas when there is an elevated amount of glucose in the blood.

Some specific foods that are rich in carbohydrates are:

1. Pasta such as spaghetti, macaroni, and pizza
2. Cereals such as bran and oat bran. These cereals are also a good supply of fiber.
3. Vegetables, such as potatoes and corn, and legumes.
4. Muffins and bagels, with whole-grain muffins (bran, oatmeal, corn) being better than white-flour muffins, donuts, and so on.
5. Whole-grain and dark breads. Whole-grain breads have more nutritional value than white-grain breads.
6. Fruits and fruit juices such as orange, banana, and apple.

Carbohydrate Loading

Carbohydrate loading is sometimes mentioned as a method to increase the amount of stored glycogen in the body. Generally there are three types of carbohydrate loading, of which only the first two are recommended, and then with caution. Carbohydrate loading should be used infrequently, and only in the sports with one main competition every few weeks, and should not be confused with the athlete's normal dietary requirement of 65 percent carbohydrates. Specific carbohydrate loading therefore is not practical for sports that have at least one competition per week.

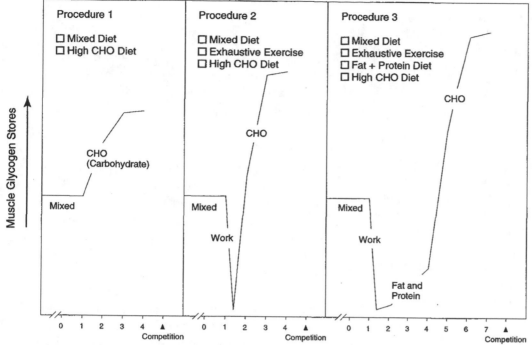

Figure 3.30: Three procedures for carbohydrate loading. Reprinted with permission from R. Bowers and E. Fox, *Sport Physiology*. (Dubuque, IA: Wm. C. Brown), 302.

The first method is to have the athlete eat a normal mixed diet for several days, followed by a high-carbohydrate diet for three or four days. During the high-carbohydrate phase, no exhaustive exercise is performed.

The second method is to follow exhaustive exercise with a few days of high-carbohydrate diet. No exhaustive exercise is performed during the carbohydrate loading.

The third type of carbohydrate loading is more controversial and should be done only once or twice a year in sports where a major competition occurs two or three times per year. In this method, three days of a low-carbohydrate, high-fat, and high-protein diet are accompanied by exhaustive exercise. This is followed by three days of a high-carbohydrate diet and light exercise.

In a study comparing the three types of carbohydrate loading, glycogen stores increased from an initial 15 grams per kilogram (g/kg) of body weight to 25 g/kg in the first method, 30 g/kg in the second method, and 50 g/kg in the third method (Bowers & Fox). The three methods are summarized in figure 3.30.

Glycogen loading, especially the third method mentioned, is not without side effects that should be considered by the coach and athlete. Since glycogen comprises three parts water to one part glycogen, increased storage of water in the muscle can result, with a weight gain of up to 11 pounds (5 kg). Muscle stiffness, nausea, and intestinal distress can also result from carbohydrate loading. All these side effects can limit performance.

In light of these side effects, it is recommended that carbohydrate loading be used selectively. A diet normally high in carbohydrates is the best nutrition for the athlete.

Fats

Fats, along with carbohydrates, supply the majority of energy for the body. (Proteins supply very small amounts.) Fats are stored as triglycerides in specialized cells in the body called "adipose tissue." Fats contain large amounts of carbon and hydrogen and relatively small amounts of oxygen. Fats do not supply energy as quickly as carbohydrates, but more energy can be stored as fat. Fats are more important as a fuel source in prolonged activity lasting more than an hour, while carbohydrates are used primarily in intense exercise of a shorter duration.

There are two types of fat sources: saturated and unsaturated. Saturated fats from animals, and coconut and palm oil, are believed to be related to incidents of atherosclerosis and cardiovascular disease, and excessive amounts should be avoided. Unsaturated fats from vegetable oils and plants are considered to be better for the athletes. As only 25 percent of the total diet should be made up of fats, the athlete should take care not to exceed this limit.

Here are some examples of fats that should and should not be included in the athlete's diet:

1. Use olive oil, canola, safflower, and sunflower oils for cooking.
2. Cut back or eliminate hamburgers, hot dogs, sausage, butter, and cheese.
3. Use low-fat cheese, margarine, yogurt, peanut butter, and salad oils.
4. Read labels to find low-fat foods.

The major problem with the fat content in the athlete's diet is that the desired percentage (25 percent) is difficult to maintain as most athletes tend to have a higher proportion of fat in their diet, to the detriment of the larger (60 percent) proportion that should be carbohydrates.

Protein

Protein, which should make up 15 percent of the athlete's diet, is essential to the body for physical growth and repair of damaged tissue. Also, the enzymes that control the chemical reactions in the body are made of proteins. Proteins are composed of chains of smaller substances called "amino acids," which are made up of carbon, hydrogen, oxygen, nitrogen, and in some cases sulfur atoms. The nitrogen content makes the protein different from carbohydrates and fat. There are twenty different amino acids, and eight of these are called "essential" because the liver cannot make these from carbohydrates, fats, and protein. Three of these essential amino acids—namely, valine, iolencine, and leucine—are essential in energy production (Brooks).

The daily requirement of protein for the average person is one gram per kilogram (g/kg) of body weight. An athlete, while training, requires 1.4 to 2.0 g/kg (Clark). The amino acids can be found in the protein of both animals and plants. Animals have a greater distribution of amino acids compared with plants, and are considered a better source. The average person with a normal diet usually consumes more than 2.0 g/kg of protein per day.

Eating an excessive amount of protein (more than 15 percent of the total diet) is not recommended. With excessive amounts of protein, the body removes the nitrogen, and the remaining amino acid is converted to fat or carbohydrates. Therefore, excessive protein cannot be stored. Excessive amounts of protein have been known to cause dehydration and constipation because the kidneys must use water to wash out the nitrogen (urea) and other waste products resulting from protein metabolism.

Since a well-balanced diet produces more than enough protein for the athlete in training, and because excessive protein cannot be stored by the body, the many protein supplements that are on the market, many making unsubstantiated claims, are unnecessary. A diet with a normal amount of protein is quite adequate for protein needs.

Some recommended sources of protein are:

1. Lean beef
2. Chicken and turkey
3. Fish, especially salmon, tuna, sardines, swordfish
4. Peanut butter
5. Beans, lentils, legumes, tofu, chili beans
6. Milk, eggs, cottage cheese

Vitamins

Vitamins are essential to the body, as parts of enzymes and coenzymes involved in the metabolism of carbohydrates and fats, but they are not a direct source of energy themselves. Vitamins are also involved in the formation of red blood cells and bone. Vitamins are not manufactured but must be ingested from the food in the diet. Some vitamins are water soluble (C and B complex) and cannot be stored, with the excess being passed in the urine. Other vitamins are fat-soluble (A, D, E, and K) and are absorbed with the fat in the stomach and small intestines. Excessive amounts are stored in the liver and fatty tissue and are not excreted in the urine.

These fat-soluble vitamins are required in small amounts and do not need to be supplied each day, but deficiencies can lead to serious illness or death. Excessive amounts, on the other hand, can be toxic.

With all essential vitamins, additional supplementation is unnecessary, and in many cases can be toxic or have side effects. The well-balanced diet can supply more than enough of the required amount of vitamins for the healthy athlete.

Water-Soluble Vitamins

VITAMIN C (ASCORBIC ACID)

Vitamin C has been advocated by some as an effective method in the prevention of the common cold, although the research is inconclusive on this topic.

It has also been hypothesized that vitamin C can be helpful for the athlete who is constantly under training stress. There is evidence that vitamin C is important in collagen synthesis, which is involved in strengthening existing and developing new connective tissue. Excess vitamin C is excreted in the urine, and the value of megadoses is not supported by conclusive research.

Sources of Vitamin C
1. Orange, tomato, apple, cranberry juice
2. Broccoli

3. Brussels sprouts
4. Tomatoes
5. Cantaloupe
6. Green peppers

B VITAMINS (THIAMINE B₁, RIBOFLAVIN B₂, AND NIACIN, PLUS OTHERS)

Thiamine (B_1), riboflavin (B_2), and niacin are important in the release of energy from food, assist in the function of the nervous system, and are a factor in the healing of skin.

Sources of B Vitamins

Thiamine— Lean beef, pork, poultry, and fish
Enriched bread

Riboflavin— Green leafy vegetables
Milk, eggs
Peas, beans
Lean beef
Fish
Whole-grain cereals, enriched breads

Niacin— Lean beef, pork, poultry, and fish
Enriched bread, whole-grain cereals
Peanut butter

Fat-Soluble Vitamins

VITAMIN A

Vitamin A is essential for healthy eyes and protects against night blindness. It is also important for healthy skin and keeps mucous membranes firm and resistant to infections.

Sources of Vitamin A
1. Peaches, apricots
2. Broccoli, spinach
3. Cantaloupe
4. Carrots
5. Sweet potatoes

VITAMIN D

Vitamin D helps build calcium and phosphorous in bones and assists the body in absorbing calcium.

Sources of Vitamin D
1. Sunlight
2. Milk
3. Eggs
4. Fish
5. Cod liver oil

VITAMIN E

There have been some claims that vitamin E is related to better athletic performance, especially in aerobic endurance events at high altitude (Kobayashi). Vitamin E does assist with tissue growth and red-cell wall integrity. There is no research on humans to substantiate that excess supplementation of this vitamin is related to improved athletic performance.

Sources of Vitamin E
1. Green, leafy vegetables
2. Wheat germ
3. Vegetable oil
4. Cereals
5. Margarine, shortening

VITAMIN K

Vitamin K is important for the clotting or coagulation of blood in cuts or any incision in the skin.

Sources
1. Milk
2. Green, leafy vegetables
3. Cabbage
4. Cereals
5. Meats

Minerals

Minerals are inorganic compounds found in small amounts throughout the body and are essential to body function.

The minerals include the so-called electrolytes, namely, sodium, potassium, and chloride; the minerals involved in bone metabolism, including calcium, phosphorus, and magnesium; and zinc and iron.

The Electrolytes—Sodium, Potassium, and Chloride

Much has been written about sport drinks as a means to replace electrolytes during and after exercise. Electrolytes are charged molecules. Most molecules are neutral, with an equal number of positive protons and negative electrons. When electrolytes are consumed in the food we eat, mostly found in fruits, vegetables, and grains, they combine with either the extracellular (outside) or the intercellular (inside) fluids (mostly water) in the body, but not in equal concentrations. Sodium ($Na+$) and potassium ($K+$) are found in the largest concentrations. Sodium is found in the extracellular fluids, and potassium is found in the intracellular fluid as shown, in figure 3.31. The balance of the concentrations of sodium and potassium inside and outside the cell are critical to life functions, especially muscle contraction.

During exercise, water moves from the extracellular fluid through the membrane into the muscle cells. This fluid is replaced in the extracellular compartment by water from the blood plasma. This movement of water across the membrane causes a difference in concentrations of the electrolytes on the inside and outside of the cell. If excessive salt (NaCl) is taken into the body, the concentration of sodium becomes greater on the outside of the cell, and water is drawn across the membrane from the inside of the cell to equalize the concentrations. This movement of water out of the cell alters the chemical reaction that produces energy (water is important for this process) and impairs muscle contraction.

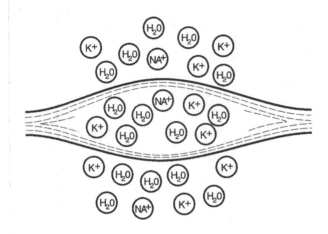

Figure 3.31: Concentration of electrolytes on either side of the cell's membrane must be balanced

A similar situation occurs when water is lost through sweating, which also disturbs the electrolyte balance. When water is lost from extracellular space and the sodium concentration is allowed to increase, water again moves from inside the cell to outside to balance the concentrations.

The electrolyte balance in the body can be kept at a normal level by the food we eat. An increase in the consumption of fruits and vegetables is the best method to replenish the electrolytes, as well as drinking as much water as is comfortable. A regular, normal salting of food is also acceptable, but excessive amounts are not necessary. Salt tablets must be consumed with at least one pint of water per tablet, and this method is not recommended. Electrolyte sport drinks are useful as they replace both electrolytes and water, although the cost may be a deterrent.

Potassium (K+) imbalance in the blood is also a problem with exercise. The rising concentration of potassium in the blood, called "hyperkalemia," is caused by potassium being released from the muscle cell and a loss of fluid from the plasma.

The best method of replacement of potassium is through the diet, with fruits, vegetables, and lean meats being the main providers. Sport drinks also include potassium.

Some food sources of sodium and potassium are:

1. Bananas, apples, apricots, oranges, tomatoes
2. Broccoli, potatoes, squash, carrots, green beans
3. Kidney beans
4. Whole-wheat bread
5. Chicken
6. Spaghetti with meat sauce
7. Raisins

Calcium, Phosphorus, and Magnesium

Calcium, phosphorus, and magnesium are important in the makeup and formation of bones and teeth.

Of the three minerals, *calcium* is the most abundant in the body. As well as being found in bones and teeth (99 percent of the total amount), a small portion plays a role in muscle contraction, transmission of nerve impulses, and the breakdown of glycogen (Williams).

A calcium deficiency can lead to a decrease in bone density, called "osteoporosis." Females with a smaller bone mass than men seem to be more susceptible. Stress fractures and muscle cramping are possibly affected by a calcium deficiency (Neilson; Williams). It has also been postulated that a calcium deficiency may have a more severe effect than normal on females who are amenorrheic, a condition where their menstrual periods have been suppressed.

Calcium can be found in dairy products and plant foods, although the absorption from dairy products is superior. Taking excess calcium is not recommended and may lead to kidney-stone formation.

Some sources of calcium are:

1. Milk
2. Cheese
3. Green, leafy vegetables
4. Egg yolk

Phosphorus, as well as being found in bones and teeth, is involved as part of the energy-producing ATP (adenosine triphosphate) and CP (creatine phosphate). Deficiencies of this mineral seem rare.

Some sources of phosphorus are:

1. Poultry
2. Fish
3. Milk
4. Meat
5. Eggs
6. Cereal
7. Grains

Magnesium is also involved in the chemical reactions related to the release of energy, muscle contraction, and the transmission of nerve impulses. As with phosphorus, deficiencies are not common.

Some sources of magnesium are:

1. Nuts
2. Whole-wheat bread
3. Green, leafy vegetables

Deficiencies of calcium, phosphorus, and magnesium can be made up by adapting the diet to include more of the foods mentioned above, and supplements are not recommended.

Iron

Iron is one mineral that hard-training athletes, especially females, must pay special attention to.

Iron is found in the red blood cells and is responsible for the oxygen-carrying capacity of the blood.

Iron is an important constituent of hemoglobin, which carries oxygen in the blood; myoglobin, which transports oxygen within the cell; and cytochromes, which are involved in the aerobic system.

Endurance athletes have been found to have low levels of iron after heavy training. When iron is at the extreme low levels, athletes may become anemic (experience reduced hemoglobin in the blood) or, more commonly, may suffer from suboptimal hemoglobin, a condition not as extreme as anemia.

Adolescents and women in their menstrual cycles are the most susceptible to iron losses, and they must take care to have the required level of iron in their diets. Iron supplements can be considered by the athlete, but should be taken only when prescribed by a doctor as overdoses can be toxic.

Iron is found in:

1. Green, leafy vegetables
2. Egg yolk
3. Liver, kidney, heart
4. Nuts
5. Dried beans
6. Red meat
7. Enriched bread and cereals

Zinc and Chromium

Research is inconclusive on the minerals zinc and chromium, but some recent work has been done on the importance of chromium in athletic performance. These minerals are found in trace amounts in the body and can be found in:

Zinc	Chromium
1. Fish	1. Fats
2. Eggs	2. Vegetable oils
3. Oatmeal	3. Wheat germ
4. Bran	4. Calf's liver
5. Nuts	
6. Green, leafy vegetables	

Water

Water is the most essential nutrient in the body. Located in both the extracellular and intracellular parts of the body, it makes up over half the body weight, over 70 percent of the muscle weight, and 80 percent of the blood.

Water replacement is essential before, during, and after exercise, as over 2 percent of the body weight can be lost through sweating. Also, water should be consumed regularly, with eight glasses or more being the minimum. Athletes should drink water frequently, at least every ten to fifteen minutes, three to six ounces at a time, during training or competition. Stomach cramps usually result from consuming too much water at one time rather than from drinking water that is too cold. A temperature range of 45°–55°F (7°–11°C) is ideal for drinking water as it has been shown that drinks at this temperature empty from the stomach faster (Bowers, Foss, & Fox).

Lack of water in the body causes reaction in muscular strength; lower plasma and blood volumes; lower oxygen consumption; decrease in work performance times; depletion of liver glycogen stores; and an increase in the amount of electrolytes lost from the body.

Water can be taken alone, but it is also found in most foods, especially in:

1. Watermelon
2. Oranges
3. Carrots
4. Pineapple
5. Apples
6. Potatoes
7. Lettuce
8. Celery

119

9. Pickles
10. Broccoli

Pre-Competition Nutrition

What and when the athlete eats before a competition is important. It should be mentioned here that an ideal pre-event meal does not compensate and provide the fuel for energy if the athlete's diet has been lacking up until that time.

The main purpose of the pre-event meal is to help provide the fuel for energy by digesting foods that can be stored as glycogen. The meal also settles the stomach and removes the feeling of hunger, as well as preventing hypoglycemia (low blood sugar), which can interfere with performance.

The following guidelines should be followed for the pre-event meal:

1. The meal should be high in carbohydrates, such as pasta, potatoes, and enriched bread, and low in fats. The meal can include small portions of protein, such as lean meat, fish, or chicken. Avoid gas-forming, greasy and spicy foods.
2. A normal-sized meal should be eaten at least three to four hours before the event. Smaller meals or snacks can be eaten two to three hours before. Liquid meals can be ingested one to two hours before. It is important that the stomach and small intestine be emptied before the competition begins. Some athletes now eat a large meal five to six hours before competition, and then have a small nutritious snack about one-half hour to two hours before. The time of the meal is more important before intense exercise than low-intensity endurance exercise. Meals should be eaten a longer time before intense exercise.
3. Avoid glucose and sugary foods less than one hour before competition. Sugary foods stimulate secretion of insulin, and the amount of glucose in the blood is actually decreased. This in turn puts a greater dependence on glycogen in the muscle, and therefore depletes the stores sooner, contributing to fatigue.
4. Drink plenty of fluids. Water and/or juices should be consumed both regularly before the competition day and on the day of the event. Four to eight glasses of water should be consumed daily, two or three glasses two to three hours before competition, and one or two glasses half an hour before the competition.

5. Eat food with which you are familiar and enjoy. Don't experiment with new foods on competition day, but rather try these foods on training days. Discomfort or a poor-tasting meal may upset the preparation for competition.
6. Some athletes may prefer liquid meals. There are several available now, including brand names such as Ensure, Ensure Plus, and SustaCal. These meals are easily digested and assist energy intake, as well as providing fluids. Do not use liquid meals for the first time on competition day. Many athletes prefer to have a full pre-event meal.

Nutrition during Competition

Water should be consumed at regular intervals (ten to fifteen minutes) throughout competition. Personal water bottles should be provided for all athletes, and they should consume small quantities whenever possible.

In events lasting longer than two hours, replacement of carbohydrates is necessary, whether the activity is continuous or intermittent. Blood glucose levels with this type of activity may have dropped to a level where the deficiency affects performance. Sport drinks or a combination of glucose and water seem to be the most popular method for supplying the added fuel necessary. The liquid should have a pleasant taste and should contain 2.5 to 10 percent carbohydrates, and electrolytes such as sodium and potassium. The normal amount ingested in these endurance events is usually 5 to 10 ounces every fifteen to twenty minutes. More than these amounts is unnecessary and could cause discomfort.

Nutrition after Training and Competition

One of the areas most neglected by athletes is when and what type of foods and liquids should be consumed after training and competition. The timing and what is ingested are very important in the recovery process.

Fluids

Fluids should be replaced as quickly as possible after competition. Water is the natural choice, as up to and sometimes more than 2 percent of the body weight is lost due to sweating, and this amount must be replaced as quickly as possible. Fruit juices and sport drinks are ideal as they also replace carbohydrates, electrolytes, and vitamins. Watery-type foods such as grapes, watermelons, oranges, and soups are also effective.

Alcohol

Alcohol consumption is not recommended as a means of fluid replacement as it has a dehydrating effect on the body. If athletes feel they would like alcohol (a couple of beers) after a competition, advise them to drink a couple glasses of water before or along with the alcoholic drinks. Alcohol is also low in carbohydrates, and there is no truth to the theory that alcoholic calories are stored as glycogen.

Carbohydrates

It is becoming increasingly clear that it is important not only to replace carbohydrates after training and competition, but to replace them within a certain time after the activity.

It is now recommended that carbohydrates should start to be replaced within one hour of competition and not longer than four hours afterward. The recommended amount is 10 grams per kilogram of body weight within the first two hours after competition, followed with same amount two hours later. This amount would range between 75 to 100 grams of carbohydrates taken twice in the first four hours. Bananas and juices are an ideal immediate source after the competition, and the typical pasta meal of spaghetti or macaroni serves to replace the carbohydrates. It is therefore recommended that athletes eat a high-carbohydrate meal within two to four hours after the competition.

Electrolytes

Electrolytes, such as sodium and potassium, can be replaced easily by fruit juices and sport drinks, as mentioned previously. Bananas are also a convenient and easily eaten food after competition. The use of salt tablets and other pill-form replacements after competition is unnecessary and not recommended.

Along with eating the proper foods after competition, it is important to rest to allow the body to restore the glycogen to its pre-event levels. An active athlete needs between eight and ten hours of sleep per night.

Caffeine

Mention should be made of the effects of caffeine, found commonly in coffee and tea, before and after competition and training. Some athletes rely on coffee before competition to pick them up, whereas others avoid it because it makes them jittery and causes discomfort.

Caffeine appears to have a short-term stimulating effect on the nervous system, which may account for the fact that some athletes feel it makes physical effort easier. However, this effect does not last and should not be a reason for an athlete to consume caffeine. Some research has shown that certain larger amounts of caffeine allow fatty acids to be mobilized and can enhance an athlete's endurance (Bowers & Fox).

It is interesting to note that caffeine in large doses is banned by the International Olympic Committee. Twelve milligrams of caffeine per milliliter of urine is enough for disqualification, but this amount would require the consumption of approximately eight cups of coffee, sixteen cola drinks, or twenty-four Anacin.

EATING DISORDERS

There appears to be an alarming increase in eating disorders among athletes, particularly females.

In weight-conscious sports such as gymnastics, figure skating, and wrestling, some athletes resort to calorie-reducing diets while they are training intensely. Some coaches have also put undue pressure on athletes to lose weight, without outlining how.

Two of the most serious eating disorders, anorexia nervosa and bulimia, have become associated with athletes in the sports mentioned above. Anorexia nervosa is an overemphasis on thinness and is characterized by a lack of eating, even to a point of starvation. Bulimia is characterized by binge eating, followed by purging the body of food by vomiting, using laxatives or fasting. Both conditions can lead to death and are quite serious.

Coaches should be aware of the signs of these two illnesses and warn their athletes against excessive and non-nutritious weight loss.

ANABOLIC–ANDROGENIC STEROIDS

The only reason for mentioning steroids is the fact that many athletes, especially in the strength and power sports such as football and throwing events in track, have heard about them and may be tempted to use them.

The first point to mention about steroids is that they are banned by the International Olympic Federation and most sports' governing bodies. They are associated with adverse side effects on the liver, cardiovascular system, and reproductive system, as well as affecting behavior.

Steroids are a derivative of the male sex hormone testosterone, secreted by the testes. The term "anabolic" refs to the building of tissue, and "androgenic" refers to the development of the male secondary sexual characteristics, which can occur also as side effects in females who use these substances.

The use of anabolic–androgenic steroids can increase body weight and muscular strength when associated with training. They do not increase aerobic power or capacity.

Coaches should look for signs that their athletes may be using steroids, such as an unnatural rapid gain of weight and strength, and changes in personality such as overaggressiveness and mood shifts.

It is important for the coach to stress that proper training methods are the best way to increase strength and weight, and that, as well as being banned, steroids have serious negative side effects which can greatly affect the athletes in their daily and future lives.

SMOKING

Smoking affects athletic performance by reducing the oxygen-carrying capacity of the blood and increasing airway resistance for the taking of oxygen into the lungs.

Oxygen combines with hemoglobin to be carried by the blood to the cells. When a person smokes, a by-product of the smoke is carbon monoxide (CO). Carbon monoxide has more than 200 times the affinity for combining with hemoglobin as oxygen does. Therefore, if both oxygen and carbon monoxide are present, carbon monoxide combines much quicker with the hemoglobin and, as a result, the oxygen-carrying capacity of the blood is reduced by as much as 10 percent with a heavy smoker.

The increased airway resistance caused by smoking can result in shortness of breath. The resistance causes the respiratory muscles to work harder to consume more oxygen. This added cost of ventilation can rob the working muscles of a percentage of their potential oxygen supply. During all-out exercise, this could lead to reduced performance, and during submaximal exercise, an increase in anaerobic metabolism may cause early fatigue.

For athletes who choose to smoke, abstaining for twenty-four hours before competing can lower the oxygen cost of ventilation by as much as 25 percent, but is still 60 percent higher than for non-smokers (Bowers, Foss, & Fox).

As well as the effect smoking has on athletic performance, it causes a greater risk of coronary heart disease and lung cancer.

MORE DETAILED PHYSIOLOGY OF THE ENERGY AND MUSCULAR SYSTEMS

Note: This section is for coaches who wish to have a more extensive understanding of the physiological basis of the energy and muscular systems of the body.

The Energy Systems

The energy to maintain life and move the body in athletic competition comes in the form of chemical energy from the foods (carbohydrates, fats, and protein) we eat. Through metabolism, the chemical release of energy provides the force to activate muscles. Although these foods we eat contain chemical energy, their molecular bonds are relatively weak and are not used directly for muscular contraction. Instead, the energy that bonds these food molecules is chemically released and stored in the form of a high-energy phosphate called "adenosine triphosphate" (ATP). ATP is comprised of adenosine, containing the compounds adenine and ribose and three simpler compounds called "phosphate groups." Assembling and disassembling ATP are facilitated by special proteins called "enzymes." ATP-ase is an enzyme which acts on the last phosphate group to split it away from the ATP molecule, as shown in figure 3.20, thereby releasing a great deal more energy than in the low-energy foods. ATP is stored and utilized by most cells in the body, including muscle and nerve cells.

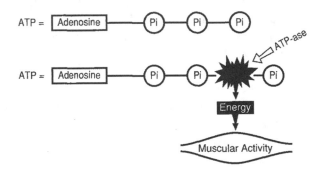

Figure 3.20: Energy release from ATP by the activation of the enzyme ATP-ase

As energy is released when ATP is broken down, energy is also required to rebuild or resynthesize ATP, as shown in figure 3.21. This energy for the resynthesis of ATP comes from three different chemical reactions in the body. Two of these chemical reactions come from the food we eat, while the other depends on a chemical compound called "creatine phosphate" (CP), which is also stored in the muscle cell.

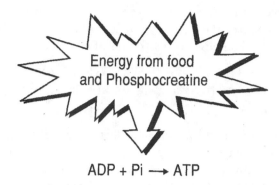

ADP + Pi $\rightarrow$ ATP

Figure 3.21: ATP resynthesis from ADP and phosphate

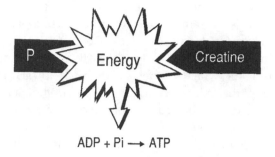

ADP + Pi $\rightarrow$ ATP

Figure 3.22: ATP resynthesis with the breakdown of creatine phosphate

The ATP that is required for the energy of muscle contraction is supplied by three different systems, one aerobic (with oxygen) and two anaerobic (without oxygen) called the "alactic," "phosphagen," or "ATP-CP" system, and the "lactic" or anaerobic glycolysis system. All three systems contribute to ATP production, but the predominant system depends on the length and intensity of athletic activity. Short, powerful muscular contractions rely on the ATP-CP system, intermediate work lasting between thirty and sixty seconds relies on the lactic system, and longer work of more than two minutes relies on the aerobic system for the product of ATP.

ATP-CP System

The ATP-CP system is utilized in high-intensity activity lasting up to ten seconds and can contribute in intense exercise lasting up to thirty seconds. The ATP in this system is stored in the muscle, along with another energy-rich compound, creatine phosphate (CP). Creatine phosphate, when broken down to creatine and with the phosphate group removed, releases a large amount of energy that resynthesizes ADP and inorganic phosphate (Pi) to ATP, as shown in figure 3.22. The enzyme creatine kinase facilitates this reaction. The ATP production in this system is the most rapid (3–6 moles per minute) of the three systems, but the total stores of both ATP and CP are small (0.6 moles). Thus this system is used for a rapid supply of ATP, but produces a limited amount. The CP concentration is about three times that of ATP, and the stores are exhausted within ten seconds of the commencement of all-out activity. The restoration of CP, however, is quite rapid as 50 percent is restored in approximately thirty seconds, 75 percent in sixty seconds, and almost all in three minutes, as shown in table 3.12. This restoration factor is important for coaches and athletes to consider when determining work-to-rest ratios.

Table 3.12: Restoration of creatine phosphate (CP) after intense exercise

Recover Time	Muscle Phosphagen Restored
Less than 10 seconds	Very Little
30 seconds	50%
60 seconds	75%
90 seconds	85%
120 seconds	95%
150 seconds	97%
180 seconds	98%

Lactic-Acid (Anaerobic Glycolysis) System

During the early minutes of intense exercise, the body is incapable of providing enough oxygen to regenerate ATP. The ATP-PC system provides the majority of the ATP in the start-up ten seconds, but after that the lactic-acid system kicks in to provide additional ATP. Glycolysis is the breakdown of glucose (simple sugar), and glycogenolysis is the breakdown of glycogen (stored carbohydrate made up of many glucose subunits). Once again enzymes enhance this reaction, and the energy necessary to make ATP is derived by splitting glucose molecules and forming a compound called "pyruvate," and releasing energy. Although this process is limited by the lack of oxygen, as each glucose molecule produces only a net gain of two ATP, the lactic-acid system can produce almost double the amount of ATP compared with the ATP-CP system (1.2 versus 0.6 moles). The rate of production of ATP, however, is less rapid than in the ATP-CP system (1.6 moles per minute compared with the ATP-CP system's 3.6 moles per minute). The chemical reactions of the lactic acid system are illustrated by the following equations:

$$C_6H_{12}O_2 \rightarrow 2C_3H_6O_3 + \text{Energy}$$
(carbohydrate)   (lactic acid)

$$\text{Energy} + 3Pi + ADP \rightarrow 3\ ATP$$

As the demand for ATP exceeds the rate provided, the pyruvate is converted to lactate. When lactate reaches a high level in the muscles, fatigue occurs. The fatigue is caused by the interior of the muscle cells becoming more acidic, which interferes with the chemical processes of the cell, as well as the buildup of inorganate phosphate. The high concentration of lactate also affects the nerve endings, causing pain. The "anaerobic threshold" is defined as the point at which the lactate starts to accumulate, which affects the movement of the muscles (usually over 85 percent maximum heart rate). The anaerobic threshold is higher for trained athletes than for the untrained.

Lactate is removed from the blood by metabolism with oxygen during recovery. Skeletal and heart muscle can aerobically metabolize lactate (approximately 72 percent), while some (19 percent) is converted to glucose in the blood, or glycogen in the liver (Bowers & Fox). Other amounts of lactate are converted to protein, carbon dioxide (CO_2), and water (H_2O). The kidneys and liver also use some small amounts as fuel.

Half of the lactate can be removed in approximately fifteen minutes, 75 percent in thirty minutes, and 95 percent in one hour.

Lactate removal is hastened by light continuous exercise (walking or jogging) as compared with no exercise or intermittent exercise (Bonen & Belcastro; Hermansen, el al.).

Light activity allows a portion of the lactate to be aerobically metabolized to supply some of the ATP for the energy required in light activity. This is an important factor for athletes performing a number of times in a short period of one day or less.

The Oxygen System

For exercise lasting longer than two to three minutes, the majority of ATP is supplied through the complete metabolism of carbohydrates and fats, and a trace amount of protein during extremely long bouts of exercise.

Aerobic metabolism begins in a similar manner to anaerobic glycolysis. The difference, however, is that, with sufficient oxygen, the pyruvate is not converted to lactate, but enters into two long series of chemical reactions called "the Kreb's cycle" and "the electron-transport system." These reactions take place in subcellular compartments called "the mitochondria," which are the powerhouse of the cell, as this is where the aerobic manufacture of ATP takes place. Approximately 39 ATP can be produced aerobically by metabolizing one molecule of glycogen. Compare this with only 3 ATP without

oxygen, using the lactic-acid system. The following equations represent the chemical reactions involved in the aerobic breakdown of 180 grams of glycogen:

$$C_6H_{12}O_6 + 6O_2 \rightarrow 6CO_2 + 6H_2O + \text{Energy}$$
$$\text{(glycogen) (oxygen)} \quad \text{(carbon dioxide) (water)}$$
$$\text{Energy} + 39 \text{ ADP} + 39 \text{ Pi} \rightarrow 39 \text{ ATP}$$

The system, however, is the least powerful of the three, with a power output of 1 mole per minute compared with 1.6 with the lactic-acid system and 3.6 with the ATP-PC system. Also of importance is the fact that no fatiguing by-products are formed with the oxygen system. The chemical reactions in the Kreb's cycle and the electron-transport system produce carbon dioxide, which is expired through the lungs, and water, which is used by the blood.

During rest, one-third of the ATP is supplied by metabolizing carbohydrates and two-thirds from fats. During physical exercise, carbohydrates become the main source of ATP, with maximum effort using totally carbohydrates for metabolism to produce ATP. As the duration of moderate exercise increases, more reliance is placed on the utilization of fat as a source of ATP. The metabolism of fat is not as efficient as carbohydrates for producing ATP. One molecule of fat has the ability to produce 140 molecules of ATP compared with 39 molecules from carbohydrates. More oxygen is required to produce ATP from fat, and the body uses carbohydrates as a faster supply in more intense exercise.

Glycogen sparing is a process whereby the body uses fats as fuel up to a certain exercise level, then uses the more limited glycogen store when the exercise level increases.

The maximal amount of energy that can be produced with aerobic metabolism is dependent on how much oxygen the body can obtain and utilize, which is designated as maximal oxygen output (MVO_2). This is usually designated in liters or milliliters of oxygen per kilogram of body weight per minute (ml/kg/min.). Top endurance athletes have MVO_2 values of 70 ml/kg/min. and higher.

Interaction of the Energy Systems

It is important to realize that all three energy sources supply a portion of ATP at all times. Short-burst activities lasting up to ten seconds rely on the ATP-CP system for the majority of the ATP, while long-endurance events rely heavily on the oxygen system. Events lasting from thirty to ninety seconds utilize the lactic-acid system to a greater degree. This interaction of the three energy systems is illustrated in figure 3.23. In many sports, all three energy systems are utilized, and it is important that the coach and athlete understand the energy systems used in their specific sport.

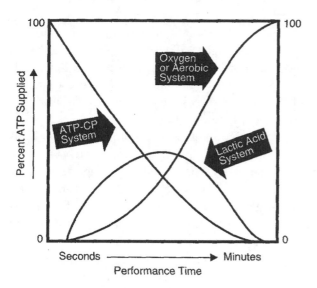

Figure 3.23: The relationship between the percentage of ATP contributed by the three energy systems

Muscle Contraction

The muscular system of the human body consists of about 600 muscles. Muscles are of three types: skeletal, smooth, and cardiac (heart). The skeletal muscles work in pairs to move the body. The muscles are attached to two or more bones by ligaments, and the bones are moved or articulated at the joints. At the end of each muscle is dense connective tissue called "the tendon." The muscles move the body in pairs of one or more muscles called "agonists" that contract and one or more muscles called "antagonists" that stretch or extend at the same time. Other muscles, usually smaller, act to anchor or steady the muscles around a joint in a movement and are called "stabilizers or fixators" and "neutralizers."

Strength development is a combination of contractile force causing movement and the ability to coordinate the agonists, antagonists, neutralizers, and stabilizers (neuromuscular coordination). The mechanized ratios of angle of pull and the length of the resistive arm is also a factor in the application of force.

Structure of the Skeletal Muscle

The three main structures of the muscle are the connective tissue, the myofibril, and the sarcomere.

The entire muscle, as shown in figure 3.24, is surrounded by connective tissue called "epimysium." The

largest subunit of the muscle, the muscle bundle, is also surrounded by connective tissue called the "perimysium." In each muscle bundle is one or more muscle fibers or cells which are also surrounded by connective tissue called "endomysium." The connective tissue provides strength and integrity to the muscles.

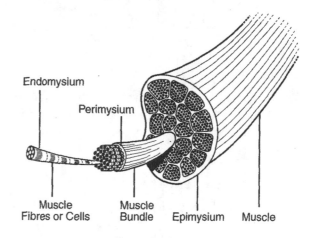

Figure 3.24: Structure of the muscle

The individual muscle fibers or cells range in length from a few centimeters to almost a meter, and extend over the entire length of the muscle. The cell membrane of the muscle fiber is called the "sarcolemma," and inside the fiber are such components as protoplasm (called "sarcoplasm" in muscle cells), nuclei, mitochondria, glycogen, ATP, and CP. The key factor that distinguishes the muscle cells from all other cells is the "myofibril." The myofibril contains two basic protein filaments— thin filaments called "actin" and thicker ones called "myosin." As well as giving skeletal muscle its striated appearance, these myofibrils are the active components in the contractile process. These protein filaments represent the site of energy utilization, where electrostatic bonds are made to facilitate muscular contraction.

The sarcomere is the smallest functional contractional unit of the myofibril and is the distance between two Z lines, as shown in figure 3.25. The alternating light (I bands) and dark (A bands) give the muscle its striated appearance. The I band contains only actin filaments that extend from the Z bands to the center of the sarcomere. The A band consists of both actin and myosin filaments. Tiny projections called "cross bridges" extend from the myosin toward the actin filaments. These cross bridges are instrumental in isotonic muscle contractions, where the muscle shortens. In the center of the A band is an area, consisting of myosin filaments, called the "H zone."

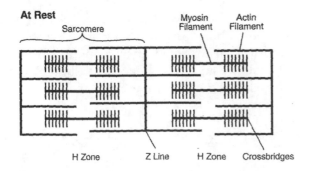

At Rest

Sarcomere · Myosin Filament · Actin Filament

H Zone · Z Line · H Zone · Crossbridges

Figure 3.25: The structure of a myofibril of the muscle with actin and myosin filaments. As the actin and myosin filaments slide over each other, the sarcomere shortens and the muscle contracts.

The Sliding Filament Theory

When a muscle develops tension and shortens, the actin filaments slide over the myosin filaments toward the center of the sarcomere. The coupling process of the actin and myosin is called "actomyosin" and is dependent on the presence of calcium ions (Ca++). When the cross bridges of the actin filaments are pulled over the myosin filaments and toward the center of the sarcomere, tension is developed, and muscle contraction occurs. When the stimulation of the muscle stops, the Ca++ is removed, and the muscle relaxes. During this process, ATP is broken down to ADP and Pi to provide the energy for contraction.

Muscle-Fiber Types

Skeletal muscle is a mixture of several types of muscle fibers. The biochemical and physical characteristics of different muscle fibers has led to the classification of the fibers as fast twitch (white Type II) and slow twitch (red Type I). Fast-twitch fibers are suited for high-intensity, short anaerobic work. These fibers have a high activity of myofibular ATP-ase, the enzyme that breaks down ATP and releases energy to cause the shortening of the muscle fiber. These fibers also have a high level of ATP and CP intramuscular stores. They also have a low aerobic capacity because of their low intramuscular stores of triglyceride, low capillary density, and low aerobic enzyme activity. These characteristics allow these fibers to develop a large amount of force per cross-sectional area in a short period of time (Fleck & Kraemer).

Fast-twitch fibers have been further subdivided into Type IIax fast oxidative glycolytic fibers (FOG), which share some of both the good anaerobic and aerobic characteristics, and Type IIx fast-glycolytic (FG) fibers,

which possess good anaerobic but poor aerobic characteristics (Staron, Hikida, & Hagerman). These subtypes of Type II fibers may be a factor in fiber type transformation due to physical training as aerobic training may cause some Type IIx fibers to transform to Type IIax fibers (Ingjer; Staron, Hikida & Hagerman).

Slow-twitch fibers are suited to endurance aerobic activities and are characterized by high aerobic enzyme activity, capillary density, mitochondrial density, and intramuscular triglyceride stores and have low fatigue levels. Table 3.13 shows the various characteristics of the three fiber types.

Most muscles in humans contain a mixture of both fast- and slow-twitch fibers. Elite athletes have a greater proportion of fiber types suited to their sports, as shown in figure 3.26. Fast-twitch fibers are predominately used in short-burst activities; slow-twitch fibers are prominent in endurance activities. The training implications are obvious. Athletes involved in short-burst activities should concentrate on training fast-twitch fibers, while endurance athletes should train in activities using slow-twitch fibers. Athletic performance in some sports requires training of both fiber types.

Table 3.13: Characteristics of fast- and slow-twitch muscle fiber

Characteristics	Slow Twitch or Slow Oxidative (SO)	Fast Twitch Fast Oxidative Glycolytic (FOG)	Fast Glycolytic (FG)
Average fiber percentage	50%	35%	15%
Speed of contraction	Slow	Fast	Fast
Time to peak tension	0.12 s	0.08 s	0.08 s
Force of contraction	Lower	High	High
Size	Smaller	Medium	Large
Fatigability	Fatigue resistant	Less resistant	Easily fatigued
Aerobic capacity	High	Medium	Low
Capillary density	High	High	Low
Anaerobic capacity	Low	Medium	High

There is no research at this time to show that there is interconversion of fast- and slow-twitch fibers with training in humans. Most evidence points to fiber-type distribution being solely determined by heredity.

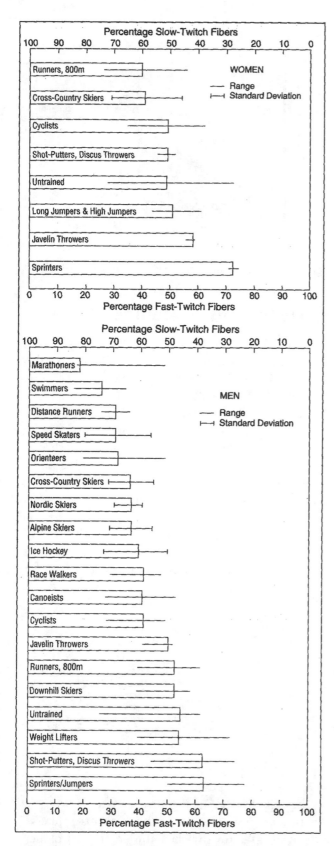

Figure 3.26: Fiber type distribution in male and female athletes. Reprinted by permission from R. Bowers and E. Fox, *Sport Physiology.* (Dubuque, IA: Wm. C. Brown), 128, 129.

Neuromuscular System

To understand how muscles contract and develop strength, it is important to understand the interaction of the muscle and the neuron system.

There are two types of nerves: sensory and motor. The sensory or afferent nerves send information such as heat, light, touch, and smell from the skin and the periphery of the body to the central nervous system or the brain and spinal cord. Motor or efferent nerves, those directly related to muscle contraction, send information from the central nervous system to the muscles.

Motor nerves, as illustrated in figure 3.27, consist of a cell body or soma, several short nerve projections called "dendrites" that carry impulses toward the soma, and long nerve fibers called "axons" which carry impulses away from the cell to the skeletal muscle. Therefore the dendrites transmit nerve impulses toward the cell, while the axons transmit impulses away from the cell body. The terminal ending of a motor neuron's axon in a skeletal muscle is called the "motor end plate" or "neuromuscular junction." Large nerve fibers like those in skeletal muscles are surrounded by a myelin sheath which is composed of lipids and proteins. Fibers with these sheaths are called "medullated fibers." Fibers without this sheath are called "non-medullated fibers." The myelin sheath is not continuous along the whole length of the fiber, but has small spaces between segments called "nodes of Ranvier." One function of the myelin sheath is to insulate the impulse in one axon from the impulse of other axons and dendrites. This prevents impulses from one muscle inadvertently reaching a different muscle.

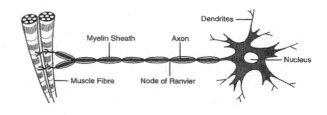

Figure 3.27: A motor neuron and muscle fibers it innervates, which together are called "the motor unit"

A nerve impulse is transmitted to the muscle in the form of electrical energy and is transmitted along the entire length of the axon. The nerve fiber, at rest, has sodium ions (Na+) concentrated heavily on the outside of the nerve cell, causing it to be electrically positive, while the inside of the nerve is negative. This difference in electrical potential is called "the resting membrane potential." With a stimulus the nerve membrane

127

becomes highly permeable to the sodium ions and they move into the nerve. This movement causes the outside of the nerve to become negative and the inside positive, a reversal called "action potential." Also a local flow of current is created at the site where the stimulus is applied and flows to the surrounding area. This current causes a reversal of polarity which, in turn, causes the action potential to be propagated along the whole length of the nerve fiber. In myelinated axons, common in skeletal muscle, the nodes of Ranvier make possible a fast type of impulse conduction called "saltatory conduction" as the action potential jumps from one node to the next. Large medullated fibers have a conduction velocity approximately ten times that of non-medullated fibers of the same size. In general fast-twitch muscle fibers are innervated by larger axons than are slow-twitch fibers.

When the nerve impulse reaches the end of the axon, it causes the release of a chemical transmitter substance called "acetylcholine," which causes an action potential in the muscle, causing the muscle to contract.

The motor unit consists of a motor neuron and all the muscle fibers it innervates. Each muscle fiber has at least one motor neuron, and the larger the number of muscle fibers in a motor unit, the greater amount of force the motor unit will produce when stimulated to contract.

The larger muscles of the leg contain as many as a thousand fibers in a motor unit, whereas the eye may contain only ten fibers per motor unit.

All the muscle fibers in a motor unit contract when stimulated, which is referred to as "the all-or-none law." Whole muscles such as the biceps, however, are made up of many motor units, and a small force generated is caused by only a small number of the motor units firing. Therefore, the more motor units within a muscle that are stimulated to contract, the greater the amount of force generated. Varying the force in a muscle is called "multiple motor-unit summation."

Different gradations of force can also be achieved by controlling the force of one motor unit. A twitch is produced when a motor unit responds to a single impulse conducted by an axon. The twitch produces a brief contraction followed by a relaxation of the motor unit. When a second impulse is received proximate to the first impulse, this causes the muscle fiber to produce more total tension rather than relaxing. A number of successive twitches creates a greater force and is called "wave summation," as illustrated in figure 3.28. The complete summation is called "tetanus" and is the maximal force the motor unit can develop.

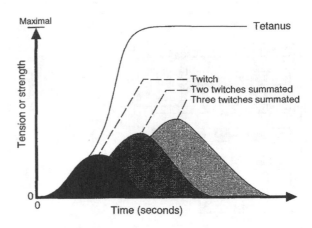

Figure 3.28: Wave summation with gradations of strength

Flexibility and Stretching

Stretching the muscle fibers involves the stretch reflex, the muscle spindles, and the Golgi tendons. Flexibility stretching is usually done slowly while plyometric contractions occur when the muscle is pre-stretched and then contracted quickly, such as in the one- or two-foot hopping or bounding motion. The primary sensor receptor responsible for detecting stretching of the muscle fiber is the muscle spindle. The muscle spindle is capable of detecting both the magnitude and rate of change in the length of the muscle fiber. The Golgi tendon, as shown in figure 3.29, located in the tendon of the muscle, is also important as it responds to excessive tension as the result of powerful contractions and stretching of the muscle. Both of these sensory receptors function at the reflex level.

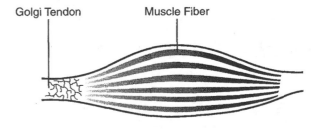

Figure 3.29: Golgi tendon.

The main function of the muscle spindle is to elicit the stretch or myotatic reflex. When the muscle fibers are slowly or rapidly stretched, the lengthening of the fibers is detected by the muscle spindle. A large number of impulses are sent to the spinal column via the afferent neurons. These neurons synapse directly with the motor neurons, which in turn send back impulses to the skeletal muscles and cause them to contract dynamically. In flexibility stretching it is important to stretch the muscle slowly in order not to initiate the myotatic reflex. In plyometrics the stretching is done rapidly to elicit the reflex.

The Golgi tendon is a receptor located in the tendon and is stimulated by tensile forces generated by the contraction of muscle fibers to which it is attached. The Golgi tendon reflex occurs when muscle tension is increased. Signals transmitted to the spinal column cause an inhibitory response to the contracted muscle, thus preventing an inordinate amount of tension from developing in the muscle. The Golgi tendon is thought to be a protective mechanism to prevent tearing of the muscle under extreme tension.

In flexibility movements it is best to stretch the muscle slowly so not to activate the stretch reflex.

Plyometrics

There are two models to explain plyometrics: a mechanical model and neurophysiological model. In the mechanical model, elastic energy is increased with a rapid stretch and then stored. When the movement is immediately followed by a concentric muscle action, the stored energy is released. The neurophysiological model involves the stretch reflex. During plyometric exercises the muscle spindles are stimulated by the rapid stretch causing a reflexive muscle action. This reflexive reaction increases the activity of the agonist muscle and thereby increases the force the muscle produces.

The stretch shortening cycle has three phases:
1. *Eccentric Phase*
   Preloading the agonist muscle where elastic energy is stored and the muscle spindles are stimulated
2. *Amortization Phase*
   Time from the end of the eccentric phase to the initiation of the concentric action
3. *Concentric Phase*
   The energy stored is used to increase the force of the subsequent movement

THE PHYSIOLOGICAL EFFECTS OF TRAINING

What happens to the body when an athlete undergoes a carefully designed training program? For the body to have a positive physiological change, the training pro-

gram must be designed to provide an effective training stimulus to elicit change with the proper adherence to the variables of training such as frequency, intensity, volume, duration, work-to-rest ratios, and recovery.

The physiological effects which occur through a scientifically designed training program can be classified into changes at the cellular level in the muscle; changes in the cardiorespiratory system, including the oxygen transport system; and other changes.

It should also be remembered that the present state of physical conditioning and the genetic endowment of the individual determine, and in some cases limit, the amount of improvement each individual can gain. For example, heredity determines the aerobic capacity (93 percent), lactic-acid system (81 percent), maximum heart rate (81 percent), and the percentage of fast- and slow-twitch fibers.

Training Adaptations in Strength Training

It has been shown that two conditions must exist for gains in strength to occur: the muscle must be overloaded, and this overload must be progressively greater as the training occurs. In other words, a stimulus must be provided to elicit a higher training state, and this stress must be progressive and at regular planned intervals.

There are two main changes that occur in the muscle through training that provide the increase in strength: one is the enlargement of the cross-section of the muscle; the other is the nervous-system adaptation.

1. Increase in Muscle Mass. Systematic strength training using the principles of overload and progressive resistance cause an increase in the cross-sectional area of the muscle as a result of a number of factors. First and foremost, the change in area is caused by an increase in the size and number of the actin and myosin filaments and the addition of sarcomeres in the existing muscle (Gordon; MacDougall, et al.). Conventional strength training in both animals and humans appears to cause a higher degree of selective hypertrophy to the fast-twitch (FT) fibers than the slow twitch (ST) fibers, although it is possible to selectively increase the cross-sectional size of either FT or ST fibers, depending on the training programs (Gonyea & Sale). An increase in the number of capillaries (Tesch, Thorsson, & Kaiser) and an increase in the size and strength of the ligaments and tendons (Fahey, Akka, & Rolph) also are factors in the increase in size of the muscle produced by a strength-training program.

2. Neuromuscular adaptation. Initial gains in strength during the first few weeks of a training program have been observed, where there has been no noticeable increases in the cross-section of the muscle (Moritani & DeVries; Costill, et al.). This increase in strength is attributed to neuromuscular adaptation (Moritani & DeVries) with improvement in synchronization of the firing of the motor units, increased activation of the contractile units, the recruiting of additional motor units, and increased neural drive to the muscle (Sale, et al.). In simpler terms, the muscle becomes more efficient through neuromuscular adaptation.
3. Increase in the capilliarization of the muscle fiber.
4. Increase in the size and strength of the connective tissue, tendons, and ligaments.
5. Increase in the fluid content within the muscle fiber.
6. Increase in the protein content and the amount of actomyosin in the muscle fiber.
7. Decrease in the amount of fat within the muscle.

Biochemical Changes within the Muscle

1. Increased capacity of alactic system (ATP-CP). Increase in the amount of CP and ATP within the muscle fiber. Increase in the enzyme activity of creative kinase, ATP-ase, and myokinase, which are involved in breaking down ATP and CP and the resynthesis of ATP.
2. Increased capacity of the aerobic system. Increase in the amount of myoglobin, which acts as a store for oxygen. Increase in the amount of glycogen stored in the muscle. Increase in the number, size, and membrane surface of the mitochondria. Increase in the level of activity of enzymes involved in the Kreb's cycle and electron-transport system. Increased oxidation of fat, including an increase of intramuscular stores of triglycerides and an increase in the release of free fatty acids from adipose tissue.

Adaption to Training of the Cardiorespiratory System

1. Increased cardiac hypertrophy (heart-muscle size). Increased ventricular cavity (pumping chamber of the heart) in endurance athletes. Increased myocardial thickness (wall of the pumping chamber of the heart).

2. Lower resting heart rate. Six to eight beats/min. to as much as thirty beats/min.
3. Lower maximum heart rate. 185–190 beats/min. for the trained versus 200 beats/min. for untrained. Age is a factor.
4. Increased stroke volume (amount of blood pumped per heart beat)

Untrained, resting	70–90 ml/beat
Untrained, exercise	100–120 ml/beat
Trained, resting	100–120 ml/beat
Trained, exercise	150–170 to 200 ml/beat

5. Increased cardiac output (total amount of blood pumped per minute. Stroke volume × heart rate). At rest, there is little difference between the trained and untrained.

Rest 4.5 liters/min.

Maximum untrained	25 liters/min.
Maximum trained	25–35 liters/min.

6. Higher tolerance of lactic-acid levels

Untrained	80–90 mg/100 ml blood
Trained	200 mg/100 ml blood

7. Blood pressure increase is less with trained versus untrained.
8. Artervenous O_2 difference. The amount of oxygen extracted from the arterial blood is greater with training; thus, the arterial venous difference is greater with the trained versus the untrained.
9. Increased ventilation efficiency. Increased breathing frequency. Increased lung volumes. Increased tidal volume. Increased diffusion of oxygen in the lungs.

Other Adaptations to Training

1. Decreased total body weight and little or no change in lean body weight.
2. Decrease in total body fat.
3. Decreased cholesterol and triglyceride levels.
4. Increased tensile strength of bones, ligaments, and tendons.

Part 4: Psychological Preparation

There are many books devoted solely to psychological preparation that can be used by both athletes and coaches. Some of these books are listed on page 141 and in the bibliography for Part 4. The purpose here is to provide an overview of the basic concepts, but coaches should do further reading in this area.

Psychology is an integral part of coaching in that how a coach schedules and organizes practices, instructs, communicates with athletes, and demonstrates how to behave, etc. are all derived from psychological principles (Vealey).

The mental-training skills discussed here are important for both the athlete and the coach. The mental skills presented include relaxation, positive self-talk, energizing, visualization, focusing (concentration), and the ideal performance state. These skills are used by athletes to develop a pre-competition and a competitive plan for mental preparation. Coaches should not only work with their athletes to develop these skills, but also use these skills themselves to better prepare for the job of coaching, which includes all the aspects of pre-event and event preparation; handling stress and pressure; decision making; relationships with athletes, friends, and loved ones; and developing the proper frame of mind to lead young men and women.

THE MENTAL-TRAINING SKILLS

The basic mental-training skills for athletes (in the order in which they are usually introduced) are relaxation, positive self-talk, energizing, visualization, and concentration. All of these psychological skills are used in developing the ideal performance state. These mental skills alone, however, will not lead to success. It is a combination of extensive physical and mental preparation which distinguishes outstanding athletes from the others.

Relaxation

Relaxation techniques are important for both the athlete and the coach. These techniques can assist in relieving the stress before competition and also allow both athletes and coaches to get a restful sleep before competitions.

The four common methods of relaxation training that are useful for athletes and coaches are:

1. Breath relaxation
2. Progressive muscular relaxation (PMR)
3. Autogenic training
4. Biofeedback
5. Imagery relaxation

Breath Relaxation

Orlick describes a very simple method of relaxation training which is used by many athletes before, during, and after competition. The procedure involves taking a deep breath with a long slow exhalation. At the same time, the athlete thinks about relaxing, and relaxes the muscles. This procedure is repeated several times and can be practiced before any stressful situation in and out of competition. It is the simplest and most often used method of relaxation.

Progressive Muscular Relaxation (PMR)

Progressive Muscular Relaxation (PMR) was developed by Edmund Jacobson in the 1930s. Its basic premise is that it is impossible to be nervous or tense when the muscles are completely relaxed. While this premise is not supported by research, PMR is effective in reducing muscle tension, which is essential for optimal sport performance. Its value, however, is in the recovery from, rather than the preparation for, competition. PMR is based on the principle of neuromuscular relaxation, where athletes are taught to tense the muscles and then relax them. Sixteen muscle groups are used initially, followed by seven, then four, and then the entire body is tensed and then relaxed. PMR is taught by a trained instructor and should be practiced three or four times per week, with effective results taking about six weeks of training. One hour per day is necessary at the beginning, but once the relaxation procedure is well learned, relaxation can be achieved in a few minutes (Nideffer).

Research supports that this method is effective in eliciting relaxation and, when used with other arousal and cognitive methods, can be associated with improved performance (Greenspan & Feltz; Onestak).

The PMR method involves the following steps:

1. Select a quiet environment with no distractions.
2. Make sure the athletes are dressed in warm, dry clothing.
3. The athletes should be well spaced from each other.
4. The athletes lie on their backs on a mat, with their arms at their sides and the palms of their hands facing slightly upwards. The calves of the legs are slightly touching, and the body is straight, with weight equally distributed. The eyes are lightly closed.
5. Muscles are contracted for five seconds and then relaxed.
6. Practice contracting and then relaxing one muscle group. Feel the muscles relax. The muscles may feel warm, tingle, or feel heavy. Concentrate on tensing and relaxing one muscle group only.
7. Practice breathing control. Do not breathe when you contract. Breathe out when you relax the muscle.
8. The exercises begin at the toes and progress to the head.
9. Use the following progression and, with the limbs, start with the left, then the right.
   — Toes curl backward (don't move ankles)
   — Toes curl under
   — Ankle bend—feet back to shins
   — Ankle stretch—point your feet
   — Knees pressed together
   — Thighs
   — Buttocks

Do eight even breaths between each exercise. Check to see if muscles are relaxed. If not, repeat the exercises.

Do twelve easy breaths.
The ankles, legs, and buttocks should be totally relaxed.

   — Stomach
   — Back. Pull shoulder blades together. Press shoulders into mat.
   — Raise your shoulders. Pull shoulders toward the feet; reach fingers as far down the thighs as possible.

Check the body and legs to determine if they are relaxed. Count twelve small, even breaths.

   — Pull the jaw down toward the neck.
   — Press your head into the mat. Do not arch.
   — Jut your jaw forward.
   — Clench your teeth.

Eight even breaths.

   — Spread lips as far apart as possible.
   — Press your tongue against the roof of your mouth. Make your tongue as big as possible.
   — Pull cheeks up and eyebrows down. Compress your eyes to the back of your head.
   — Wrinkle your forehead. Eyes are closed.

Twelve small, even breaths.
Check whole body for heaviness.
Twelve slow breaths.

   — Finish by moving each part of your body, starting from the toes up. Sit, kneel, stretch, and then stand (adapted from Coaching Association of Canada).

Autogenic Training

Autogenic (self-generated) training includes a system of standard exercises designed to return the mind and body to homeostasis. The basis of the exercises is passive concentration or self-hypnosis, and beneficial effects can occur without noticeable physical sensations. Athletes begin with three to five standard exercises repeated for thirty to sixty seconds. The athlete then activates and repeats another set of exercises. After about six months of daily practice, the athlete typically repeats commands for:

1. Heaviness: "My right arm is heavy. . . . My left arm is heavy. . . . Both arms are heavy. . . . My right leg is heavy. . . . My left leg is heavy. . . . Both legs are heavy."

2. Warmth: "My right arm is warm. . . . My left arm is warm. . . . Both arms are warm. . . . My right leg is warm. . . . My left leg is warm. . . . Both legs are warm."
3. Heartbeat: "My heartbeat is calm and regular."
4. Respiration: "My breathing is calm and regular."
5. Solar Plexus: "My solar plexus is warm."
6. Forehead: "My forehead is cool."

The athlete maintains a passive concentration and sees the statement as if it is written, says the command sub-vocal, and feels the area of the body where the statement is directed.

Autogenic training is used primarily in the recovery time between competitions.

Biofeedback

Biofeedback, short for biological feedback, training is the use of instruments to make usually unknown physiological processes, such as muscle tension or blood flow, available to the athlete so they can bring the system under voluntary control. The instruments transform the electrical signals, then amplify them and transmit them to a light or sound display. The goal of biofeedback is to eliminate the use of the equipment once the processes are learned. Commonly used biofeedback modalities include skin temperature, electromyography, heart rate, and electrodermyography (Wilson & Cummings).

Skin temperature is an indirect measure of blood flow. Some athletes express their increased tension by unknowingly vasoconstricting their arterioles, which reduces blood flow to the extremities and can easily be detected in cold hands or feet. Reduced blood flow impedes the transportation of oxygen to working muscles, as well as the removal of waste products.

Electromyography (EMG) measures the number of active muscle action potentials at a specific site. Although athletes are generally aware of major muscle tension, most underestimate or are unable to eliminate the smaller amounts of muscle tension that can interfere with flexibility or small motor skills or cause unnecessary fatigue.

Electrodermyography (EDR) measures the sweat response of the body, which is an indirect measure of emotional involvement. Under stress of any nature, most individuals record an almost instantaneous change in sweat, thus EDR is often used to teach athletes how to cope with thoughts or moods that may affect their performance.

Heart rate can be used to determine the total cardio-vascular response of the athlete. Although the heart rate is most responsive to the physical load, some athletes have significant increases in heart rate merely from thoughts of competition or competitors.

Electroencephlography (EEG) is a measure of the amount of brain activity. Specific seeds and locations of brain waves are associated with specific actions of the brain. For example, fast brain waves, beta waves, usually indicate a very busy brain, while alpha waves are a more relaxed attention. Depression is associated with waves in one area of the brain, while happiness produces a different pattern in another area of the brain. Although EEG can be used with athletes, it takes considerable training and sophisticated equipment to obtain meaningful data, thus its use is currently limited in sport.

With some training, coaches and athletes can use biofeedback to learn to fine tune performance or decrease the amount of time necessary to learn relaxation or energizing skills.

Visualization/Imagery Relaxation

Imagery relaxation involves the athlete visualizing an environment or setting which is very pleasing and relaxing, such as waves on a beach or a picturesque mountain. The place must conjure up a good, relaxing feeling. The image must be vivid, and usually in color. The athletes must practice this visualization in a quiet place, and not only see the scene, but hear the sounds (e.g., waves lapping) and smell the air, for the image to be successful for relaxation. More information in visualization techniques is provided on pages 135–136.

Other methods for relaxation training include meditation, yoga, hypnosis, and physical means such as hot tubs, saunas, showers, and massage.

Positive Self-Talk

Talking to oneself in a positive manner is a confidence booster for athletes, and there is some evidence of its effectiveness. Rushall and colleagues did a study with elite cross-country skiers, using three types of self-talk. One method included task-like terms such as "uphill," "quick," and "grip"; another method included positive, self-assertive statements such as "feel strong" and "feel great"; and a third method included emotional mood words such as "drive" and "blast." All three methods used showed a 3 percent increase in performance, as opposed to a control group who used no self-talk and showed no increase in performance times.

Positive self-talk is an important way for the athletes to gain assurance that they can accomplish what they want to do. Athletes should be reminded of their strengths and their past successes.

As important as positive self-talk is, the opposite, that is, negative self-talk, can be very destructive to an athlete before and during competition. When athletes are stressed, they are more likely to engage in negative self-talk. Some types of negative thoughts for athletes include worrying about performance, self-criticism, self-blame, losing, being preoccupied with physical stress, dislike of teammates, and dislike of the coach.

The athlete must first recognize that he or she has negative thoughts that can affect performance. Martens describes some steps the athlete can use to try to eliminate negative thoughts.

1. Discuss with the athlete whether the negative thoughts are disruptive for performance.
2. Try to identify the causes of negative thoughts.
3. Be able to stop or park the negative thoughts immediately.
4. Develop positive-self-talk thoughts to replace the negative ones.
5. Practice these self-talk skills in training, and then in competition.

Ellis and Grieger described irrational beliefs that many athletes have, and suggested ways of counteracting these beliefs.

The old adage of controlling what you can control and not worrying about what you can't control defi-

Belief	Counteraction
1. I must not make errors or do poorly.	1. Doing things well is satisfying, but I am going to make some errors.
2. You should blame people who act unfairly or are not kind to you.	2. Even though I feel I have been treated unfairly, I should not blame others for my performance.
3. A bad experience in my past has to keep determining my behavior and feelings today.	3. A bad experience in my past should not affect my behavior today. I can change things by working hard.
4. People and events should be the way I want them.	4. People are going to act the way they want, not the way I want.
5. I must be loved and approved by every important person in my life.	5. It is nice to have the approval of everyone, but I can still work and enjoy myself without it.

nitely applies to self-talk. Self-talk should be confined to the positive and to the task. Athletes and coaches should identify both the positive and the negative self-talk they use, and work to eliminate the negative.

Energizing (Arousal)

"Energizing" (frequently called arousal) refers to the psychological feeling that an athlete has reserve energy to call upon. It is a positive feeling that leads to confidence and an ability to cope with and control the situation. Energizing is affected by things we do and things we think as the athlete prepares for competition.

Botterill lists a number of ways to energize:

1. *Energize by doing exercise.* A good-warm up or physical exercise on a game day can be energizing as long as it is not so demanding on the energy systems as to create fatigue. A short exercise session of about fifteen to twenty minutes gets the body and the circulation moving and creates a positive feeling in the body.
2. *Stretching.* A good scientific stretching program stretching the major muscle groups, and holding the stretch for fifteen to twenty seconds not only energizes the body, but also reduces tension.
3. *Read and react drills.* By working the skills of the game using simple read-and-react drills with hand–eye and foot–eye coordination, drills can energize the athlete.
4. *Tense and relax muscles.* Alternate tensing and relaxing different muscle groups.
5. *Showers and massage.* Temperature contrasts and physical massage can both energize and relax the athlete.
6. *Music.* Music can be relaxing or energizing. Energizing music is usually upbeat, rock-type music, but different types of music affect people differently. Some teams have a team theme song which has an energizing effect on the athletes.
7. *Videotapes.* Videotapes of positive highlights of team success accompanied by upbeat music can have an energizing effect on athletes. The videos should not be longer than ten minutes to keep the athletes' attention.
8. *Pep talks.* The coach or a respected member of a team can give an inspirational talk to the athletes to energize them. The pep talk should be used selectively, in situations when it appears the athletes are not energized. This can be when the opponent is taken lightly or the athletes appear fatigued. The pep

talk should be short and delivered with enthusiasm and meaning.

9. *Verbal interaction with the athletes and coaches.* Positive statements among athletes and coaches, such as "Here we go," "Let's get it done," "Show time," and "Let's do it," are examples of good interaction that helps athletes energize.

10. *Energize by thinking*
    — Visualizing and imagining. Develop a positive image in your mind about performing successfully and overcoming all obstacles.
    — Focus on positive cues and activities or rituals. Focus on cue words and phrases such as "Blast off," "Intensity," "Power to spare." Use positive mental rehearsal of the skills.
    — Park negative thoughts and concentrate on positive thoughts.

11. *Take energy from your environment.* Focus on energy from spectators, teammates, the sun and wind, and so on.

12. *Energy from faith.* Some athletes energize from their faith and beliefs in religion or related ways of life. Lectures in the areas of positive thinking and motivation have been known to energize athletes.

13. *Goal setting.* Positive goal setting by athletes and teams are methods of energizing if the goals are attainable and both short- and long-term.

Inverted U

The "inverted **U**" refers to the point where being over-energized can be detrimental to performance. Athletes must be energized to perform well, and this level must be reached by the athlete. Being overenergized can result in the athlete being psyched-out instead of psyched-up. The inverted **U**, as illustrated in figure 4.1, is familiar to most coaches, but what is important to note is that the arousal level varies with the type of task being performed. Also, each athlete has a different arousal or energizing level. Martens notes that most athletes reach their peak performance when their psychic energy is high but their stress level is low. Therefore, coaches must try to teach athletes that psychic energy is important, but that the athletes must also keep their stress levels low by using various means of relaxation and focusing skills.

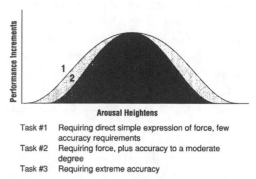

Task #1 Requiring direct simple expression of force, few accuracy requirements
Task #2 Requiring force, plus accuracy to a moderate degree
Task #3 Requiring extreme accuracy

Figure 4.1: The inverted-U principle of arousal with various types of tasks.

Figure 4.1: The inverted-U principle of arousal with various types of tasks.

It should be mentioned here that some experts have been critical of the inverted U theory, as they feel it is far too simplistic to account for the complex relationship between arousal and performance (Raglin; Weinberg).

Energizing is a skill that must be practiced regularly to be effective. The athletes should learn to be self-energized, and psychologists and coaches can assist with this process.

Visualization/Imagery

A number of terms have been used to describe the process of visualizing a performance, including "imagery," "mental rehearsal," "visual motor behavior rehearsal (VMBR)," "cognitive behavior modification," and "success visualization."

"Visualization" refers to a process where an athlete sees himself or herself experiencing a movement or skill. This visualization can also involve any or all senses, including the kinesthetic sense of body position.

In a survey done with top athletes, 98 percent of them reported doing some type of visualization practice before competing (Nideffer). Visualization is used to help athletes learn motor skills, rehearse strategies and reactions in competition, see success (visualize best performance), familiarize with the competition site and possible distractions, and generally mentally prepare for competition.

Sport psychologists have identified two types of visualization: internal and external. "Internal visualization" refers to seeing the movement or skill performed through your own eyes. "External visualization" refers to seeing documentation of your performance done with a camera or video machine. The research done in this area has shown the internal method to be superior to the external, but both methods can and should be used.

Does visualization practice work in perfecting skills and planning strategy moves in a sport? A number of research studies support the premise that it does. Associated with these studies is the concept that visualization, coupled with relaxation training, is even more effective (Suedfeld & Bruno).

Kolonay and Lane studied the effectiveness of basketball free-throw success with visualization, relaxation, and a combination of visualization and relaxation. The combination method was the most successful. Davis noted that there was a significant relationship between performance in professional hockey and visualization.

Reviews of the literature by Richardson, Corbin, Martens, and Williams, Rippon, Stone, & Annett support the position that visualization in a sport setting is effective.

It is important for both coaches and athletes to realize that visualization is a learned skill and must be practiced, as are physical skills, to get improvement. Cox suggests some steps to develop general visualization skills:

1. Find a quiet place where you will not be disturbed, assume a comfortable position, and relax completely.
2. Practice imagery by visualizing a circle that fills the visual field. Make the circle turn a deep blue. Repeat the process several times, imagining a different color each time. Allow the images to disappear. Relax and observe the spontaneous imagery that arises.
3. Create the image of simple three-dimensional glass. Fill it with a colorful liquid, add ice cubes and a straw. Write a descriptive caption underneath.
4. Select a variety of scenes and develop them with rich detail. Include sport-related images such as a swimming pool, tennis courts, and a beautiful golf course. Practice visualizing people, including strangers, in each of these scenes.
5. Imagine yourself in a sport setting of keen interest to you. Visualize and feel yourself successfully participating in the scene. Relax and enjoy your success.
6. End the session by breathing deeply, opening your eyes, and adjusting to the external environment.

Martens uses three main steps in developing visualization skills specifically for sport:

1. Sensory Awareness
2. Vividness
3. Control Ability

"Sensory awareness" refers to the athlete becoming more aware of what he or she feels, sees, and hears when performing a sport skill alone or in a team situation.

This past experience in being more aware of body position, timing, movement patterns, and so on in these situations helps the athlete to better visualize these movements in the future.

"Vividness" allows the athlete to develop distinct images, feeling all the senses, sound, smell, touch, as well as the visual. The vividness exercise allows the athlete to imagine the images more exactly in a setting mimicking the actual sport situation.

"Control ability" refers to the manipulation of the images to produce a successful sport movement or strategy. The athlete visualizes the movement done correctly with a successful outcome.

To practice visualization away from the sport setting, the athlete should be in a relaxed state in a pleasant environment. It is important that the athlete have a set routine for practicing the visualization skills and be motivated to train. Visualization can also be used when the athlete is injured or unable to practice because of weather, facility problems, and so on.

Visualization can be used to evoke concentration and, more commonly, to rehearse sport-specific situations such as a one-on-one in ice hockey, a penalty shot in soccer, or a pass-coverage situation in football. It also can be used to overcome anxiety related to a certain facility or venue.

When mentally rehearsing for the development of a skill, athletes can use visualization in three ways:

1. To practice the performance
2. To preplay the performance
3. To replay the performance

In practicing the performance, the athletes mentally practice the skill they have performed in the past. Preplay visualization occurs immediately before the skill is performed, as a diver would do immediately before the dive. Replay visualization is done immediately following a skill, when an athlete reviews mentally the motions performed. Golfers tend to mentally review the swing after the ball has been hit.

It is important for the coach to sell the idea of visualization training to the athlete. As mentioned earlier, most high-level athletes engage in some form of visualization training. Very few athletes, however, practice visualization skills in a systematic way throughout their training. In the discussion of periodization of the mental-training program that follows, a systematic program is suggested.

Coaches can use visualization as well as the athletes. Visualizing reactions to certain situations which occur in an athletic contest are commonly used by coaches. Visualization, coupled with relaxation, can also help the coach to alleviate stress during the competitive season.

Concentration (Focusing)

The ability to focus or concentrate during a competition with pressure and distractions often separates the top athletes from those with a similar level of physical skill. Certain cues become important, and the athlete must be able to discriminate between the relevant and the irrelevant ones.

"Centering" refers to focusing on one point or directing your thoughts internally for a moment to mentally check and to adjust your breathing and level of muscle tension. The concept comes from the martial arts and refers to a feeling of being calm, relaxed, receptive, and clear (Nideffer). The point that is consciously attended to is the center of gravity, which is located just below and behind the navel.

To be centered is to have the knees slightly bent, muscles loose, and breathing slower and slightly deeper than normal. The feet are apart, one slightly ahead of the other. The body is in a balanced position and able to move in any direction. Athletes and coaches are familiar with centering that involves lowering the center of gravity, frequently called "the ready position."

Centering is a combination of a physical positioning and a psychological feeling. Nideffer lists some cue words associated with centering, as illustrated in table 4.1. These cue words relate to both the positive and the negative physiological feelings that can affect the ability of the athlete to be centered.

Physical Feelings		Psychological Feelings	
Positive	Negative	Positive	Negative
Loose	Tight	Controlled	Beaten
Relaxed	Tense	Confident	Scared
Solid	Shaky	Powerful	Weak
Balanced	Unsteady	Commanding	Dominated
Strong	Weak	Calm	Upset
Light	Heavy	Tranquil	Panicked
Energetic	Tired	Peaceful	Worried
Effortless	Hard	Easy	Rushed
Fluid	Choppy	Clear	Confused
Smooth	Awkward	Focused	Overloaded

Table 4.1: Positive and negative physical and psychological feelings associated with centering

When an athlete is centered, he or she is ideally physically positioned for the particular performance setting. Becoming physically centered requires attention to breathing and refocusing. The athlete should feel confident and in control when in the centered position.

Dimensions of Attention

Nideffer described two types of attention to be applied to a sport situation, as shown in figure 4.2. The "width of attention" refers to whether we have a narrow focus or a broad focus of attention in a sport. A quarterback in football must have a broad focus of attention to spot the various pass receivers, whereas a baseball player must have a narrow focus when concentrating on hitting the ball.

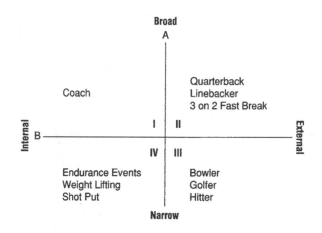

Figure 4.2: Two-dimensional model for attention in sport

The "direction of attention" refers to whether the focus is directed toward the external environment and things going on around us, or internally toward the thoughts and feelings.

In most sports, there is a time for both broad or narrow and internal or external focus. Martens expands on Nideffer's model, as shown in figure 4.3, to illustrate that the athletes must be capable of all the dimensions of focusing.

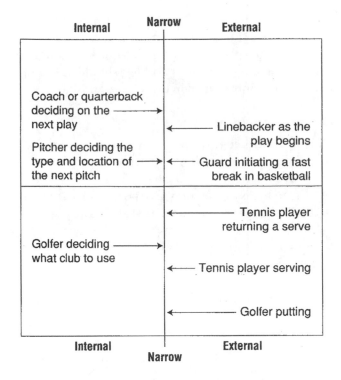

Figure 4.3: Internal and external attention focuses shown as dichotomous rather than continuous. Reprinted by permission from R. Martens, *The Coaches Guide to Sport Psychology*. (Champaign, IL: Human Kinetic Publishers), 141.

The coach and athlete should analyze the attentional demands of the sport and determine the cues and their order. Keep the number of cues to a minimum.

Martens outlines some guidelines for improving concentration skills:

1. The sport should be analyzed to determine whether the attention should be broad or narrow and internal or external.
2. External attention should focus on a few discernible cues that an athlete can learn to respond to.
3. Internal attention should concentrate on positive and constructive thoughts.
4. Concentrate on the forms and execution of the skill, not the outcome.
5. Minimize distractions early when learning skills, but later add competition-like distractions.

Refocusing

Athletes should develop a plan to refocus when events do not go as planned and unexpected distractions occur. Develop a "what if" list so every type of distraction, and an appropriate response, is thought of beforehand. If a distraction occurs before the execution of a skill, shift focus, relax, then refocus. The athlete should always concentrate on only what can be controlled, and events that are out of the athlete's control, such as facility problems and late starts to events, should not be focused on. The athlete should be able to "park" any negative distraction and refocus.

THE IDEAL PERFORMANCE STATE

The psychological study of how athletes feel when they give their best performances has received attention from Maslow, Ravizza, Csikszentmihalyi, Loehr, and Willams and Krane.

Loehr asked athletes to describe their internal feelings and experiences when they performed well and when they performed poorly. Athletes described their psychological feelings when they had high energy and positive feelings as alert, lively, energetic, stimulated, vigorous, enthused, and high in team spirit. When their high energy was accompanied by negative feelings, they described themselves as fearful, nervous, anxious, angry, frustrated, upset, and vengeful. Low energy accompanied by pleasant feelings was described as tired, weary, exhausted, and low in desire. Low energy accompanied by negative thoughts produced feelings such as bored, disinterested, annoyed, irritated, and lacking motivation. Obviously the athlete wishes to have high energy and positive thoughts, and these characteristics are prevalent when athletes perform their best.

Loehr draws the following conclusions from his research:

1. An ideal performance exists for every athlete.
2. An athlete's performance is directly related to how he or she feels inside. When an athlete feels right he or she can perform right.
3. The components of the Ideal Performance State are the same for all athletes in all sports.

Loehr concludes from an analysis of hundreds of reports of top athletes that the following distinct feelings are present when an athlete performs optimally:

- Physically relaxed
  — looseness of muscles
- Mentally calm
  — feeling of inner calmness
- Low anxiety
  — feeling of lack of pressure
- Optimistic
  — feeling positive with no negative thoughts

- Effortless
  - mind and body working in harmony
- Automatic
  - performed without thought, played by instinct
- Focused
  - attending to the relevant aspects of play and blocking out the irrelevant
- Self-confident
  - calm, poised, inner belief in oneself
- In control
  - in total control of the situation
- Alert
  - heightened awareness, ability to read the situation
- Energized
  - most important: feelings of joy, challenge, determination, power, and intensity

THE PERIODIZATION OF MENTAL TRAINING

The integration of mental training with components of the physical, technical, and tactical training in the annual plan is not done well by most coaches. Mental skills, like physical skills, and must be practiced for improvement and should be integrated into the various phases of the annual plan. Mental preparation is improved by using the five basic mental skills of relaxation, positive self-talk, energization, visualization, and concentration, as illustrated in figure 4.4 (Bacon).

Not all athletes respond in the same manner to mental training and, according to a study by Seabourne, Weinberg, Jackson, and Swimm, subjects who were able to choose the mental skills that they felt comfortable with improved as much as those who had programs designed for them.

The need for coaches to establish periodization for mental training is essential, as many of the books on psychological preparation do not relate the material to the training schedule or training phases (Bacon).

The psychological preparation can be divided into: basic mental skills, sport-specific mental skills, and individual competition strategies. As was pointed out in the discussion on periodization in Part 2, the annual plan is divided into pre-competition (general and specific), competition, and transitional phases.

Relaxation

The ability to relax the body and/or mind to an appropriate level.

- centering
- progressive relaxation training (PRT)
- autogenic training
- meditation
- breath control
- biofeedback
- stress management

Positive Self-Talk

The ability to stay positive and eliminate inappropriate negative thoughts or feelings.

- positive thinking
- positive affirmations
- thought stopping
- positive thought control
- rational emotive therapy
- stress inoculation training (SIT) (relaxation + positive self-talk)
- cue words

Energization

The ability to raise physical and/or mental activation to an appropriate level

- music
- psychic energy management
- self-regulation
- energy control
- energizing cue words
- rapid tensing and relaxing of muscles
- physical exertion
- quick deep breaths
- visualize energizing scenes

Visualization

The ability to imagine (sight, feel, etc.) scenes to enhance effectiveness.

- imagery
- mental rehearsal
- mental practice
- visuo-motor behavior rehearsal (VMBR)
- self-hypnosis (relaxation + visualization + positive suggestions)

Concentration

The ability to focus on the appropriate thing, while blocking out irrelevant distractions.

- centering
- meditation
- focusing
- attention control training (ACT)

Figure 4.4: The five basic mental skills and their related techniques

General Preparation

In the general preparation phase, after an initial measuring of mental skills using assessment tools such as the TAIS (Nideffer), Competitive Reflections Form (Orlick), or the Self Assessment Questionnaires (Suinn), the acquisition of various mental skills can take six to eight weeks of practicing three to five times per week for fifteen to thirty minutes a day. Williams suggests relaxation skills should be taught first, followed by positive self-talk, energizing, visualization, and concentration.

Specific Preparation

In the specific-preparation phase, the emphasis shifts to applying the mental skills to specific requirements of the sport in simulations during practice. In the pre-competitive phases, the athlete applies these learned skills to the actual competition, both in the preparation and in actual performance in the exhibition or non-league competitions.

Pre-Competitive

In the pre-competitive phase, the athlete should work on both psychological and physical preparation. Psychological preparation should be concerned with pre-event routines, including concentration, relaxation, energizing, and visualization skills in progressively more challenging situations in exhibition or non-league play. The preparation also should include the physical logistics of pre-competition meals, stretching and warm-up, getting equipment ready, getting to the competition site, talking with the coaches, and so on.

Competitive

During the competitive phases, the athlete refines the various mental skills in competitions, preparing for peaking in the final competition or, in team sports, the playoffs. Visualization to prepare for opponents, and relaxation and positive self-talk to manage stress, along with concentration skills during the competitions, are developed during this competition period.

After a competition is over, there should be some type of analysis of the performance of the team and the athletes. It is always a question whether coaches should talk about the performance immediately after the contest or wait until the next training session. Most coaches have a few words after a competition and reserve the more detailed analysis for the next training session. Some coaches prefer to wait until the next day for comments, when they have had time to analyze the performance, usually with the aid of video. Comments on

work effort usually can be made immediately following the competition.

Post-competition analysis usually falls into four categories, especially in team sports: played well and won, played poorly and won, played well and lost, and played poorly and lost.

Taper

In the tapering (unloading) phase, before the final competition, mental skills can play a role in lowering stress, enhancing confidence, and focusing on the task at hand (Bacon).

A well-thought-out mental training plan developed in conjunction with the various phases of the annual physical training schedule can greatly assist the athlete to perform at his or her maximum potential. The mental-training objectives are summarized in table 4.2.

Table 4.2: Summary of objectives for mental preparation in the annual plan (Coaching Association of Canada)

Phase	Mental-Training Objectives
General	1. Evaluation of mental skills
	2. Learn basic mental skills in a quiet setting
Specific Preparatory	1. Adapt and practice mental skills in sport-specific situations
	2. Use mental skills to help attain training objectives
	3. Maintain basic mental skills
Pre-competitive	1. Develop and practice focus plan
	2. Use focus plan in simulations
	3. Maintain basic mental skills
Competitive	1. Evaluate and refine focus plan
	2. Use mental skills to prepare for specific opponents and competitions
	3. Use mental skills for stress management
Unloading	1. Use mental skills to aid regeneration and lower stress
Transition	1. Recreational activities to maintain fitness and prevent staleness

Sport psychologist T. Orlick suggests that the coaches meet with the athletes early in the training to begin to develop mental-training preparation plans and to begin to practice the various mental-training skills. He suggests three early mental-preparation meetings, with the first meeting coming early in training, the next three days later, and the third two weeks later. The goals of the three meetings should be:

1. To develop a pre-competition plan
2. To develop a competition focus plan
3. To develop a refocus plan to deal with distractions and keep focused
4. To develop a communication plan to facilitate team harmony and open discussion of problems

The first meeting might include a discussion of the importance of mental preparation and training for it; setting goals; and reflecting on previous competition, that is, the mental state for best performance and worst performance, and so on. The second meeting would develop the pre-competition, competition, and refocusing mental-preparation plans, as well as a discussion of team harmony. The third meeting would set out the plans for practicing the mental-preparation skills and incorporating them into the yearly, monthly, and weekly plans (discussed below). Like physical skills, the mental-preparation skills must be practiced, and focusing, imagery, and relaxation should be used in training as well as competition.

For further information on psychological preparation, coaches and athletes can consult the following:

M. Anshel. *Sport Psychology: From theory into practice.*
R.H. Cox. *Sports Psychology: Concepts and Applications.*
D. Kraus. *Mastering your inner game.*
L. Leith. *The Psychology of Coaching Team Sports.*
R. Martens. *Coaches' guide to sport psychology.*
S. Miller. *Hockey Tough.*
A. Moran. *The psychology of concentration in sport performers.*
S. Murphy. *The sport psych handbook.*
R. Nideffer. *Psyched to win.*
Athletes' guide to mental training.
T. Orlick. *In pursuit of excellence.*
Psyching for sport: Mental training for athletes.
Psyching for sport: Mental training for coaches.
R. Singer. *Handbook of sport psychology.*
R. Vernacchia, R. McGuire, & D. Cook. *Coaching mental excellence.*
J. Williams & V. Krane. *Psychological characteristics of peak performance.*

THE PERIODIZATION OF STRESS

Intensity of training and competitions are the major causes of stress for an athlete. Other factors such as crowd, peers, family, and pressure from the coach also must be considered. The amount of stress varies throughout the training year, as shown in figure 4.5. Stress is the lowest in the preparation period, although testing and the selection period can raise stress levels. The stress levels undulate in the competitive period, with alternate competition and development microcycles. Regeneration from highly stressful competitions and the unloading prior to competitions are both important factors in the planning process relative to stress levels (Bompa).

MOTIVATION

Motivation can be defined as the psychological force that drives a person to perform. It also has been described as a direction and intensity of purpose involved in a task or a way of life. To understand an athlete, the coach must understand both his or her needs and motivation. Maslow's hierarchy of needs is one of the better-known theories of what motivates people. This theory states that people are motivated and satisfy their needs according to a system of priorities. The priorities are divided into two general categories: deficiency needs, such as thirst, hunger, sex, security, and safety, which are the first priority, and growth needs, such as belongingness, love, self-respect, ego, and self-actualization, which are the second priority. The theory postulates that, once one need is satisfied, the person moves up the hierarchy to the next-highest need.

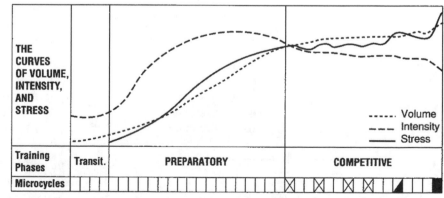

Figure 4.5: Stress curve during the monocycle. Reprinted by permission from T. Bompa, *Theory and Methodology of Training*. (Dubuque, IA: Kendall/Hunt), 176.

Most athletes have their deficiency needs satisfied, and their reason for competing is usually concentrated on the growth needs. Athletes have many reasons for competing, among them satisfaction of accomplishment, pleasure in participating, admiration earned, and a feeling of being part of a group and belonging (Vernacchia, McGuire, & Cook). Many athletes are motivated by success, or sometimes by a fear of failure. Cratty applied psychologist Murray's needs to the athletic situation, as shown in table 4.3.

Table 4.3: Application of Murray's list of needs to the sport situation

MURRAY'S LIST OF NEEDS	BEHAVIOR IN ATHLETIC SITUATION
1. Need for prestige, enhancement of the self, achievement.	1. The athletic contest usually provides this for the athlete.
2. Need to defend status, avoid humiliation, and overcome defeat.	2. Coaches appeal to this need prior to important contests when facing opponents who have defeated and/or humiliated them.
3. Need to affiliate, form affectionate relationships with others, be friendly and cooperative.	3. Many athletes join teams to satisfy this motive. Coaches use this with phrases such as "For the good of the team."
4. Need to acquire inanimate objects, arrange things, keep things tidy.	4. The concern for both athletes and coaches with rules, organization, collection of trophies.
5. Need to explore, ask questions, satisfy curiosity.	5. Athletes depending on coach's rationale for training programs, tactics, etc.
6. Need to exercise power over others, dominate or be submissive to others.	6. Many sports by their very nature demonstrate this motive. Football linemen fighting for territory, wrestlers, boxers, tennis, and any one-on-one matches illustrate this motive.

An often-asked question is "What, if any, is the coach's role in motivating the athlete?" There are two extreme answers to this question. One is that the athlete has total responsibility for motivation; the other is that the coach has the full responsibility for motivation. In reality, the coach's role is usually somewhere in between these extremes, as the athlete should be self-motivated, even though the coach plays an important role in the motivation process.

The coach can play an important role in motivation in the following ways:

1. *Selection.* Selecting athletes who are highly self-motivated and enjoy participating in the sport is one of the most important means to ensure group motivation. The athlete should also care about the program and his or her teammates. This selection process is important for both the coach and the athlete in terms of both individual and team motivation. Highly motivated athletes can make the coach's role in motivation less important, as well as making the job of the coach much easier and definitely more enjoyable.

2. *Efficient, well-run training sessions.* Well-thought-out and organized practices are a motivating factor for athletes. Workout programs in which athletes are scientifically trained and which they enjoy motivates them. In contrast, poorly run practices lead to boredom and lack of motivation on the part of the athlete (see "Planning the Practice," in Part 2).

3. *Good teaching and reinforcement.* When athletes are learning and are reinforced and given feedback on how they are doing, their motivation level tends to rise. Good coaches are good teachers, and athletes usually respond well and are motivated by them.

4. *Communication.* The coach should continually communicate with his or her athletes to understand what they are thinking and to understand what motivates each of them. Regular meetings, formal or informal, should be held with the athletes frequently to discuss any problems that may affect his or her motivation. Alternatively, a coach should make sure to speak to each athlete at every training session, whether it is just a greeting or a short conversation. Specific problems should be dealt with immediately, and the athlete should feel the coach is approachable.

5. *Fun and variety.* Include fun drills in each practice, and arrange for other enjoyable activities during the year. Vary your training programs and include other

activities. If the athletes are not enjoying what they are doing, their motivation level is usually affected.

6. *Pep talks.* Pep talks have their place and, in some situations, can be effective. Pep talks should be used when the coach feels the athletes' motivation is low, such as when they are competing against an inferior opponent or are physically fatigued. Pep talks should be short and to the point. Regular talks using the same theme are not usually effective.

7. *Punishment/Fear.* Regularly resorting to the use of fear and punishment as motivators is not recommended. There are times, however, when fear of what punishment a coach can deliver has been known to motivate athletes. Usually punishment is employed as a tactic when athletes are not putting forth enough effort, and it can be in the form of verbal berating or a tough physical workout. Not all athletes respond well to this type of motivational tactic, and coaches should be very selective about using this method.

8. *Short- and long-term goals.* Both short-term and long-term goal setting is a motivator for the athlete. The goals should be attainable, and the athlete should be given feedback about his or her progress toward meeting these goals.

9. *Extrinsic rewards.* Medals, trophies, stars on football helmets, money, points for performance, and so on are all motivating factors. Behavior modification developed by the psychologist B.F. Skinner uses external reinforcement to change behavior using extrinsic rewards. Extrinsic rewards tend to lose some of their value once a need is satisfied or if they are used excessively, and coaches must make sure that these rewards are meaningful to the athletes.

10. *Intrinsic rewards.* Athletes must develop their own intrinsic rewards, such as self-satisfaction, accomplishment, work ethic, doing your best, and enjoyment of the sport. Few highly paid professional athletes play only for the money. The feeling of accomplishment and being the best one can be has a greater value than the extrinsic reward of money.

11. *Responsibility, control, and discipline.* The coach should try to assist the athletes in developing their own feeling of responsibility and control of their lives, as related not only to their athletic training and competition but also to their life in general. Helping an athlete to control his or her life in a disciplined manner leads to self-motivation, which is what every coach should strive for. Curfews and penalties for being late are not necessary if this self-motivation is present.

The reasons for participating in sport, and the particular motivation for competing, vary from athlete to athlete. The self-motivated athlete is the ideal person to coach. However, not all athletes have the same level of self-motivation, and it is important that the coach assist athletes to become self-motivated, which is one of the most important roles the coach can play.

GOAL SETTING

Goal setting is important for athletes, coaches, and teams. Guidelines for goal setting were presented in Part 1 (pages 14–15) relating to the coach/athlete relationship. Athletes should have both short- and long-term goals depending on the sport they are participating in. Short-term goals can be week to week and long-term goals can be yearly or even longer. Goal setting can be divided into outcome goals and process goals. Outcome goals are achieved through competition results which are measurable, and self-improvement goals which may or may not be measurable depending on the sport. Process goals are the means about which the athlete is going to achieve the set goals such as number of training days, skill and fitness improvement, attitude, motivation, and working well with teammates and coaches. Outcome goals and process goals are both important and process goals are very important in the day-to-day development of the athlete.

Athletes who use goal setting effectively tend to:
- be more committed and motivated day to day
- concentrate better on the task
- definition of success is clearer
- coping mechanisms are better because process is as important as winning and losing
- have achievable, challenging targets as individuals and as a group
- show higher levels of self-confidence
- show appreciation for group as well as individual goals
- emphasize on the "Be the best you can be" goal motto every training or competition day

Part 5:Motivational Slogans and Sport Quotations

Author's note: These slogans have been collected over many years, and many of the sources unfortunately have not been identified.

Success

Nine Principles of Success

1. Have a Dream
   — create a vision for the future
2. Develop a Plan
   — organize your thinking
3. Control Your Focus
   — don't do too many things at once
4. Take Personal Initiative
   — act as if it all depends on you
5. Practice Self-Discipline
   — don't be distracted, stay on target
6. Learn to Budget
   — put your time, energy, and money behind your plan
7. Show Enthusiasm
   — it's contagious
8. Enjoy Yourself
   — laughter is healing
9. Go for It!
   — keep the faith, no matter what.

The Way to Success: Pay the Price

Preparation	Each day, each practice, each game.
Attitude	Always positive: "I will be a success"
You	Nobody else but you can do it for you as an athlete and a student.
Team	Put the team goals ahead of personal goals.
Help	Others to be successful, care about others.
Effort	Success only comes to those who put in the effort both in sport and school.
Pressure	Believe you can handle any pressure placed upon you.
Responsible	Be responsible and accountable for all that you do.
Intensity	Be totally focused in on what you are trying to accomplish.
Commitment	Be committed to being a success.
Execute	Be disciplined in what you do— execute the offense, the defense, the game plan.

—*Ian Percy*

Winner vs Loser

1. When a *winner* makes a mistake, he says, "I was wrong"; when a *loser* makes a mistake, he says, "It wasn't my fault."
2. A *winner* credits good luck for winning, even though it isn't good luck. A *loser* blames bad luck for losing even though it isn't bad luck.
3. A *winner* works harder than a loser and has more time; a *loser* is always too busy to do what is necessary.
4. A *winner* goes through a problem; a *loser* goes around it and never past it.
5. A *winner* shows he's sorry by making up for it; a *loser* says, "I'm sorry," but does the same thing the next time.
6. A *winner* knows what to fight for, and what to compromise on; a *loser* compromises on what he shouldn't and fights for what isn't worthwhile fighting about.

7. A *winner* says, "I'm good, but not as good as I ought to be"; a *loser* says, "I'm not as bad as a lot of other people."
8. A *winner* would rather be admired than liked, although he would prefer both; a *loser* would rather be liked than admired, and is even willing to pay the price of mild contempt for it.
9. A *winner* respects those who are superior to him, and tries to learn something from them; a *loser* resents those who are superior to him, and tries to find chinks in their armor.
10. A *winner* feels responsible for more than his job; a *loser* says, "I only work here."
11. **A *winner* never quits! A *quitter* never wins!**

Attitude

The longer I live, the more I realize the impact of attitude on life. Attitude, to me is more important than facts. It is more important than the past, than education, than money, than circumstances, than failures, than successes, than what other people think or say or do!

It is more important than appearance, giftedness, or skill. It will make or break a company ... a home ... a team. The remarkable thing is we have a choice every day regarding the Attitude we will embrace for that day. We cannot change our past. We cannot change the inevitable.

The only thing we can do is play on the one string we have—and that is our Attitude. I am convinced that life is 10 percent what happens to you and 90 percent how you react to it.

And so it is with you.

WE ARE IN CHARGE OF OUR ATTITUDES!

Characteristics of the Non-assertive Person

He confuses the goal of being liked with being respected.

He is conditioned to fear being disliked or rejected.

He is unable to recognize the difference between being selfish in the bad sense and in the good sense.

He allows others to maneuver him into situations he doesn't want.

He is easily hurt by what others say and do.

He feels inferior because he is inferior.

He limits his experiences and doesn't use his potential.

Characteristics of the Assertive Person

He acts in a way that shows he respects himself, is aware than he cannot always win, and accepts his limitations.

He strives, in spite of the odds to make a good try. Win, lose or draw, he maintains his self-respect.

He feels free to reveal himself: "This is me. This is what I feel, think, and want."

He can communicate with people on all levels: strangers, friends, family. Communication is open, direct, honest and appropriate.

He has an active orientation to life. He goes after what he wants—in contrast to the passive person who waits for things to happen.

Slogans for Success

When you can't change the direction of the wind, adjust your sails.

When giving advice, it's best to make it brief.

Encouragement from a good coach can turn an athlete's life around.

Most things important to know are difficult to learn.

Conscience and reason will have the last word. Passion will have the last deed.

Don't judge those who try and fail. Judge only those who fail to try.

Behold the turtle. He makes progress only when he sticks his neck out.

The great challenge of life is to decide what's important and to disregard everything else.

A diamond is a chunk of coal that made good under pressure.

It's not hard to make decisions when you know what your values are.

You see things that are and say, "Why?" But you dream things that never were and say, "Why not?"

Praise in public, criticize in private.

Be humble—a lot was accomplished before you were born.

Don't be afraid to take big steps. You can't cross a chasm in two small jumps.

Challenges can be stepping stones or stumbling blocks. It's just a matter of how you view them.

Even if you are on the right track, you'll get run over if you just sit there.

When bad times come, you can let them make you bitter or use them to make you better.

Every great achievement was once considered impossible.

In the confrontation between the stream and the rock, the stream always wins—not through strength but by perseverance.

In the game of life, even the 50-yard seats don't interest me. I came to play.

Dream what you dare to dream. Go where you want to go. Be what you want to be.

The only limits are those of vision.

They can who believe they can.

Accept the challenges so that you may feel the exhilaration of victory.

Success is a dream turned into reality.

Some people dream of worthy accomplishments, while others stay awake and do them.

Success is a journey, not a destination.

Attitude is a little thing that makes a big difference.

The race is not always to the swift, but to those who keep running.

No one can predict to what heights you can soar. Even you will not know until you spread your wings.

Keep your face to the sunshine and you cannot see the shadows.

In the middle of every difficulty lies opportunity.

You cannot discover new oceans unless you have the courage to lose sight of the shore.

Do not fear the winds of adversity. Remember: A kite rises against the wind rather than with it.

Pride is a personal commitment. It is an attitude that separates excellence from mediocrity.

Excellence is the exceptional drive to exceed expectations.

In the end, the only people who fail are those who do not try.

When you lose, don't lose the lesson.

I've learned that you never get rewarded for the things that you intended to do.

I've learned that I still have a lot to learn.

Learn to listen. Opportunity sometimes knocks very softly.

Strive for excellence, not perfection.

Remember that overnight success usually takes many years.

Remember that winners do what losers don't want to.

What your mind can conceive and your heart can believe, your body can achieve.

The road to success is always under construction.

Luck is when preparation meets opportunity.

Failure isn't fatal and success isn't final.

Our greatest glory is not in never falling but in rising every time we fall.

Success is determined by how determined you are to succeed.

Most things are difficult before they are easy. The difference between playing to win and playing not to lose is often the difference between success and mediocrity.

Winners see what they want to happen. Losers see what they want to avoid.

When you lose say little. When you win say less.

You play a game with the head and heart.

It is better to try and fail than to fail to try.

Your attitude will determine your altitude.

You can't build a reputation on what you are going to do.

An idea is only as good as its execution.

Giving up reinforces a sense of incompetence. Going on gives you a commitment to succeed.

Only those who have the patience to do simple things perfectly will acquire the skill to do difficult things easily.

Most people fail not because they aim too high—but because they aim at nothing.

All people are created with an equal opportunity to become unequal.

Doing the best that you are capable of is victory, and doing less is defeat.

Be thankful for adversity—it separates the winners from the quitters.

You are what you are when no one is around.

Remember when you are not practicing, somewhere someone is, and when you meet him, he will win.

Those who profit most are those who give the most.

A winner credits good luck for winning, even though it isn't good luck. A loser blames bad luck for losing, even though it isn't bad luck.

A winner never quits. A quitter never wins.

When the going gets tough, the tough get going.

The amount of success you are able to achieve through wisdom will be in direct proportion to the effort expended in acquiring it.

A nice thing about the future is that it comes one day at a time.

The trouble with not having a goal is that you can spend your life running up and down the field and never score.

You cannot push someone up the ladder unless they are willing to climb themselves.

Whatever the mind can conceive and believe, it can achieve.

Attitude is an inner concept. It is the most important thing you can develop in your life. *Wayne Dyer*

Nothing ever built arose to touch the skies unless some man dreamed that it should, some man believed that it could, and some man willed that it must. *Charles Kettering*

To do what others cannot do is talent. To do what talent cannot do is genius. *Will Henry*

Strange how much you got to know before how little you knew. *Duncan Stuart*

He didn't know it couldn't be done…so he did it.

Nothing great was ever achieved without enthusiasm. *Ralph Waldo Emerson*

To be what we are, and to become what we are capable of becoming, is the only end of life. *Robert Louis Stevenson*

The reward of a task well done is in being called to do a bigger one.

Once in a century a man may be ruined or made insufferable by praise. But surely, once in a minute, something generous dies for want of it. *Erich Fromm*

In the long run, people hit only what they aim at. Therefore, they had better aim at something high. *Henry David Thoreau*

Press on: nothing in the world can take the place of persistence. Talent will not; nothing is more common than unsuccessful individuals with talent. Genius will not; unrewarded genius is almost a proverb. Education will not; the world is full of educated derelicts. Persistence and determination alone are important. The slogan "press on" has solved, and always will solve, the problems of the human race.

We see obstacles when we take our eyes off our goals.

Every noble work is at first impossible. *Thomas Carlyle*

Chance favors the prepared mind. *Louis Pasteur*

Life does not require that we become the biggest or the best, only that we try.

They won because they refused to become discouraged by their defeats.

He can who thinks he can, and he can't who thinks he can't. This is an inexorable, indisputable law. *Orison Marden*

The only thing that stands between a man and what he wants from life is often merely the will to try it and the faith to believe that it is possible. *Richard Devos*

The first and most important step toward success is the feeling that we can succeed. *Nelson Boswell*

A man is literally what he thinks. *James Allen*

The only limit to our realization of tomorrow will be our doubts of today. *Franillin Roosevelt*

The barrier between success is not something which exists in the real world; it is composed purely and simply of doubts about ability. *Mark Caine*

Failure is the only opportunity to move intelligently to begin again. *Henry Ford*

The greatest mistake a man can make is to be afraid of making one. *Elbert Hubbard*

The difference between greatness and mediocrity is often how an individual views a mistake. *Nelson Boswell*

No man fails who does his best. *Orison Marden*

If you don't know where you are going, how can you expect to get there? *Basil Walsh*

The only limits, as always, are those of vision. *James Broughton*

Success doesn't come to you ... you go to it. *Marua Collins*

If it is meant to be, it is up to me. *Sherry Bassin*

Whether you think you can or think you can't—you are right. *Henry Ford*

In order to succeed we must first believe we can. *Michael Korda*

I found that I could find the energy, that I could find the determination to keep on going. I learned that your mind can amaze your body, if you just keep telling yourself, I can do it, I can do it, I can do it. *Jon Erickson*

We can do only what we think we can do. We can be only what we think we can be. We can have only what we think we can have. What we do, what we are, what we have, all depend upon what we think. *Robert Collier*

He who loses wealth loses much; he who loses a friend loses more; he who loses courage loses all. *Cervantes*

The trouble with opportunity is that it always comes disguised as hard work.

Winners forget they are in a race. They just love to run.

Even if you're on the right track, you'll get run over if you just sit there. *Will Rogers*

Take your job seriously, not yourself. *Newt Gingrich*

For want of a nail the shoe was lost; for want of a shoe the horse was lost; and for want of a horse the rider was lost, being overtaken and slain by the enemy, all for want of care about a horseshoe nail. *Benjamin Franklin*

People don't care about how much you know until they know how much you care.

When all is said and done, more is said than done.

To be what we are, and to become what we are capable of becoming is the only end in life.

The difference between good and great is taking care of the little things.

What you do speaks so loud I can't hear what you say. *Ralph Waldo Emerson*

The man who believes he can do something is probably right, and so is the man who believes he can't. *Andrew Jackson*

Life is like a ten-speed bike: Most of us have gears we never use. *Charles Schulz*

Try to be the kind of person your dog thinks you are.

Only those that have the patience to do simple things perfectly will acquire the skill to do difficult things easily.

An optimist sees an opportunity in every catastrophe. A pessimist sees a catastrophe in every opportunity.

Good habits are hard to form but easy to live with.

Bad habits are easy to form but hard to live with.

The measure of a person's real character is what they would do if they know they would never be found out. *Thomas MacAuley*

A positive attitude is not a destination. It is a way of life.

People who win many have been counted out several times, but they didn't hear the referee. *H.E. Janson*

Intelligence is defined as the ability to adjust.

Fame is a vapour, popularity is an accident, money takes wings, those who cheer you today may curse you tomorrow. The only thing that endures is character.

Adversity makes some people break and makes others break records.

Without a risk there can be no challenge, without challenge there can be no reward. *Dave Mancuso*

Success comes before work only in the dictionary.

The golden opportunity you are seeking is in yourself. It is not in your environment, not in luck or chance, or the help of others; it is in yourself alone.

If what you did yesterday seems important, then you haven't accomplished anything today.

The minute you start talking about what you are going to do if you lose, you have lost. *George Schultz*

He that is good for making excuses is seldom good for anything else. *Ben Franklin*

Spectacular success is preceded by spectacular although invisible mental preparation.

Excellence can be attained if you care more than others think is wise. Risk more than others think is safe. Dream more than others think is practical. Expect more than others think is possible.

Success is never final. Failure is never fatal.

Hold yourself responsible for a higher standard than anyone expects from you.

Live intelligently in the present to prepare for the future.

Those who are upset by criticism admit they deserve it. *Cornelius Tacitus, Roman historian*

Your character is defined by your actions, not merely by your thoughts. Your actions represent who you are, while your thoughts only represent what you would like to be.

Attitudes are contagious, is yours worth catching?

We are what we repeatedly do.

Excellence, then, is not an act, but a habit. *Aristotle*

Success is a matter of luck, ask any failure. *Earl Wilson, columnist*

The will to win is easy. The will to prepare to win is more difficult.

It is all too easy to become focused on yesterday's success rather than today's challenges. *James A. Belasco and Ralph C. Stayer*

To listen well is as powerful a means of influence as to talk well.

Success, like self-worth, is something that must be determined by each individual according to the standards, beliefs and values that they use to guide their life. *John Wooden*

Every one of us always acts, feels and behaves in a way that is consistent with our self-image—regardless of the reality of that image. *Psycho-cyber 2000*

By having adversity in life we can see in others and in ourselves who quits and those who won't quit, and in the end adversity will make winners of those who won't quit.

What lies behind us and what lies before us are tiny matters compared to what lies within us. *Ralph Waldo Emerson*

Courage is resistance to fear, mastery of fear—not absence of fear. *Mark Twain*

What the superior man seeks is in himself: what the small man seeks is in others. *Francois de La Rochefoucauld*

Slogans for Leadership

After victory—beware of too much good staying in your hand. It will fast corrupt and warm worms. *Emerson*

Whilst he sits on the cushion of advantages he goes to sleep. When he is pushed, tormented, defeated, he has a chance to learn something. *Emerson*

You cannot manage men into battle, you manage things; you lead people. *General Murray Hopper*

Leaders are like eagles. They don't flock—you find them one at a time.

Leadership is an attitude before it is an ability.

The speed of the leader determines the rate of the pack.

Real leaders are ordinary people with extraordinary determination.

Be a leader: Remember the lead sled dog is the only one with a decent view.

Accept the fact that regardless of how many times you are right, you will sometimes be wrong.

Be decisive even if it means you'll sometimes be wrong.

Don't use time or words carelessly. Neither can be retrieved.

I believe some of us must assume leadership, I believe young people thirst to be led to better themselves. Life is hard and success is survival. Leaders inspire us. Leaders show us the way. *Frank Leahy, college football coach*

You don't become a leader because you say you are. It's much more what you do than what you say. *Sparky Anderson, professional baseball coach*

A successful leader has to be innovative. If you are not one step ahead of the crowd, you soon will be a step behind everyone else. *Tom Landry, professional football coach*

The players don't want to see me rushing around and screaming. They want to believe I know what I am doing. *Tom Landry*

If it doesn't work, I'll take the blame. You need that courage to be a good coach. *John McKay, professional football coach*

If you set up an atmosphere of communication and trust, it becomes a tradition. Older team members will establish your credibility with newer ones. Even if they don't like everything about you, they'll still say, "He's trustworthy, committed to us as a team." *Mike Krzyzewshi, college basketball coach*

Slogans for Teamwork

Coming together is a beginning; keeping together is progress; working together is success. *Henry Ford*

Teamwork is the ability to work together toward a common vision, the ability to direct individual accomplishment toward organizational objectives. It is the fuel that allows common people to attain uncommon results.

Teamwork is the collective talents of many individuals.

It's amazing what a team can accomplish when no one cares who gets the credit. *John Wooden, college basketball coach*

Together everyone achieves more.

Two stone cutters were asked what they were doing. The first said, "I'm cutting this stone into blocks." The second replied, "I'm on a team that's building a cathedral."

There is no I in the word team.

When you come to practice, you cease to exist as an individual. You're part of a team. *John Wooden, college basketball coach*

Teamwork: divides the tasks and doubles the successes.

Together
Everyone
Achieves
More

By union the smallest states thrive/ By discord the greatest are destroyed. *Sallust*

Together we shall achieve victory. *General Eisenhower*

The name on the front of the jersey is more important than the one on the back. *Sign on a team dressing room door*

Key Ingredients to Team Success

Team: "We are not a collection of talented players, we are a team"

Attitude:
  A. Always positive and supportive—helpful.
  B. No back-stabbing.
  C. Team before self: "There is no I in Team."
  D. A willingness to learn and listen—nobody's perfect.
  E. A desire to improve.
  F. Total commitment to school, work, family, and your sport.
  G. Hard work.
  H. Respect for teammates, coaches, equipment room staff, manager, team room, and staff.

Discipline:
  A. Always be on time—most often early and never late.
  B. Do the little fundamental skills well—excellent technique.
  C. No short cuts in drills.
  D. All drills done at top speed and maximum intensity.
  E. No talking when coach is speaking—pay attention.
  F. Hustle from one drill to the next.

Execution:
  A. Don't be lazy in the execution of the system.
  B. Don't accept mediocre execution: "PERFECT PRACTICE MAKES PERFECT PERFORMANCE."

Defense:
  A. We can only win if all players play great defense.
  B. Defense must be played as the way the defensive system is taught.

Are you playing for your name in the paper, or your name on the trophy? Are you playing for the name on the back of your sweater or the name on the front of the sweater? *Sherry Bassin, manager, professional hockey*

Being together as a team is more important than winning. If you're not together as a team, any success you have is not going to last. Achieve togetherness, achieve unity of purpose, and success will follow. *Pat Riley, professional basketball coach*

Disease of Me—The greatest obstacle to teamwork
Seven factors of how selfish individuals can easily bring down an entire team:
1. Inexperience in dealing with sudden success
2. Chronic feelings of underappreciation
3. Paranoia over being cheated out of one's rightful share
4. Resentment against the competence of others
5. Personal effort mustered solely to out-achieve a teammate
6. A leadership vacuum resulting from the formation of cliques and rivalries
7. Feelings of frustration even when the team performs successfully

Pat Riley, Successful N.B.A. coach and General Manager, Miami Heat

Code of Commitment
- To prepare every day as best we can
- To play with discipline at all times
- To support each other
- To never let ourselves be outworked
- To follow the game plan to the best of our ability
- To pay the price necessary to win

Kamloops Blazers (Western Junior Hockey League)

Coaching and Sport Quotations

Winning without arrogance, losing without alibi. *Grantland Rice*

Confidence is contagious, as is lack of confidence. *Vince Lombardi, professional football coach*

The harder you work, the harder it is to surrender. *Vince Lombardi*

If you don't respect yourself that's your problem. If you don't respect the game, that's my problem. *Kevin Costner, in the movie* Bull Durham

Life is 10 percent what happens to me and 90 percent how I react to it. *Lou Holtz, college football coach*

I always turn to the sports page first…It records people's accomplishments, the front page nothing but man's failure. *Earl Warren, former chief justice, United States Supreme Court*

In baseball and in business, there are three types of people. There are those who make it happen, those who watch it happen, and those who wonder what happened. *Tommy Lasorda, professional baseball coach*

We aren't where we want to be, we aren't where we ought to be, but thank goodness we aren't where we used to be. *Lou Holtz, college football coach*

When you think of the Forty-Niners, you think of their tradition. When you think of all the good teams of the past, like the old Steelers, the old Raiders, they all had identity. We will have identity. We want men who will stand up and be counted. Men who will make something happen. *Jerry Glanville, professional football coach*

If you accept losing, you can't win. *Vince Lombardi*

Confidence comes from hours and days and weeks and years of constant work and dedication. *Roger Staubach, former professional football player*

There is no substitute for work. It is the price of success. *Earl Blaik, college football coach*

Winning isn't everything, but making the all-out effort to win is the most important thing. *Vince Lombardi*

I will demand a commitment to excellence and to victory and that is what life is all about. *Vince Lombardi*

Failure is good. It's fertilizer. Everything I've learned about coaching I've learned by making mistakes. *Rick Pitino, college basketball coach*

It's what you learn after you know it all that counts. *John Wooden, college basketball coach*

If you recruit good players and they play well, you're a genius… So for a year or two you'll be called a genius. Sometimes a "genius manager" will recruit bad players, who play poorly, which will make people wonder how come a genius got so dumb so fast. *Whitey Herzog, professional baseball coach*

A team should be an extension of the coach's personality. My teams are arrogant and obnoxious. *Al McGuire, college basketball coach*

You have to improve your club, even if it means letting your grown brother go. *Tim McCarver, former baseball player*

People are human. If you're going to criticize them, compliment them first. *Bum Phillips, professional football coach*

Deep down, your players must know you care about them. This is the most important thing. I could never get away with what I do if the players felt I didn't care. They know, in the long run, I'm in their corner. *Bo Schembechler, college football coach*

A lifetime contract for a coach means, if you're ahead the third quarter, moving the ball, they can't fire you. *Lou Holtz, college football coach*

If you make every game a life-and-death proposition, you're going to have problems. For one thing, you'll be dead a lot. *Dean Smith, college basketball coach*

Tackle your hardest job first. Usually when we are faced with a number of projects to work on, we take the easiest or the most rewarding one first. Start with a job you really don't want to do. Once you get it out of the way, everything else will seem easy. *Red Auerbach, general manager, professional basketball*

There are certain qualities that you look for in people, whether you are on a football team or in business. You look for people who are committed, devoted and doing the best job. Talent isn't going to matter either. I'll take the guy who is out breaking his butt over a guy with talent in a close situation every time. I may get my butt beat a few times, but in the long run, I'll win because I'll have a guy with more character. *Mike Ditka, professional football coach*

The will to prepare to win is infinitely more important than the will to win. A team that is really willing to prepare is the team that has the best chance to win and wants to win. *Bobby Knight, college baslletball coach*

Winning isn't everything, but it beats anything that comes in second. *Bear Bryant, college football coach*

Sustain a family life for a long period of time and you can sustain success for a long period of time. First things first. If your life is in order, you can do whatever you want. *Pat Riley, professional basketball coach*

Next year is not about winning another championship or having one more ring or developing bigger reputations. It's about leaving footprints. *Pat Riley*

Success is not a sometimes thing. In other words, you don't do what is right once in awhile, but all the time. Success is a habit. Winning is a habit. *Vince Lombardi*

Success is perishable and often outside our control. In contrast, excellence is something that's lasting, dependable and largely within a person's control. *Joe Paterno, college football coach*

To get people to do what they don't want to do in order to achieve what they want to achieve. That is what coaching is all about. *Tom Landry, former professional football coach*

I don't ask our athletes how many of them want to win. The question I ask is can you live with losing, can you live with failure, can you live with mediocrity. *Lou Holtz*

Remember the five P's: proper preparation prevents poor performance.

Hard work beats talent: unless talent works.

Everyone has the will to win, but few have the will to prepare to win. *Bobby Knight, college basketball coach*

I like to have a closely knit team. I like players to do things together off the court. I like to show them I care about their problems. I want them to know that they and winning come first. *Bob Cousy, former professional basketball player and coach*

Don't mistake activity for achievement—practice the right way. *John Wooden, former college basketball coach*

Over the years, I have become convinced that every detail is important and that success usually accompanies attention to little details. It is this, in my judgment, that makes for the difference between champion and near champion. *John Wooden*

You must dedicate yourself to a far-reaching goal and sacrifice to reach it. You must enjoy what you do. Reach beyond your abilities; recognize that no talent, without hard work, can make you a winner. *George Allen, former professional football coach*

A team can only do as much as it believes it can do.

I'm never too busy to talk with any of those guys [former players]. A player-coach relationship ought to last a lifetime. *Mike Krzyzewski, college basketball coach*

It's hard for truly great players to understand how difficult the game is for players with less ability than they themselves have. *Del Harris, professional basketball coach commenting on great players becoming coaches*

The only things that are going to change you from where you are today to where you are going to be five years from now are the people you meet and the books you read. *Lou Holtz*, The Fighting Spirit

Success is perishable and often outside our control. In contrast, excellence is something that's lasting, dependable, and largely within a person's control. *Joe Paterno, football coach*

All the rings, all the color, all the money and all the display linger in the memory only a short time and are soon forgotten. But the will to win, the will to excel, these are the things that endure and are so much more important than any of the events that occasion them.

Winning is a habit. Unfortunately, so is losing.

Nobody can achieve perfection, but in the pursuit of perfection, one can obtain excellence. *Vince Lombardi*

The duration of an athletic contest is only a few minutes, while the training for it may take many weeks of arduous work and continuous exercise of self-effort.

The real value of sport is not the actual game played in the limelight of applause, but the hours of dogged determination and self-discipline, carried out alone, imposed and supervised by an exacting conscience.

The applause soon dies away, the prize is left behind, but the character you build up is yours forever.

There is nothing more unequal than the equal treatment of unequals. *Ken Blanchard*

Glossary of Terms

A Band   Area located in the center of the sarcomere containing both actin and myosin.

Actin   A protein involved in muscle contraction contained in the myofibril of the muscle.

Action Potential   The electrical activity developed in a muscle or nerve cell during activity or depolarization.

Adenosine diphosphate (ADP)   A complex chemical compound which, when combined with norganic phosphate, forms ATP.

Adenosine triphosphate (ATP)   A complex chemical formed with the energy released from food and stored in all cells, particularly muscles. The energy released from the compound allows the muscles to perform work.

Aerobic   In the presence of oxygen.

Afferent Nerve   A neuron that conveys sensory impulses from a receptor to the central nervous system.

Agonistic Muscle   A muscle directly engaged in a muscle contraction and working in opposition to the action of other muscles.

All-or-None Law   A stimulated muscle or nerve fiber contracts a nerve impulse completely or not at all.

AMI   The Athletic Motivation Inventory developed by Tutko, Ogilvie, and Lyon for measuring eleven personality traits.

Anabolic   Tissue building.

Anaerobic   In the absence of oxygen.

Anaerobic Glycolysis   The incomplete chemical breakdown of carbohydrate. The anaerobic reactions release energy for the manufacture of ATP, and lactic acid is also produced (also known as the lactic-acid system).

Anaerobic Threshold   The intensity of workload or oxygen consumption in which anaerobic metabolism is accelerated.

Androgenic   Substance that possesses masculinizing properties.

ATP-CP System   An anaerobic energy system in which ATP is manufactured when phosphocreatine is broken down.

Axon   Nerve fiber.

Back Extensor   Muscles involved in straightening the back.

Ballistic   Dynamic muscular movements.

Barbell   A bar with varying weights attached at the ends, usually held with both arms.

Biceps Brachii   Elbow flexor of the upper arm.

Biopsy   Removal and examination of human tissue.

Blood Glucose   The level of sugar in the blood.

Body Building   A sport in which muscle size, definition, and symmetry determines the winner.

Capillary   A fine network of small vessels located between arteries and veins.

Carbohydrate   A chemical compound containing carbon, hydrogen, and oxygen. A basic food stuff, it comes in the form of starches, cellulose, and sugars.

Carbohydrate Loading   A method used to increase the glycogen stores in the body by manipulating the diet.

Cardiac Output   The amount of blood pumped by the heart in one minute.

Cardiorespiratory Endurance   The ability of the heart and lungs to take in and transport adequate amounts of oxygen to the working muscles allowing activities involving large muscle groups to be performed over long periods of time.

Catell 16 PF   Catell's Personality Factor Questionnaire measuring the sixteen source traits of personality.

Central Nervous System   The spinal cord and brain.

Circuit Training   A conditioning program consisting of a number of exercise stations.

Concentration   The ability to focus on the appropriate thing while blocking out irrelevant distractions.

Creatine phosphate (CP)   A chemical compound stored in muscle, which, when broken down aids in manufacturing ATP.

Cross Bridges   Extensions of myosin.

Detraining   Reversal of adaptation to exercise.

Dumbbell   Small weights of fixed resistance, usually held in one hand.

Eccentric Contraction   The muscle lengthens while contracting and tension is developed.

Efferent Nerve   A neuron that conveys motor impulses away from the central nervous system to an organ of response such as a skeletal muscle.

Electrolyte   A substance that ionizes in solution and is capable of conducting an electrical current.

Electron   A negatively charged proton.

Endomysium   A connective tissue surrounding a muscle fiber or cell.

Energization   The ability to raise physical and/or mental activation to an appropriate level.

Energy   The capacity to perform work.

Energy System   One of three metabolic systems involving a series of chemical reactions resulting in the manufacture of ATP and the formation of waste products.

Enzyme   A protein compound which speeds up a chemical reaction.

Epimysium   A connective tissue surrounding the whole muscle.

Estrogen   Female androgen.

Exercise Recovery   The performance of light exercise during recovery from exercise.

External Imagery   Visual imagery in which athletes watch themselves perform.

Extracellular   Outside the cell.

Extrinsic Motivation   External rewards such as trophies and money.

Fartlek Training   Speed play where the athlete varies the pace from fast sprints to slow jogging—usually performed in the countryside using hills.

Fast-Twitch (FT) Fiber   A muscle fiber characterized by fast contraction time, high anaerobic capacity, and low aerobic capacity, all making the fiber suited for high-power-output activities.

Flexibility   Range of motion about a joint (static flexibility) or opposition or resistance of a joint to motion (dynamic flexibility).

Food Stuff   A substance suitable for food. Protein, carbohydrate, and fat are examples.

Free Weights   Weights not part of an exercise machine, such as barbells and dumbbells.

Glucose   Simple sugar.

Glycogen   The form in which glucose (sugar) is stored in the muscles and liver.

Glycogen Loading   An exercise-diet procedure that elevates muscle-glycogen stores.

Glycogen Sparing   The diminished utilization of glycogen when using other fuels. If fat is used to a greater extent for fuel, then glycogen is spared.

Glycogenesis   The manufacture of glycogen from glucose.

Glycogenolysis   Metabolic breakdown of glycogen.

Glycolysis   The incomplete breakdown of glycogen. In anaerobic glycolysis (lactic-acid system), the end product is lactic acid. In aerobic glycolysis, the end product is pyruvic acid.

Goal Setting   The process of setting goals in order to increase motivation and achieve results.

Golgi Tendon Organ   A proprioceptor located within the muscle tendon.

Hamstrings   Muscles on the back of the thigh that flex the knee and extend the hip.

Heat Cramp   The initial signs of painful muscle contractions caused by prolonged exposure to a hot environment.

Hemoglobin   A complex molecule found in red blood cells, which contains iron (heme) and protein (globin) and is capable of combining with oxygen.

Hollow Sprints   Bouts of running with two sprints interspersed with a period of jogging or walking (hollow period).

Hyperplasia   An increase in the number of cells in a tissue or organ.

Hypertrophy   An increase in the size of a cell or organ.

Imagery   Use of visualization to imagine situations.

Initiating Structure   A leadership style in which patterns of organization, communication, and procedures are well established.

Intermittent   Work exercises performed with alternate periods of relief.

Internal Imagery   Kinesthetic imagery in which the subject is within its own body while performing.

Interval Training   An exercise program in which the body is subjected to short but regularly repeated periods of work stress interspersed with adequate periods of relief.

Intrinsic Motivation   An internal desire to achieve success.

Ion   Electrically charged particle.

Isokinetic Contraction   Contraction in which the tension developed by the muscle while shortening at a constant speed is maximal over the full range of motion.

Isometric Contraction (Static)   Contraction in which tension is developed, but there is no change in the length of the muscle.

Isotonic Contraction   Muscle contraction in which the muscle shortens with varying tension while lifting a constant load. Also referred to as dynamic contraction and concentric contraction.

Karvonon Method   A procedure to determine the intensity of training using heart rates.

Kreb's Cycle   A series of chemical reactions occurring in the mitochondria in which carbon dioxide is produced and hydrogen ions and electrons are removed from carbon ions (oxidation).

Lactic Acid   A fatiguing metabolite of the lactic-acid system resulting from the incomplete breakdown of carbohydrate.

Lactic Acid System   An anaerobic energy system in which ATP is manufactured when glucose (sugar) is broken down to lactic acid. Used in high-intensity work lasting less than two minutes.

Macrocycle   A phase of training 2–6 weeks long.

Mental Practice   Practicing a physical skill mentally or cognitively without overt movement of the limbs or body.

Metabolism   The sum total of the chemical changes or actions occurring in the body.

Microcycle   A phase of training of approximately one week.

MMPI   Minnesota Multiphasic Personality Inventory.

Motor Unit   An individual motor nerve and all the muscle fibers it innervates.

Multiple Motor Unit Summation   The varying of the number of motor units contracting within a muscle at a given time.

Muscle Cell (Muscle Fiber)   The basic contractile unit. May be fast or slow twitch.

Myofibril   The part of a muscle fiber containing two protein filaments, myosin and actin.

Myoglobin   An oxygen-binding pigment similar to hemoglobin that gives the muscle fiber its red color. It acts as an oxygen store and aids in the diffusion of oxygen.

Myosin   A protein involved in muscular contraction.

Nerve   A cordlike structure that conveys impulses from one part of the body to another.

Neuron   A nerve cell consisting of a cell body (soma) with its nucleus and cytoplasm, dendrites, and axons.

Nodes of Ranvier   Those areas on a medullated nerve that is devoid of a myelin sheath.

Nutrition   The process of assimilating food.

Obliques   Muscles on the side of the abdominal area.

Overload   To exercise a muscle or muscle group with a resistance greater than that which it encountered previously, usually maximal or near maximal.

Oxygen System   An aerobic-energy system in which ATP is manufactured when food (principally sugar and fat) is broken down. The most abundant supply of ATP comes from this system and is the prime energy source during long-endurance activities.

Performance Routines   Planned sequence of mental or physical steps designed to assist the athlete in focusing attention upon relevant stimuli.

Perimysium   A connective tissue surrounding a fasciculus or muscle bundle.

Periodization   A planning process which structures training into phases.

Personality   The dynamic organization of psychological systems that determines an individual's uniqueness.

Personality Trait   A relatively stable personality disposition to respond to the environment in predetermined ways.

Phosphagen System   See ATP-CP System.

Phosphagens   A group of compounds that yield inorganic phosphate and release energy when broken down. ATP and CP are phosphagens.

Plyometrics   A quick powerful movement using a pre-stretch or counter movement. Also called the stretch-shortening cycle.

Positive Self-Talk   The ability to stay positive and eliminate inappropriate negative thoughts or feelings.

Progressive Resistance   Overloading a muscle or group of muscles consistently throughout the duration of a weight-resistance exercise.

Psychological Profile   Based upon a number of inventories, the profile is a distinct pattern of responses that a particular group of subjects, such as elite athletes, displays.

Pyruvic Acid   Chemical precursor of lactic acid.

Refocusing   The process of returning attention to a relevant stimuli after being distracted.

Reinforcement   A reward that is given so that the rewarded action will be repeated.

Relaxation The ability to relax the body and/or mind to an appropriate level.

Relief Interval The time between work intervals as well as sets in an interval-training program.

Repetition Maximum (RM) The maximum load that a muscle group can lift in one attempt.

Resistance Training The use of various methods or equipment to provide an external force against which to exercise.

Sarcolemma The muscle cell membrane.

Sarcomere The distance between two lines; the smallest contractile unit of skeletal muscle.

Self-talk A form of verbal self-affirmation.

Set A group of work and relief intervals in interval training. In weight training the total number of repetitions performed consecutively without resting.

Slow Twitch Fiber (ST) A muscle characterized by slow contraction time, low anaerobic capacity, and high aerobic capacity.

Social Cohesion The degree to which members of a team like one another and enjoy one another's company.

Specificity of Training Principle underlying construction of a training program for a specific activity or skill.

Speed Play (Fartlek) An exercise program alternating fast and slow running over natural terrains. An informal method of interval training.

Sprint Training System of short high-powered sprints designed to increase the capacity of the anaerobic system.

Stabilizer Muscles that anchor or stabilize the position of a limb.

Static Contraction See Isometric Contraction (Static).

Steroid A derivative of the male sex hormone testosterone, which has the masculine qualities.

Strength The maximal pulling force of a muscle.

Stress The non-specific response of the body to any demand made on it.

Stretch or Myotatic Reflex The reflex that responds to the rate of muscle stretch. This reflex has the fastest response to a stimulus (muscle stretch).

Synapse The connection or junction of one neuron to another.

Synergist Muscle A muscle that actively provides an additive contribution to the agonist muscle during a muscle contraction.

Task Cohesion The degree to which members of a group work together to achieve a specific and identifiable goal.

Testosterone The male sex hormone secreted by the testicles. It possesses masculinizing properties.

Tetanus The maintenance of tension of a motor unit at a high level as long as the stimulus continues or until fatigue sets in.

Training Frequency The number of times per week for the training workout.

Trait Relatively stable personality disposition.

Triglycerides The storage form of fatty acids.

Universal Behaviors A certain set of leadership behaviors believed to be possessed by all successful leaders.

Universal Traits A certain set of personality traits believed to be possessed by all successful leaders.

Visualization The ability to imagine (sight, feel, etc.) scenes to enhance effectiveness.

Vitamin Organic nutrients in the presence of which important metabolic reactions occur.

Volume A quantitative element in training. In weight training it relates to the total of sets, repetitions, and load.

Warm-Down An exercise performed at the end of a training workout to stretch the muscles joints and tendons and assist in removing any accumulated lactic acid from the muscles and blood.

Work Application of a force through a distance.

Work-to-Relief Ratio In an interval training program, the ratio of the duration of the work interval to the duration of the relief interval.

Z Line A protein band that defines the distance of one sarcomere in the myofibril.

Bibliography

Part 1: Self Management

Argue, L. (1979, October). A father's wish. p. 192, *Reader's Digest*.

Botterill, C. (1992). Goal setting with athletes. *Scientific Periodical on Research and Technology in Sport* (BU-1). Ottawa: Coaching Association of Canada.

Carron, A.V. (1980). *Social psychology of sport*. Ithaca, NY: Movement.

Christina, R.W., & Corcos, D. (1988a). *Coaches' guide to teaching skills*. Champaign, IL: Human Kinetics.

Christina, R.W., & Corcos, D. (1988b). *Coaches' guide to teaching sport skills*. Champaign, IL: Human Kinetics.

Coaching Association of Canada (1992a). *Coaching Theory Level 1*. National Coaching Certification Program. Ottawa: author.

Coaching Association of Canada (1992b). *Coaching Theory Level 2*. National Coaching Certification Program. Ottawa: author.

Coaching Association of Canada (1992c). *Coaching Theory Level 3*. National Coaching Certification Program. Ottawa: author.

Coaching Association of Canada (2007). Competition Introduction. Reference Material. Parts A and B. Ottawa.

Coaching Association of Canada (2007). *Teaching and Learning*. Reference Material. Part B Competition–Introduction. Ottawa.

Coaching Association of Canada (2007). *Planning a Practice*. Reference Material. Part A Competition–Introduction. Ottawa.

Cosentino, E (1995). Lecture. Toronto: York University.

Covey, S. (1990). *Principle centered leadership*. New York: Simon & Schuster.

Cratty, B.J. (1983). *Psychology in contemporary sport*. Englewood Cliffs, NJ: Prentice-Hall.

Dorrance, A. and Averbach. (2002) *The Vision of a Champion*. Chelsea: Clock Tower Press.

Douglass, M., & Douglass, M. (1980). *Manage your time, manage your work, manage yourself*. New York: AMACOM, A Division of the American Management Association.

Dryden, K. (1983). *The game*. Toronto: HarperCollins.

Dubin, A. (1990). *Dubin Commission of Inquiry into the use of drugs and banned practices intended to increase athletic performance*. Ottawa: Coaching Association of Canada.

Dungy, T. and Whitaker, N. (2007). *Quiet Strength*. Carol Stream, IL: Tyndele House Pub. Inc.

Fiedler, EE. (1967). *A theory of leadership effectiveness*. New York: McGraw-Hill.

Fiedler, EE. (1974). The contingency model—new directions for leadership utilization. *Contemporary Business, 4*, 65–79.

Fischer, S. (1994). *NHL Coaches: The Best Coaching Legends from Lester Patrick to Pat Burns*. Whitby, Ont: Donalds Broad.

Gallon, A. (1980). *Coaching: Ideas & ideals*. Boston: Houghton Mifflin.

Gambetta, V. (2007). *Athletic Development: The Art and Science of Functional Sports*. Champaign IL: Human Kinetics.

Gazes, P., Sovell, B., & Dellastatious, J. (1969, October). Continuous radioelectrocardiographic monitoring of football and basketball coaches during games. *American Heart Journal, 78*, 509–512.

Gillet, W (1972). What is a coach? Lecture notes. Ohio State University.

Gould, D., Udry, E., Tuffey, S., and Loehr, J. (1996). *Burnout in Competitive Junior Tennis Players: A Quantitative Psychological Assessment*. The Sport Psychologist 10, 322–340.

Halliwell, W. (1994). Mental preparation for coaches. In *Proceedings: International Coaching Symposium, Quebec City* (pp. 217–225). Ottawa: Canadian Hockey Association.

Hanel, F., Martin G., & Koop, S. (1983). Fieldtesting of a self-instructional time management manual with managerial staff in an institutional setting. *Journal of Organizational Behavior Management, 4,* 81–96.

Hemphill, J.K., & Coons, A.E. (1957). Development of the leader behavior description questionnaire. In R.M. Stogdill & A.E. Coons (eds.), *Leader behavior: Its description and measurement.* Columbus: Ohio State University Press.

Hersey, P., & Blanchard, K.H. (1977). *Management of organizational behavior.* Englewood Cliffs, NJ: Prentice-Hall.

Holly, M. (2004). *Patriot Reign.* New York, NY: HarperCollins.

Husman, B., Hanson, D., & Walker, R. (1970). The effect of coaching basketball and swimming upon emotion as measured by telemetry. In G. Kenyon (ed.), *Contemporary psychology of sport,* Second International Congress of Sport Psychology (pp. 287–291).

Iso-Ahola, S.E., & Hatfield, B. (1986). *Psychology of sports.* Dubuque, IA: Wm. C. Brown.

Jackson, P. (1995). *Sacred hoops.* New York: Hyperion.

Johnston M. and R. Walter (2004). *Simply the Best: Insights and Strategies from Great Hockey Coaches.* Surrey, BC.

Jones, J., Wells, L., Peters, R., & Johnson, D. (1982). *Guide to effective coaching: Principles and practice.* Boston: Allyn & Bacon.

Kahn, R.I., & Katz, D. (1960). Leadership practices in relation to productivity and morale. In D. Cartwright & AT. Zander (eds.), *Group dynamics.* Evanston, IL: Row, Peterson.

Keller, LA (1982). *The interscholastic coach.* Englewood Cliffs, NJ: Prentice-Hall.

Kolbenschlag, M. (1976). Tranquilizers, towel drawing, tantrums: All part of work stress. *The Physician and Sports Medicine, 4,* 97, 99, 101.

Kozell, C.E. (1985). *Coaches' guide to time management.* Champaign, IL: Human Kinetics.

Kroll, W. (1982). Competitive athletic stress factors in athletes and coaches. In L.P. Zaichkowsky & W.E. Sime (eds.), *Stress management for sport* (pp. 1–10). Peston, VA: American Alliance for Health, Physical Education, Recreation and Dance.

Krzyzewski, M. and Phillips, D. (2000). *Leading with the Heart.* New York, NY: Warner Books Inc.

Maraniss, D. (1999) *When Pride Still Mattered.* Lombardi. New York, NY: Simon and Schuster, Inc.

McClements, J., & Botterill, C.B. (1978, November). *Goal setting and performance.* Canadian Society for Psycho-Motor Learning and Sport Psychology Congress, Toronto, Ontario.

McKenzie, B. (1993). *Many faces of Burns.* Toronto: *Toronto Star,* May 9, G-1.

Marshall, J. & Chambers, D. (1992). *Sport profile.* Toronto: Self Management Resources.

Martens, R. (1990). *Successful coaching.* Champaign, IL: Leisure.

Martin, D. (1993). *Team think.* New York: Penguin.

Massengale, J. (1975). *The principles and problems of coaching.* Springfield, IL: Charles C. Thomas.

Miller, D. (1974). *Coaching the female athlete.* Philadelphia: Lea & Febiger.

Neal, P. (1978). *Coaching methods for women.* Reading, MA: Addison-Wesley.

Neil, P., & Tutko, T. (1975). *Coaching girls and women: Psychological perspectives.* Boston: Allyn & Bacon.

Parcells, B. and J. Caplan (1995). *Finding a Way to Win: The Principles of Leadership, Teamwork, and Motivation.* New York: Doubleday.

Paterno, J. (1989). *Paterno by the book.* New York: Random House.

Percival, L. (1971). The coach from the athlete's viewpoint. In *Proceedings: International Symposium on the Art and Science of Coaching* (pp. 285–325). Toronto.

Pyke, F. (1980). *Towards better coaching.* Canberra, Australia: Australian Coaching Council.

Roberts, W. (1987). *Leadership secrets of Attila the Hun.* New York: Warner.

Ryan, R. and D. Yaeger (2011). *Play Like You Mean It: Passion, Laughs, and Leadership in the World's Most Beautiful Game.* New York, NY: Doubleday.

Saban, N. and B. Curtis (2007). *How Good Do You Want to Be.* New York, NY: Ballantine Books.

Sabock, R. (1979). *The coach.* Philadelphia: W.B. Saunders.

Schula, D. and K. Blanchard (1995). *Everyone's a Coach.* Grand Rapids, MI: Zondervan Pub. House.

Smith, Bell, G and J. Kilgo (2004). *The Carolina Way: Leadership Lessons from a Life of Coaching.* New York: Penguin.

Smith, J. Kilgo and S. Jenkins (2002). *A Coach's Life.* New York: Random House.

Stogdill, R.M. (1950). *Leadership, membership and organization.* Psychological Bulletin, 47, 1–14.

Stogdill, R.M. (1948). Personal factors associated with leadership: Survey of literature. *Journal of Psychology, 25,* 35–71.

Taylor, J. (1974). *How to be an effective coach.* Ottawa: Coaching Association of Canada.

Tutko, T, & Richards, J. (1971). *Psychology of coaching*. Boston: Allyn & Bacon.

Walsh, B. (1993, January/February). *To build a winning team*. Harvard Business Review.

Walton, G. (1992). *Beyond winning*. Champaign, lL: Leisure.

Warren, W. (1988). *Coaching and winning*. West Nyack, NY: Parker.

Wilson, v., Haggerty, J., & Bird, E. (1989, September). Burnout in coaching. *Scientific Periodical on Research and Technology in Sport*. Ottawa: Coaching Association of Canada.

Part 2: Team Management

Baley, J.A., & Mathews, D.L. (1984). *Law and liability in athletes, physical education and recreation*. Boston: Allyn & Bacon.

Black, H.C. (1979). *Black's law dictionary*. St. Paul, MI: West.

Blanchard, K., & Schula, D. (1995). *Everyone's a coach*. Grand Rapids, MI: Zondervan.

Bompa, T (1984, April, May). Peaking for major competitions—parts 1 and 2. *Scientific Periodical on Research and Technology in Sport*. Ottawa: Coaching Association of Ontario.

Bompa, T (1993). *Periodization of strength*. Toronto: Veritas.

Bompa, T (1994). *Theory and methodology of training*. Dubuque, IA: Kendall/ Hunt.

Bridges, E.J., & Roquemore, L. (1992). *Management for athletic/sport administration*. Decatur, GA: ESM.

Bronzan, R., & Stotlar, D. (1992). *Public relations and promotions in sport*. Daphne, AL: American Sports Academy.

Bucher, C., & Dritee, M. (1993). *Management of physical education and sport*. St. Louis, MI: Mosby Year Book.

Bucher, C.A. and M.L. Kootee (1998) *Management of Physical Education and Sport*. 11th ed. Boston: McGraw-Hill.

Bukharina, G. (1977). Stades de l'entrainement: Preparation des jeunes conveurs (russe). Legkaya Ati., 8.

Chambers, D. (1993). Developing the self managed athlete. In *Proceedings: Roger Neilson's Coaches Clinic* (pp. 17-27). Windsor, Ontario.

Chambers, D. (1995). Building an Effective Program. In *Proceedings: Advanced II*. The National Coaching Certification Program. Ottawa: Canadian Hockey Association.

Coaching Association of Canada (1994). *Coaching assessment workbook, Level 3 Theory*. Ottawa.

Coaching Association of Canada (2007). Reference Material A and B, Competition Introduction. Ottawa.

Deegan, A. (1979). *Coaching: A management skill for improving individual performance*. Reading, MA: Addison-Wesley.

Dyba, W. (1996). *Men's volleyball weekly practice plan*. Toronto: York University.

Fletcher, T, & Rockler, J. (1990). *Getting publicity*. Vancouver, BC: Self Counsel.

Francis, C. (1992). *The Charlie Francis training system*. Ottawa: TBLI.

Glover, D. and D. Miduva (1992). *Team Building Through Physical Challenges*. Champaign, IL: Human Kinetics.

Glover, D. and D. Miduva (1995). *More Team Building Challenges*. Champaign, IL: Human Kinetics.

Hughes, C. (1982, February). From planning to implementation-some coaching principles. *Scientific Periodical on Research and Technology in Sport*. Ottawa: Coaching Association of Canada.

Kotter, J. (1991). *"What leaders really do": Managers as leaders*. Cambridge, MA: Harvard Business School, Publishing Division.

Leith, L. (1990). *Coaches' guide to sport administration*. Champaign, IL: Leisure.

Leith, L.M. (1983, February). The coach as manager-administrator. *Scientific Periodical on Research and Technology in Sport*. Ottawa: Coaching Association of Canada.

Loehr, J.E. (1983, January). The ideal performance state. *Scientific Periodical on Research and Technology in Sport*. Ottawa: Coaching Association of Canada.

Lyons, W. (1981). Bryant at mark he doesn't care about. *The Charlotte Observer*, Nov. 13, C-15.

MacIntyre, C. (1982). *Planning the sport program*. Ottawa: Coaching Association of Canada.

Marshall, J., & Chambers, D. (1992). *Sport profile*. Toronto: Self Management Resources.

Martens, R. (1980). *Coaches' guide to sport psychology*. Champagne, IL: Human Kinetics.

Martens, R. (1990). *Successful coaching*. Champaign, IL: Human Kinetics.

Martin, D. (1993). *Team think*. Toronto: Penguin.

Nesbitt, K. (1982). *Fundraising made easy*. Ottawa: Coaching Association of Canada.

Nideffer, R.M. (1976). Test of attentional and interpersonal style. *Journal of Personality and Social Psychology*, 34: 397-404.

Orlick, T (1986). *Coaches' training manual to psyching for sport*. Champaign, IL: Leisure.

Pipe, A. (1983, December). The making of a champion: Chemistry or coaching? *Scientific Periodical on Research and Technology in Sport*. Ottawa: Coaching Association of Canada.

Quick, T. (1992). *Successful team building*. New York: American Management Association.

Russell, K. (1989, January). Athletic talent. *Scientific Periodical on Research and Technology in Sport*. Ottawa: Coaching Association of Canada.

Samela, J., & Regnier, G. (1983, October). A model for sport talent detection. *Scientific Periodical on Research and Technology in Sport*. Ottawa: Coaching Association of Canada.

Seaboume, T.G., Weinber, R.S., Jackson, A., & Suinn, R.M. (1985). Effect of individualized, nonindividualized, and packaged intervention strategies on karate performance. *Journal of Sport Psychology, 2*, 318-336.

Stoddart, I. (1982). *Marketing your sport to others*. Ottawa: Coaching Association of Canada.

Suinn, R.M. (1986). *Seven steps to peak performance*. Toronto: Hans Huber.

Tharrett, A.J., K.J. McInnis and J.A. Peterson. J.A. (2007). *ACSM's Health/Fitness Facility Standards and Guidelines*. 3rd ed Champaign IL: Human Kinetics.

Walton, G. (1992). *Beyond winning*. Champaign, IL: Human Kinetics.

Williams, J.M. (1986). Integrating and implementing a psychological skills training program. *Applied Sports Psychology*. Palo Alto, CA: Manfield.

Wise, G. (1996). *General monthly plan for ice hockey*. Toronto: York University.

Wise, S. (1996). *Three week plan for 100 and 200 meter sprints*. Toronto: York University.

Yessis, M. (1990). *Soviet training methods*. New York: Barnes & Noble.

Part 3: Physical Preparation

Albert, M. (1995). *Eccentric Muscle Training in Sports and Orthopedics*. New York: Churchill Livinstone.

Alter, M. (1990). *Sport stretch*. Champaign, IL: Human Kinetics.

Asmussen, E., & Mazin, B. (1978). A central nervous component in local muscular fatigue. *European Journal Applied Physiology, 38*, 9–15.

Atha, J. (1981). *Strengthening muscle. Exercise and Sport Sciences Reviews, 9*, 1–73.

Bacon, T. (1989). The planning and integration of mental training programs. *Scientific Periodical on Research and Technology in Sport, 10*, 1, Ottawa: Coaching Association of Canada.

Baechle, T., & Groves, B. (1992). *Weight training: Steps to success*. Champaign, IL: Human Kinetics.

Baechle, T., Earle, W. and Wathen, M. (2008). *Resistance Training Essentials of Strength Training and Conditioning* 3rd ed., Champaign, IL: Human Kinetics.

Baechle, T. and R. Earle (2006). *Weight Training Steps to Success*, 3rd ed., Champaign, IL: Human Kinetics.

Baechle, T. and Earle R. eds. (2008). *Essentials of Strength Training and Conditioning*, 3rd ed., Champaign, IL: Human Kinetics.

Balyi, I. (1991). Quadrennial and double quadrennial planning of athletic training. In *Training Tips*, 141.

Blimkie, C. Altitude and performance. *Scientific Periodical on Research and Technology in Sport*. Ottawa: Coaching Association of Canada.

Blimkie, C. Heat stress and athletic performance: Survival of the sweatiest. *Scientific Periodical on Research and Technology in Sport*. Ottawa: Coaching Association of Canada.

Blimkie, C.J.R. (1989). Age and sex associated variation in strength during childhood: anthrompetric, morphologic, neurologic, biomechanical, endocrinologic, genetic and physical correlates. In C. Gisolfi & D. Lamb (eds.), *Perspectives in exercise science and sports medicine: Youth exercise and sport* (2, pp. 99–163). Indianapolis, IN: Benchmark.

Bompa, T. (1993a). *Periodization of strength*. Toronto: Veritas.

Bompa, T. (1993b). *Power training for sport*. New York: Mosaic.

Bompa, T. (1994). *Theory and methodology of training*. Dubuque, IA: Kendall Hunt.

Bompa, T. and M. Carrera (2005). *Periodization Training for Sports*. Champaign, IL; Human Kinetics.

Bompa, T. and D. Chambers (2003) *Total Hockey Conditioning*. Toronto: Key Porter Books.

Bompa, T, and Haff, G. (2009). *Periodization Theory and Methodology of Training*, 5th ed. Champaign, IL; Human Kinetics.

Bonen, A., & Belcastro, A. (1976). Comparison of self-selected recovery methods on lactic acid removal rates. *Med. Sci. Sports, 8*,176–178.

Bowers, R., Foss, M., & Fox, E. (1988). *Physiological basis of physical education and athletics*. Dubuque, IA: Wm. C. Brown.

Bowers, R., & Fox, E. (1992). *Sports physiology*. Dubuque, IA: Wm. C. Brown.

Boyle, M. (2004). *Functional Training for Sports*. Champaign, IL: Human Kinetics.

Brook, G., & Fahey, T. (1987). *Fundamentals of human performance*. New York: Macmillan.

Brooks, G.A. (1987). Amino acid and protein metabolism during exercise and recovery. *Medicine and Science in Sports and Exercise, 19* (5), 50–156.

Brown, L. and V Ferrigano (2005). *Training for Speed, Agility and Quickness*. Champaign, IL; Human Kinetics.

Brynteson, P., & Sinning, W.E. (1973). The effects of training frequencies on the retention of cardiovascular fitness. *Medicine and Science in Sports and Exercise, 5*, 29–33.

Campbell, C.J. Information on jet lag. *Scientific Periodical on Research and Technology in Sport, W-2*. Ottawa: Coaching Association of Canada.

Cardinal C. (1990). *Annual training and competition plan for juvenile volleyball players (16–17)*. Montreal: University of Montreal.

Charters, P. (1992). Strength training for athletes. Lecture. Toronto: York University.

Chu, D. (1998). *Jumping into Plyometrics*, 2nd ed., Champaign, IL: Human Kinetics.

Chu, D. and Potach P. (2008). *Plyometrics Training. Essentials of Strength Training and Conditioning*, 3rd ed., Champaign, IL: Human Kinetics.

Church, J.B., M.S. Wiggins, EM. Moode, and R. Crist (2001). *Effect of warm-up and flexibility treatments on Vertical Jump Performance*. J. Strength Condo Res. 15(3); 332–336.

Cinique, C. (1989). Massage for cyclists: The winning touch? *The Physician and Sports Medicine, 17* (10): 167–170.

Clark, H., ed. (1974). Development of muscular strength and endurance. *Physical Fitness Research Digest*. President's Council on Physical Fitness and Sports. Washington, D.C., U.S. Government Printing Office, Series 4, No. 2, January.

Clark, N. (1990). *Sports nutrition guidebook*. Champaign, IL: Leisure.

Clark, N. (2008). *Sport Nutrition Guidebook*. Champaign, IL: Human Kinetics.

Clarke, D.H. (1973). Adaptations in strength and muscular endurance resulting from exercise. In J.H. Wilmore (ed.), *Exercise and sports sciences reviews 1* (pp. 73–102). New York: Academic.

Coaching Association of Canada (1992a). *Coaching Theory Level 1*. National Coaching Certification Program. Ottawa: author.

Coaching Association of Canada (1992b). *Coaching Theory Level 2*. National Coaching Certification Program. Ottawa: author.

Coaching Association of Canada (1992c). *Coaching Theory Level 3*. National Coaching Certification Program. Ottawa: author.

Coaching Association of Canada (2007). Competition Introduction Reference Material Part A and Part B, Ottawa.

Costill, D. (1986). *Inside running: Basics of sports physiology*. Indianapolis, IN: Benchmark.

Costill D.L., Coyle, E.E, Fink, W.E, Lesmos, G.R., & Witzmann, E.A. (1979). Adapting in skeletal muscle following strength training. *Journal of Applied Physiology, 46*, 96–99.

Coyle, E.E, Martin, W.I-I., Sinacor, D.R., Joyner, M.J., Hagber, J.M., & Holloszy, J.O. (1984). Time course of loss of adaptations after stopping prolonged intense endurance training. *Journal of Applied Physiology, 57*, 1857–1864.

DeLorme, T., & Watkins, L. (1948). Techniques of progressive resistance exercise. *Archives of Physical Medicine, 29*, 263–273.

Drinkwater, B.L., & Horvath, S.M. (1972). Detraining effects in young women. *Medicine and Science in Sports, 4*, 91–95.

Edgerton, V.R. (1978). Mammalian muscle fiber types and their adaptability. *American Zoologist, 18*, 113–125.

Ehret, E, & Scanlon, L. (1988). *Overcoming jet lag*. Argonne National Laboratory. Toronto: Berkeley.

Eisenman, P., Johnson, S., & Benson, J. (1990). *Coaches' guide to nutrition and weight control*. Champaign, IL: Human Kinetics.

Fahey, T.D., Akka, L., & Rolph R. (1975). Body composition and U02 max of exceptional weight trained athletes. *Journal of Applied Physiology, 39*, 559–561.

Fleck, S.J., & Kraemer, W.J. (1987). *Designing resistance training programs*. Champaign, IL: Human Kinetics.

Fleck, S.J., & Schutt, R.C. (1985). Types of strength training. *Clinics in Sports Medicine, 4*, 159–168.

Fleck, S.J. and W.J. Kramer (2003). *Designing Resistance Training Programs*, 3rd ed., Champaign, IL: Human Kinetics.

Fleck, S.J. and W. Kramer (2007). *Optimizing Strength Training*. Champaign, IL: Human Kinetics.

Francis, C., & Patterson, P. (1992). *The Charlie Francis training system*. Ottawa: TBLE

Frederick, A. and C. Frederick (2006). *Stretch to Win*. Champaign, IL: Human Kinetics.

Gambetta, V. (2007). *Athletic Development*. Champaign, IL: Human Kinetics.

Goldenberg, L. and P. Twist (2007). *Strength Ball Training*. Champaign, IL: Human Kinetics.

Gonyea, W.J., & Sale, D. (1982). Physiology of weight lifting exercise. *Archives of Physical Medicine and Rehabilitation, 63*, 235–237.

Gordon, E. (1967). Anatomical and biochemical adaptations of muscle to different exercises. *Journal of American Medical Association, 201*, 755–758.

Hahn, A.G. (1993). The effect of altitude training on athletic performance at sea level—A review. *Scientific Periodical on Research and Technology in Sport*. Ottawa: Coaching Association of Canada.

Harre, D. (1982). *Principles of sport training*. Berlin: Sportverlag.

Hartman, J., & Tunnemann, H. (1988). *Fitness and strength training*. Berlin: Sports Verlag.

Hatfield, P.C., & Drotee, M.L. (1978). *Personalized weight training for fitness and athletics from theory to practice*. Dubuque, IA: Kendall/Hunt.

Hermansen, L., et al. (1975). Lactate removal at rest and during exercise. In H. Howalf & R Poortmans (eds.), *Metabolic adaptation to prolonged physical exercise*, (pp. 101–105). Basel: Birkhauser, Verlag.

Holt, C. (1986). *Stretching for sport*. Ottawa: Coaching Association of Canada.

Hunter, G.R (1985). Changes in body composition, body build and performance associated with different weight training frequencies in males and females. *National Strength and Conditioning Association Journal, 1*, 26–28.

Ingjer, F. (1979). Effects of endurance training on muscle fiber ATP-ase activity, capillary supply and mitochondria content in man. *Journal of Physiology, 294*, 419–432.

Jackson, A., Jackson, T., Hnatck, J., & West, J. (1985). Strength development: Using functional isometrics in an isotonic strength training program. *Research Quarterly for Exercise and Sport, 56*, 234–237.

Jefferys, I. (2008). *Warm-up and Stretching. Essentials of Strength Training and Conditioning*, 3rd ed. Champaign, IL: Human Kinetics.

Kobayashi, Y. (1974). *Effect of vitamin E on aerobic work performance in man during acute exposure of hypoxic hypoxia*. Unpublished doctoral dissertation, University of New Mexico.

Komi, P. Klissouras, v., & Karvinen, E. (1973). Genetic variation in neuromuscular performance. *Int. Z. angew. Physiol., 31*, 289–304.

Knapik, J.J., B.H. Jones, C.L. Bauman and J.M. Harris (1992). *Strength, Flexibility and Athletic Injuries*. Sports Med. 146: 277–288.

Kraemer, W.J. (1983). Detraining the bulked up athlete: Prospects for lifetime health and fitness. *National Strength and Conditioning Association Journals, 5*, 10–12.

Kraemer, W., & Fleck, J. (1993). *Strength training for young athletes*. Champaign, IL: Human Kinetics.

Kuehn, L. (1983, June). Managing and monitoring heat stress in sport. *Scientific Periodical on Research and Technology in Sport*. Ottawa: Coaching Association of Canada.

McArdle, W.D., EJ. Katch and V.I. Katch. *Exercise Physology: Energy, Nutrition and Human Performance*, 6th ed. Baltimore: Lippincott, Williams and Wilkins.

McDonagh, M. & Davies, C. (1984). Adaptive response of mammalian skeletal muscle to exercise with high loads. *European Journal of Applied Physiology, 52*, 139–155.

MacDougall, J., Sale, D., Moroz, J.R, Elder, G., Sutton, J., & Howard, H. (1979). Mitochondria volume density in human skeletal muscle following heavy resistance training. *Medicine and Science in Sports, 11*, 164–166.

MacDougall, J., Wenger, H., & Green, H. (1991). *Physiological testing of the high-performance athlete*. Champaign, IL: Human Kinetics.

McMorris, R.O., & Elkins, E.C. (1954). A study of production and evaluation of muscle hypertrophy. *Archives of Physical Medicine and Rehabilitation, 35*, 420–426.

Matveyev, L. (1981). *Fundamentals of sport training*. Moscow: Progress.

Milner-Brown, H.S., Stein, R.B., & Yemin R. (1973). The orderly recruitment of human motor units during voluntary contractions. *Journal of Physiology, 230*, 359–370.

Morehouse, C. (1967). Development and maintenance of isometric strength of subjects with diverse initial strengths. *Research Quarterly, 38*, 449–456.

Moritani, T., & DeVries, H. (1979). Neural factors versus hypertrophy in the time course of muscle strength gain. *American Journal of Physical Medicine, 82*, 521–524.

Moritani, T., & DeVries, H. (1980). Potential for gross hypertrophy in older men. *Journal of Gerontology, 35*, 672–682.

National Strength and Conditioning Association. Position Statement: *Explosive Plyometric Exercises*. NSCAJ 15(3): 16, 1993.

Neilson, K.L. (1986). Injuries in female distance runners. In B.L. Drinkwater (ed.), *Female endurance athletes* (pp. 149–161). Champaign. IL: Human Kinetics.

Newton, H. (2006). *Explosive Lifting for Sport*. Champaign, IL: Human Kinetics.

Ozolin, N. (1971). *Athlete's training system for competition*. Moscow: Phyzkultura Sport.

Poliquin, C. (1988, August). Variety in strength training. *Scientific Periodical on Research and Technology in Sport*. Ottawa: Coaching Association of Canada.

Poliquin, C. (1991). Training for improving relative strength in sports. *Scientific Periodical on Research and Technology in Sport*. Ottawa: Coaching Association of Canada.

Poliquin, C. (1992). *Strength training: an introduction to methods and principles*. Video. Ottawa: Coaching Association of Canada.

Portman, M. (1985). *The planning and peliodization of training and competition program*. Ottawa: Coaching Association of Canada.

Radcliffe, J., & Farentinos, R. (1988). *Plyometrics: Explosive power training*. Champaign, IL: Human Kinetics.

Radcliffe, J. (2005). *High Powered Plyonetrics*. Champaign, IL: Human Kinetics.

Ramsay, J.A., Blimkie, C.J.R., Smith, K., Gavner, S., MacDougall, J.D., & Sale D.G. (1990). Strength training effects in prepubescent boys. *Medicine and Science in Sports and Exercise, 22*, 605–614.

Rasch, P., & Morehouse, L. (1957). Effect of static and dynamic exercise on muscular strength and hypertrophy. *Journal of Applied Physiology, 11*, 29–34.

Rhodes, T., & Twist, P. (1990). *The physiology of ice hockey*. Vancouver: University of British Columbia Press.

Sale, D. (1981, March). Specificity in strength training: A review for coach and athlete. *Scientific Periodical on Research and Technology in Sport*. Ottawa: Coaching Association of Canada.

Sale, D.G. (1989). Strength training in children. In C.V. Gisolfi & D.R. Lambs (eds.), *Perspectives in exercise and sport science* (pp. 165–216). Carmel, IN: Benchmark.

Sale, D.G., MacDougall, J.D., Upton, A.R.M., & McComas, A.J. (1983). Effects of strength training upon motor neuron excitability in man. *Medicine and Science in Sports and Exercise, 15*, 57–62.

Saltin, B., & Hermansen, L. (1967). Glycogen stores and prolonged severe exercise. In G. Blix (ed.), *Nutrition and physical activity*. Uppsala, Sweden: Almquist and Weksells.

Sandler, D. (2010). *Fundamental Weight Training*. Champaign, IL: Human Kinetics.

Sewall, L., & Micheli, L.J. (1986). Strength training for children. *Journal of Pediatric Orthopedics, 6*, 143–146.

Sharkey, B. (1986). *Coaches' guide to sport physiology*. Champaign, IL: Human Kinetics.

Sharkey, B. (1993). *Coaches' guide to sport physiology*. Champaign, IL: Human Kinetics.

Shaw, T. (1992). *Never look back*. Video. Cranston, RI: MF Athletic.

Sobey, E. (1980). *The complete circuit training guide*. Mountain View, CA: Anderson World.

Staron, R.S., Hagerman, Ee., & Hikida, R.S. (1983). Reevaluation of human fast-twitch subtypes evidence for a continuum. *Histo chemistry, 78*, 33–39.

Tesch, P.A., Thorsson, A., & Kaiser, P. (1984). Muscle capillary supply and fiber type characteristics in weight and power lifters. *Journal of Applied Physiology: Respiratory, Environmental and Exercise Physiology, 56*, 35–38.

Vrijens, J. (1978). Muscle strength development in the pre and post pubescent age. *Medicine and Sport, 11*, 152–158.

Waldman, R., & Stull, G. (1969). Effects of various periods of inactivity on retention of newly acquired levels of muscular endurance. *Research Quarterly, 40*, 393–401.

Weltman, A., Janney, C., Rians, C.B., Strand, K., Berg, B., Tippett, S., Wise, J., Cahill, B.R., & Katch F.I. (1986). The effects of hydraulic-resistance strength training in prepubertal males. *Medicine and Science in Sports and Exercise, 18*, 629–683.

Williams, M.H. (1985). *Nutritional aspects of human physical and athletic performance*. Springfield, IL: Charles C. Thomas.

Wilmore, J.H. (1974). Alterations in strength, body composition and anthrometric measurements consequent to a 10 week weight training program. *Med. Sci. Sports, 6*, 133–138.

Wilmore, J.H., & Costill, D.L. (1988). *Training for sport and activity*. Dubuque, IA: Wm. C. Brown.

Wright, J.E. (1980). Anabolic steroids and athletics. In R.S. Hutton & D.I. Miller (eds.), *Exercise and Sport Science Review* (pp. 149–202). The Franklin Institute.

Yessis, M. (1990). *Soviet training methods*. New York: Barnes & Noble.

Part 4: Psychological Preparation

Abraham, A., and Collins, D. (1998). Examining and Extending Research in Coach Development. *Quest, 50,* 59–79.

Anshel, M.H. (1997). *Sport Psychology: From Theory into Practice.* Scottsdale, Arizona: Gorsuch Pub.

Bacon, T. (1989). The planning and integration of mental training programs. *Scientific Periodical on Research and Technology in Sport.* Ottawa: Coaching Association of Canada, 10, 1.

Benson, H., Beary, J.E, & Carol, M.P. (1974). The relaxation response. *Psychiatry, 37,* 37–46.

Bompa, T. (1994). *Theory and methodology of training.* Dubuque, IA: Kendall Hunt.

Botterill, C. (1986, December). Energizing. *Scientific Periodical on Research and Technology in Sport.* Ottawa: Coaching Association of Canada.

Botterill, C., & Winston, G. (1984, August). Psychological skill development. *Scientific Periodical on Research and Technology in Sport.* Ottawa: Coaching Association of Canada.

Carron, A.V., and Hausenblas, H.A. (1998). *Group Dynamics in Sport,* 2nd ed. Morgantown, WV: Fitness Information Technology.

Chevalier, N. (1983, October). Understanding the imagery and mental rehearsal processes in athletics. *Scientific Periodical on Research and Technology in Sport.* Ottawa: Coaching Association of Canada.

Cohn, P.J. (1991). *An Exploratory Study of Peak Performance in Golf.* The Sport Psychologist, 5.

Corbin, C. (1972). Mental practice. In W.P. Morgan (Ed.) *Ergogenic aids and muscular performance* (pp. 94–118). New York: Academic.

Cox, R. (1994). *Sport psychology: Concepts and applications.* Dubuque, IA: Wm. C. Brown.

Cox, R.H. (1994) *Sport Psychology Concepts and Applications.* Duguque, LA.: Brown and Benchmark.

Cox, R.H. (2002). *Sport Psychology, Concepts and Applications.* New York, N.Y., McGraw-Hill.

Cratty, B. (1989). *Psychology in contemporary sport.* Englewood Cliffs, NJ: Prentice-Hall.

Csikszentmihalyi, M. (1979). The flow experience. In D. Goleman & R. Davidson (eds.), *Consciousness: Brain, states of awareness, and mysticism.* New York: Harper & Row.

Davis, H. (1990). Cognitive style and non-sport imagery in elite hockey performance. *Perceptual and Motor Skills, 71,* 795–80l.

Ellis, A. & Grieger, R. (1977). *Handbook of rational-emotive therapy.* New York: Springer.

Gavon, E. (1984). *Mental training for peak performance.* Lansing, NY: Sport Science Associates.

Gould, D., & Udry, E. (1994). Psychological skills for enhancing performance: Arousal regulation strategies. In *Med. Sci. Sports Exercise, 26* (4), 478–485.

Gould, D. (1998). *Applied Sport Psychology: Personal Growth for Peak Performance.* J.M. Williams ed., Mountain View, CA. Mayfield.

Greenspan, M.J., & Feltz, D.L. (1989). Psychological interventions with athletes in competitive situations: A review. *The Sport Psychologist, 3,* 219–236.

Haslam, I. (1990). A conceptual framework for planning imagery training. *Scientific Periodical on Research and Technology in Sport.* Ottawa: Coaching Association of Canada.

Jackson, P. (1995). *Sacred hoops.* New York: Hyperion.

Kolonay, B. (1977). The effects of visual motor behavioral rehearsal on athletic performance. Unpublished master's thesis, Hunter College, New York.

Kolonay, B. (1977). The effects of visual motor behavioral rehearsal on athletic performance. In R. Martens, *Coaches' guide to sport psychology.* Champaign, IL: Human Kinetics.

Krauss, D. (2001). *Mastering Your Inner Game.* Champaign, IL: Human Kinetics.

Lane, J.E. (1980). Improving athletic performance through visual-motor rehearsal. In RM. Suinn (ed.), *Psychology in sports: Methods and applications* (pp. 316–320). Minneapolis, MN: Burgess.

Leith, L. (2003). *The Psychology of Coaching Team Sports.* Toronto: Sports Book Publisher.

Loehr, J. (1983, January). The ideal performance state. *Scientific Periodical on Research and Technology in Sport.* Ottawa: Coaching Association of Canada.

Lueinberg, R.S., and Gould, D. (1999). *Foundations of Sport and Exercise Psychology,* 2nd ed. Champaign, IL: Human Kinetics.

Mahoney, M., & Averner, M. (1977). Psychology of the elite athlete: An exploratory study. *Cognitive Therapy and Research, 1,* 135–141.

Martens, R. (1982, September). Paper presented at the Medical and Scientific Aspects of Elitism in Sport Conference, Brisbane, Australia. In R. Martens, *Coaches' guide to sport psychology.* Champaign, IL: Human Kinetics.

Martens, R. (1987). *Coaches' guide to sport psychology*, Champaign IL: Human Kinetics.

Martens, R., Vealey, R.S. and Burton, D. (1990) *Competitive Anxiety in Sport*. Champaign, IL: Human Kinetics.

Martin, G., & Lumsden, J. (1999). *Coaching: A behavioral approach*. St. Louis, MI: Times Mirror-Mosby.

Martin, K.A., Moritz, S.E., and Itell, C.R. (1999). Imagery Use in Sport: A Literature Review and Applied Model *The Sport Psychologist, 13,* 245–268.

Maslow, A. (1965). Humanistic science and transcendent experiences. *Journal of Humanistic Psychology, 5*(2): 219–226.

Mikalachki, A. (1969). *Group cohesion reconsidered*. London, Ontario: School of Business Administration, University of Western Ontario.

Miller, S. (2003). Hockey Tough. Champaign, IL: Human Kinetics.

Moran, A.P. (1996). *The Psychology of Concentration in Sport Performers*. Itove, U.K., Psychology Press Publishers.

Murphy, S. (2005). *The Sport Psych Handbook*. Champaign, IL: Human Kinetics.

Nideffer, R. (1976). *The inner athlete*. New York: Thomas Y. Crowell.

Nideffer, R.M. (1981). *The ethics and practice of applied sports psychology*. Ithaca, NY: Mouvement.

Nideffer, R. (1985). *Athletes' guide to mental training*. Champaign, IL: Human Kinetics.

Nideffer, R. (1992). *Psyched to win*. Champaign, IL: Leisure.

Onestak, D.M. (1991). The effects of progressive relaxation, mental practice, and hypnosis on athletic performance: A review. *Journal of Sport Behavior, 14,* 247–282.

Orlick, T. (1986a). *Psyching for sport: Coaches' training manual*. Champaign, IL: Leisure.

Orlick, T. (1986b). *Psyching for sport: Mental training for athletes*. Champaign, IL: Leisure.

Orlick, T. (1990). *In pursuit of excellence*. Champaign, IL: Human Kinetics.

Ravizza, K. (1977). Peak experiences in sport. *Journal of Humanistic Psychology, 17,* 35–41.

Richardson, A. (1967a). Mental practice: A review and discussion (Part 1). *Research Quarterly, 38,* 95–107.

Richardson, A. (1976b). Mental practice: A review and discussion (Part 2). *Research Quarterly, 38,* 263–273.

Rohnke, K. (1986). *Silver bullets: A guide to initiation problems*. Adventure Games and Trust Activities, Project Adventure.

Rohnke, K. (1988). *The bottomless bag*. Project Adventure.

Rushall, B. (1981, December). On-site psychological preparations for athletes. *Scientific Periodical on Research and Technology in Sport*. Ottawa: Coaching Association of Canada.

Rushall, B.S., Hall, M., & Rushall A. (1988). Effects of three types of thought content instructions on skiing performance. *The Sport Psychologist, 2,* 283–297.

Scannel, E., & Newstrom, J. (1987). *More games trainers play: Experimental learning exercises*. Toronto: McGraw-Hill.

Schubert, F. (1988). *Psychology: From start to finish*. Toronto: Sport Books.

Schultz, J.H., & Luthe, W. (1959). *Autogenic training: A psychophysiological approach to psychotherapy*. New York Grune & Stratton.

Seabourne, T., Weinberg, A., Jackson, A., & Suinn, R. (1985). Effect of individualized, non individualized, and packaged intervention strategies on karate performance. *Journal of Sport Psychology, 7,* 40–50.

Seppo, E., & Hatfield, B. (1986). *Psychology of sports*. Dubuque, IA: Wm. C. Brown.

Singer, R. (1993). *Handbook of sport psychology*. Champaign, IL: Human Kinetics.

Suedfeld, P., & Bruno, T. (1990). Flotation and imagery in the improvement of athletic performance. *Journal of Sport and Exercise Physiology, 12,* 308–310.

Suinn, R. (1986). *Seven steps to peak performance*. Toronto: Hans Huber.

Syer, J. and Connelly, C. (1998). *Sporting Body, Sporting Mind: An Athlete's Guide to Mental Training*. London, U.K., Simon & Schuster.

Tutko, T., & Richards, J. (1971). *Psychology of coaching*. Boston: Allyn & Bacon.

Tutko, T., & Umberto, T. (1976). *Sports psyching*. Los Angeles, CA: J.P. Tarcher.

Tutko, T. (1976) Sport Psyching: *Playing Your Best Game All the Time*. New York, N.Y.: J.P. Tarcher.

Vealey, R.S. (1994). Current status and prominent issues in sport psychology interventions. In *Med. Sci. Sports Exercise, 26,* 495–502.

Vernacchia, R., McGuire, R., & Cook, D. (1996). *Coaching mental excellence*. Portola Valley, CA: Wade.

Weinberg, R.S. (1999). Anxiety and motor performance: Where to go from here? In *Anxiety Research, 2,* 227–242.

Williams, J. (1986). Integrating and implementing a psychological skills program. In *Applied Sport Psychology*, ed. J.M. Williams, 301–324. Palo Alto: Mayfield.

Williams, J.D., Rippon, G., Stone, B.M., & Annett, J. (1995). Psychophysiological correlates of dynamic imagery. In *British Journal of Psychology, 86,* 283–300.

Williams, J.M. and V. Krane (1998). Psychological Characteristics of Peak Performance. In: *Applied Sport Psychology: Personal Growth to Peak Pelformance.* J.M. Williams, ed. Mountain View, CA: Mayfield, pp. 158–170.

Part 5: Quotations

Chambers, D. and P. Klavora (2008). *The Great Book of Inspiring Quotations.* Toronto, ON: Sports Books Publisher.

Index